Praise for Onward to Chicago

"Larry A. McClellan makes an important contribution to our knowledge of the Underground Railroad in one of its principal hubs. He paints a full picture in this lively and engaging book that will be of interest to both experts and general readers."
—**Keith Griffler**, author of *The Freedom Movement's Lost Legacy: Black Abolitionism Since Emancipation*

"In *Onward to Chicago*, Larry A. McClellan captures the lives of the freedom seekers and the activists who aided them in northeastern Illinois in all of their humanity and complexity. Furthermore, he upends our usual interpretation of the Underground Railroad by showing the agency exerted by the freedom seekers and the vital roles played by Black abolitionists, Black churches, and Black communities in this struggle for liberty."
—**Roy E. Finkenbine**, coeditor of *Black Abolitionist Papers, 1830–1865*

"McClellan's research is meticulous and thorough. This study traces the Underground Railroad enterprise in Chicago and surrounding areas, revealing the true scope of the soul-crunching, human work involved in securing freedom for enslaved people and their families."
—**Jennifer Harbour**, author of *Organizing Freedom: Black Emancipation Activism in the Civil War Midwest*

ONWARD TO CHICAGO

Onward to Chicago

Freedom Seekers and the
Underground Railroad in
Northeastern Illinois

Larry A. McClellan

Southern Illinois University Press
Carbondale

Southern Illinois University Press
www.siupress.com

26   25   24   23   4   3   2   1

Cover illustration: Photo from mural created by an Underground Railroad
Arts Project at Oberlin High School. Used by permission of the City
Council, Oberlin, Ohio. Photo courtesy of Tanya Rosen-Jones

Library of Congress Cataloging-in-Publication Data
Names: McClellan, Larry A., author.
Title: Onward to Chicago : freedom seekers and the Underground
Railroad in northeastern Illinois / Larry A McClellan.
Other titles: Freedom seekers and the Underground
Railroad in northeastern Illinois
Identifiers: LCCN 2022054100 (print) | LCCN 2022054101 (ebook) |
ISBN 9780809339259 (paperback) | ISBN 9780809339129 (ebook)
Subjects: LCSH: Underground Railroad—Illinois. | Fugitive slaves—Illinois—
History—19th century. | Antislavery movements—Illinois—History—19th
century. | Abolitionists—Illinois—History—19th century. | African American
abolitionists—Illinois—History—19th century. | Chicago (Ill.)—History—
19th century. | Illinois—History—1778-1865.
Classification: LCC E450 .M1295 2023 (print) | LCC E450 (ebook) |
DDC 973.7/115—dc23/eng/20221123
LC record available at https://lccn.loc.gov/2022054100
LC ebook record available at https://lccn.loc.gov/2022054101

Printed on recycled paper ♻

SIU
Southern Illinois University System

This book is dedicated to the memory
of Eliza and John Little and all those who escaped
from enslavement and traveled to and through
Chicago and northeastern Illinois
on their way to freedom.

Then we came on barefooted all the way to Chicago.
My feet were blistered and sore and my ankles swollen,
but I had to keep on.
There was something behind me driving me on.

—Eliza Little, Freedom Seeker from Tennessee, 1841
   In Drew, *Narratives of Fugitive Slaves*.

CONTENTS

Contents

ILLUSTRATIONS, MAPS, AND TABLES

Illustrations

Maps

Tables

ONWARD TO CHICAGO

The Great Chicago Exodus

APRIL 1861. FOR REFUGEES from slavery who settled in Chicago and for those stopping on their way to Canada, the fear of capture and return was supposedly distant and unlikely. In March, Abraham Lincoln had been sworn in as President. Yet in the early days of April, urgent news spread through the African American community in Chicago. Free Black residents, along with long-settled and newly arrived refugees were raising the alarm. Chicago was no longer safe; it was essential for those identified as fugitives to get to Detroit and then quickly to Canada. Within four days, over four hundred left, and in two weeks, more than three hundred others joined the exodus. In these few days more than half of Chicago's Black population was gone.[1]

After Lincoln's election in November 1860, South Carolina headed for secession, soon followed by six other states. By March of 1861, the entire nation, already fractured, was following the tension in Charleston—what would happen with Fort Sumter? The fort, as an outpost of the United States Army, sat in the range of South Carolina's guns and militia. Was the country falling into some sort of war among the states? "Civil War the Great Danger," was the March 14th headline in the *Chicago Journal*.[2]

In his inaugural address on March 4th, Lincoln started by assuring the South that his intent was not to overturn slavery, that, in fact, the laws for the return of fugitive slaves were in place and to be followed. Congruent with this affirmation, in scattered places across the North, Federal agents were making final efforts toward appeasement, gathering up fugitive slaves to be returned to their owners.

Russell A. Jones was the new federal marshal in Chicago, an appointment Lincoln announced on March 15th. A long time Lincoln supporter and

ironically nominated to this position by congressman and radical abolitionist Owen Lovejoy, Jones proved to be far more enthusiastic about the Fugitive Slave Act than any had foreseen. Near the end of March, Jones declared
that he had "fellows of the right kidney" who were willing to follow orders
and capture all fugitives in the city, "guaranteeing promptness and dispatch
in so doing."[3]

Then, on April 3rd, at 6:00 a.m., the Harris family was forced awake, their
three children screaming as they were carried downstairs by deputies. Living
in the second level of a small home on South Clark Street near Jackson Bou-
levard, the Harris's had been in Chicago a little over a month, after escaping
from a farm outside St. Louis. As the arrest happened, a large crowd gathered
outside their home and called for vengeance against those involved. A private detective named Hayes, who was himself a fugitive slave, was in the area
and, suspected of betraying the Harris family, he was attacked by the crowd.[4]

Word spread that the family was taken to a depot where Marshal Jones
conveniently arranged for a special train to whisk them away. Some incensed
residents gathered at the train station, while others sought to intercept the
train and rescue the family. Although they could not stop it from leaving,
shots were fired at the train as it moved from the station. It carried the marshal's deputies, the Harris family, and two men from St. Louis claiming ownership of the family. In court in Springfield the next day, they were declared
fugitives and sent to St. Louis on the night train.[5]

This brutal and rapid act focused and intensified the fears of fugitives in
transit, settled refugees, and free people of color across Chicago. Over the
next several days and nights, hundreds simply packed up and left, traveling
by train, over land, and on ships leaving for Detroit. Some were observed
leaving on foot, following train tracks heading for Detroit. The *Chicago Journal* warned: "We advise every colored fugitive in the city to make tracks for
Canada as soon as possible. Don't delay a moment. Don't let grass grow under your feet. Stand not upon the order of your going but go at once. You are
not safe here and you cannot be safe until you stand on English soil.... *Strike
for the North Star.*[6]

Reviewing the actions of Marshal Jones, the *Chicago Tribune* noted that in
the few weeks since his appointment, "in saloons and bar-rooms about town,
the zealous Federal officer is praised, but good men and humane men hang
their heads." The paper declared that because of the eager "man-hunting," many
Black residents who lived in Chicago for years were now quickly departing.[7]

Among the hundreds in transit, thirty fugitives were concealed aboard a lake schooner, to carry them around Michigan to Detroit and Canada. After the immediate initial departures, the most pressing task was aiding freedom seekers with limited resources. Longtime Underground Railroad activists negotiated for a fast, final train to freedom. On April 4th, 5th, and 6th, prominent Black abolitionist leaders met with church pastors, Black and white, and with white abolitionist colleagues and friends to help others leave the city. They met in the offices of Chicago attorney L. C. Paine Freer to organize fundraising and sign a contract with the Michigan Southern Railroad. The meeting included Freer's close friend, John Jones, other key leaders from the Black community, and additional longtime white activists.[8]

The flurry of activity culminated on Sunday, April 7th. The day started with religious services at the Zoar Baptist Church, the forerunner of Chicago's Olivet Baptist Church and the congregation of John and Mary Jones and other leading Black abolitionists. Thereafter, freedom seekers and their friends were "going from door to door, bidding each other good-bye and mingling their congratulations and tears." For several blocks around the Michigan Southern depot, the streets were filled "with an excited multitude of colored people of both sexes. Large numbers of white people also gathered. . . ." The loading process moved quickly under the leadership of several Black men assisted by some white men. One hundred and six people squeezed in the cars of the Michigan Southern. "Each car was supplied with a cask of water, . . . boiled beef, hams, beans, bread, and apples. Some of the party were old, but most of them were young men in their prime. . . . There were quite a number of young families going to save the children from sharing the fate of a slave mother." It cost two dollars apiece to send them to Detroit. They were packed into four freight cars attached to the back end of a passenger train. It was a crowded ride to freedom.[9]

Newspapers across the country carried the details of this remarkable exodus. Articles from the *Chicago Tribune* and the *New York Times* were copied and paraphrased by other papers including reports in Michigan, Pennsylvania, Ohio, Iowa, and Massachusetts; even a small article in the Salt Lake City *Mountaineer*. The *Chicago Journal* referred to it as the "Exodus of the Colored Population to Canada"; the *National Republican* in Washington, DC, headlined: "Great Stampede of Fugitive Slaves for Canada." Curiously, in an issue filled with news about Fort Sumter and the outbreak of hostilities, the *Weekly Standard* of Raleigh, North Carolina, used the ancient Arabic reference to Muhammad's flight from danger to present an account of the train trip of April 7th under the headline, "The Slave Hegira from Chicago – Flight of Over One Hundred Fugitives."[10]

In these intense, early April days in 1861, the *Great Chicago Exodus* made public the semisecret networks of the Underground Railroad in Chicago. The pressing need to support those in immediate danger brought to the forefront skills and experience gained from more than twenty years assisting fugitives on their way to freedom. For decades, the Chicago region had played a significant role in the movement of freedom seekers from the South, and now, its role was all in the open.[11]

Freedom Seekers and
the Underground Railroad

I N ILLINOIS, AS WAS the case across America, from the onset, people held
in the bondage of slavery, identified and treated as property, constantly
sought means for resistance and escape. In response to these efforts, over
time and across the state and the country, diverse groups of African American and white collaborators managed to devise a variety of ways to assist these
freedom seekers.

Until recently, historical research and stories related to the Underground
Railroad have focused on the conductors, stations, and routes and by implication, and occasionally explicitly, have portrayed fugitive slaves as passive
victims in desperate need of help. Of course, as was the case in Chicago at the
onset of the Civil War, these "fugitives" were in fact a remarkable collection
of individuals, families, and small groups who made courageous choices to
leave their enslavement, to liberate themselves, and seek freedom where they
could find it. From this recognition comes the reference to fugitive slaves as
"freedom seekers" to help shift our understanding of their decisions and journeys. Margaret Washington writes: "I reject the term 'fugitive,' and use it only
in quotations or as an allegation. I prefer to represent Black people fleeing
bondage as self-emancipated freedom seekers, rather than as criminals." In
addition, Cheryl LaRoche, author of *The Geography of Resistance, Free Black
Communities and the Underground Railroad*, refers to those escaping as "self-
liberators," and "freedom seizers."[1] In these pages, "freedom seeker" refers to
those individuals, families, and groups seeking to liberate themselves from
chattel slavery. Closely connected to these freedom seekers were free people
of color living in northeastern Illinois carrying the knowledge of slavery from
their own lives and the experiences of family and friends.[2]

Just as referring to freedom seekers underscores the deep intention of enslaved persons to liberate themselves, Jennifer Harbour suggests the use of "emancipation activism" as a way to underscore the all-encompassing activity of Black leadership in Chicago and elsewhere. Emancipation is not simply something bestowed by white political leaders but rather is freedom sought and gained by the struggle of Black individuals, families, and communities "as a vigorous, aggressive, tenacious group." Although our focus here is on the movement of freedom seekers and the networks of response to that movement, none of these dynamics can be understood separately from an interrelated set of commitments. For Black communities and leaders, emancipation meant not only freedom from slavery but also claiming their full humanity and their rights as citizens. Thus, building community and institutions, creating avenues for education, struggling against Black codes, demanding legal and political rights, destroying slavery, connecting with national leaders and movements, and participating in the Underground Railroad were all essential, interrelated ingredients for emancipation activists.[3]

These interconnecting commitments in Chicago as elsewhere, serve then as compelling reminders that in contrast with white abolitionists who actively supported freedom seekers as one of a number of public "causes" they pursued, the work of Black leadership was an all-encompassing, constant struggle in many directions to gain full freedom, full equality, and their full humanity. In addition, the broad experience of Chicago's Black leadership supports LaRoche's identification of the "Colored Conventions" held at state and national levels in the 1840s and 50s as being of particular importance as environments for strengthening collaboration on networks of assistance.[4]

A common issue in the stories of the Underground Railroad is the use of encounters with freedom seekers as the occasions to tell heroic and romanticized stories of white abolitionists. The travelers serve simply as the objects of rescue in the detailed stories of their rescuers. Two of the most well-known pre-Civil War Illinois abolitionist stories are the trial of John Hassock and the Ottawa abolitionists, who assisted Jim Gray to escape, and the journey of John Brown with fugitives from western Missouri across Iowa and Illinois and on to Canada. In contrast to the traditional focus of these stories, these pages emphasize the journey and challenges for Jim Gray and the actions of Jim and Narcissa Daniels in seeking out John Brown along with the responses of Black abolitionists in Chicago when they all arrived. This new focus shifts attention from the actions of white men to the agency of freedom seekers.

This shift is also occurring in other areas where writers are examining Black experience and agency in our national history and are seeking to affirm deeply human stories. One example is in the work of Deirdre Cooper Owens examining the origins of gynecology in the United States. A significant source of early nineteenth-century research involved experimentation on enslaved women. Owens recasts the traditional white male origins in research using Black enslaved women to include the crucial and creatives roles played by these women in the original work. Seen not simply as objects in the research, she seeks to "present these women as complicated, whole, and fully human."[5]

The emphasis on the wholeness and agency of enslaved persons is deeply expressed in the mid-twentieth-century writings of African American author and anthropologist Zora Neale Hurston. She wrote that culturally, many Americans carry a "willful ignorance of the complexities of non-white people," and in much of earlier American writing, "it is assumed that all non-Anglo-Saxons are uncomplicated stereotypes. Everybody knows all about them."[6]

Not only does this book tell the complex and deeply human stories of freedom seekers, but it also underscores that the Underground Railroad did not shape the movement of freedom seekers; rather it was the decisions and movement of freedom seekers that gave shape to what became the networks known as the Underground Railroad. Keith Griffler offers the pointed assessment: "The Underground Railroad did not organize the flight from slavery but was organized by it." Thus, in the title of this book, and in other contexts, it is useful, again and again, to see these stories and this history as freedom seekers *and* the Underground Railroad, with the latter always informed by the former.[7]

As clarity about the role of freedom seekers grows, so does recognition of the significant and often central leadership provided by free and self-liberated persons of color, who often intentionally settled in places to be of assistance to others seeking their freedom. Griffler presents the crucial role played by Black individuals, families, and small communities in the Ohio River valley who were on the "front line," assisting freedom seekers who engaged with other Black communities and with sympathetic white people on their way north. In Illinois, their travels led some freedom seekers to several well-established Black communities and other points of refuge on the way to the Chicago region. Both Griffler and LaRoche look at communities in Ohio, Indiana, and Illinois, with most of the travelers in Illinois heading toward the

Chicago region.[8] Crucial to Black leadership was the growth of Black African Methodist Episcopal and Baptist churches and the web of human and social connections they fostered and nourished.

The wider understanding of the initiative and determination in the actions of families and individuals seeking freedom is part of a fuller picture of American slavery and reactions to it, as found in a range of newer books and other media. Attention to the "peculiar institution" that sits at the core of America's story ranges from general overviews to a greater focus on the political, social, and economic impacts of slavery and on the growth of the networks of the Underground Railroad in regions and nationally.[9]

Over the past twenty years, in the national literature on the Underground Railroad, little attention is paid to the impact of events in Illinois and particularly in Chicago. In recent efforts to create a fresh picture of these networks of collaboration, there are useful new interpretations of this national experience of civil disobedience, but often Illinois is not discussed. Today, across Illinois, most public discussions and educational materials focus on the Underground Railroad outside of Illinois, with particular focus on activities in eastern states and the work of Harriet Tubman and Frederick Douglass. These are, of course, great stories; however, there is so much in Illinois that must be seen.

Fergus Bordewich's *Bound for Canaan: The Underground Railroad and the War for the Soul of America* (2005), a very solid overview of the American experience, contains only a handful of references to Illinois. Frost and Tucker's *A Fluid Frontier* (2016), written about the Detroit region, includes a map with Chicago but shows no flow of movement for freedom seekers from there, and has almost no discussion of the Chicago region as part of the journey for some. In Foreman, *et.al., The Colored Convention Movement* (2021) does not mention the conventions held in Illinois in 1853 and 1856. However, the role of Illinois in the national story is in some recent works including La-Roche, *Geography of Resistance* (2014), Blackett, *The Captive's Quest for Freedom* (2018), Harbour, *Organizing Freedom* (2020), and Masur, *Until Justice Be Done* (2021).

This lack of attention is ironic given that it was in Illinois that Dred Scott and his family were "almost free"; abolitionist Elijah Lovejoy was murdered; several independent Black towns were established by former slaves and free people of color; and Abraham Lincoln and Stephen A. Douglas debated the future of the country. In addition, Illinois had a longer border with slave states than any other state in the North; the Ohio and Mississippi Rivers provided hundreds of miles of porous borders with the slave states of Kentucky and Missouri.

In exploring what actually happened with freedom seekers in northeastern Illinois, most of the existing materials reflect stories that were repeated in various late nineteenth-century and early twentieth-century Chicago histories. These Underground Railroad stories focused on the actions of white participants, almost always white *men*, with some brief mention of the assisted, and often bewildered, fugitives. A particularly clear example is in an extended article on the Underground Railroad in the early twentieth-century editions of the *Historical Encyclopedia of Illinois* tied to various county histories. Several paragraphs provide detail on people and events in Chicago, but all the individuals named are white people. It portrays a situation of dedicated white people helping passive runaways. To move beyond existing traditional accounts, resources used in this book include newspapers of the period (e.g., *Chicago Tribune, Chicago Democrat, Western Citizen, Joliet Democrat, New York Times*), the personal papers and recorded stories of key abolitionists (e.g., John Jones, Philo Carpenter, Zebina Eastman), other collections of primary sources, cycles of stories about fugitive slaves in various histories of Chicago and counties in the region, family records from persons involved in assisting freedom seekers, and reports from persons settling in Canada who escaped through Illinois and Chicago (including interviews conducted by Benjamin Drew in 1856, presented in *The Refugee: or the Narratives of Fugitive Slaves in Canada*).[10]

The harsh realities in Illinois meant that for those escaping slavery and for those officially "free," their daily lives were always complicated by demeaning and restrictive Black codes, ongoing threats of kidnapping, and the increasing punitive activities fostered by Federal legislation concerning "fugitive slaves."

It has been extraordinarily challenging to sift out actual events from the often-romanticized material to build a more complete and accurate picture. Throughout this book, my focus is on the journeys of freedom seekers and the people and places where they found assistance. Materials from memoirs, family memories, church-related sources, and locally printed pieces have been useful for focusing on personal and eyewitness accounts. In the late nineteenth and early twentieth centuries, a wide variety of county histories and related books (e.g., biographical albums) were published across Illinois. These sources often contain extended articles on the work of the Underground

Railroad. Focused almost entirely on the "heroic" work of white abolitionists, these sources are nonetheless useful since they point to significant participants in the work and, on occasion, reflect first-person accounts and memories of events involving freedom seekers. In this book, when possible, these
sources are reinforced by census data. Census data has also uncovered the
settlement of Black individuals and families across northeastern Illinois in
the 1830s, 1840s, and 1850s.

There is a significant amount of material found in newspaper accounts.
Often, these accounts can be reinforced by census records and other sources
identifying the participants in the articles. However, it is crucial to recognize
that there is a wide range in the usefulness and value of newspaper accounts
regarding "fugitives" and the Underground Railroad. These accounts range
from those that are obviously embellished and romanticized to some that
contain remarkable first-person accounts. In addition, there are significant
differences contained in those from before and after the Civil War.

Newspaper accounts from before the Civil War provide a rich range of
source material. In papers from across Illinois, notices related to sought and
caught fugitive slaves often contain details about individuals and not only their
place of enslavement but also indicators of where they were headed. As early as
1834, such notices appeared in Chicago papers. From the early 1840s forward,
Chicago and regional newspapers carried specific accounts of freedom seekers
coming to the city and surrounding communities and their encounters with
courts, kidnappers, and residents who gave them assistance. Along with these
accounts, and often within them, are expansions and observations intended to
reinforce the horrors of slavery and the demands to abolish it. This type of article was particularly common in the *Western Citizen*, the fiercely abolitionist
newspaper established in Chicago in 1843, which regularly offered embellished
accounts to reinforce opinions and spur calls to action.

There were also occasions when activists would deliberately "celebrate"
their actions to both strengthen and perhaps mystify what they were up to.
See, for example, an announcement from the *Chicago Tribune* in 1854 under
the headline, "Passengers on the Underground Railroad":

Its trains run through our streets regularly, but notwithstanding its passenger business has increased at a rate equal to that of any other "upper
ground" road, we hear of no speculation in its stock, or even an opinion
as to dividends. We can assure its friends, and the public, that its business,

above all expectations, is still increasing at a most astonishing rate.... A large corps of trusty conductors has been secured, the stations well fitted up, and the officers and passengers on the road furnished with "irons" to be used against all who may have the audacity to interfere with trains or passengers.[11]

While acknowledging the distinct goals of activists to report, to celebrate, or to mystify the Underground Railroad to readers, it is important to still recognize the value of newspaper accounts as resources for understanding the movement of and encounters with freedom seekers. Often these accounts are strengthened by material from other sources, and they provide a base for further research and inquiry. For this book, it is appropriate to cautiously trust the antebellum newspaper sources and provide supporting documentation whenever possible.[12]

Following the Civil War, some Underground Railroad accounts are found within obituaries, generally in those of white participants, but some are also found in those of Black activists. These obituaries look back to times of engagement with freedom seekers and contain a few accounts of specific encounters. References to the Underground Railroad can also be found in sources related to abolitionists' reunions and in historical summaries of the "old days." Most often these are a kind of "celebration history" that is generalized and most likely inflates claims of involvement. As indicated earlier, the work of white activists was often romanticized and was occasionally reported as law-breaking high adventure.

Later, whenever veterans gathered, there were war stories to tell and claims to make about connections with the illegal networks. This sensibility is certainly reflected in the words of John Beveridge who, while serving as governor of Illinois, spoke to the Abolitionists' Convention in 1874, a reunion of his fellow veteran abolitionists in Chicago. In reflecting back on events before the Civil War, he declared, in the romantic language of the day, that the Underground Railroad was

Chartered not by law, but in moral conviction;
Engineered not by science, but through charity;
Constructed not with money, but out of love;
Freighted not with commerce, but with downtrodden humanity;
Operated not for the benefit of stockholders, but for the escape of
the fugitive fleeing from the hand of his oppressor.[13]

At the National Anti-Slavery Reunion, in Chicago in 1874, only a few African Americans were present or invited. Although John Jones was part of the planning committee, he was not visible during the actual four days of the gathering. The lack of Black involvement, combined with the general racism of the time, meant that from the 1870s forward, the work of the Underground Railroad in and around Chicago was seen as an overwhelmingly white venture. This book aims to challenge and change that interpretation.

In 1898, Wilbur Siebert, a long-time professor at The Ohio State University, published his massive (478 page) text, *The Underground Railroad from Slavery to Freedom*—a useful, although limited, source for research. He was among the first to clarify that the railroad-related terms like *stations*, *agents*, and *conductors* were simply "figurative," although they were useful and helped "mystify the minds of the public." From the beginning, he understood that the movement of freedom seekers ranged from their independent actions to their engagement with well-organized networks of assistance.[14]

Contrary to these understandings, by the start of the twentieth century, the popular perception regarded the Underground Railroad in Illinois as having been extremely well organized for many years with regular routes across the state. In a school text of the time, *The Story of Illinois and Its People* (1910), declarative sentences recounted that "by 1835 there were regular lines of travel from the Ohio and Mississippi rivers, northward toward Chicago and Milwaukee, where negroes were smuggled aboard boats bound for Canada. . . . The negroes were concealed in one place, sometimes for a week, in order to throw their pursuers off the track. The hiding place was usually the cellar, the attic, or a secret room. . . . Fugitives were sent on usually at night, either by wagon or foot, with careful directions where to find their next friend, and how to signal him, by tapping on the window."[15]

These notions of regularity were often reinforced using maps with delineated routes. In his 1898 book, Siebert presented a number of examples of these maps. These maps are helpful as visual conceptions of the activity called the Underground Railroad, but routes were far from regular. The dilemma, of course, as reflected in the Illinois section of his national map, was that the maps served to reinforce a reality for regularized routes that did not exist. The routes on the map also reinforced the notion that these were established and regular *over time*, when in fact, the movement of freedom seekers and the places of specific support developed and changed over the years.[16]

As this book presents, the movement of freedom seekers and the support provided evolved over time. The eventual well-established networks were the result of responding to the movement and the expressed need for assistance coming from freedom seekers. At the beginning and throughout the years of operation of the Underground Railroad, there were individuals, families, and small groups traveling on their own. Many received only sporadic or onetime assistance. Others connected only with Black families, living across the state and in Chicago, and with congregations of Baptist and African Methodist Episcopal churches. There were also many others who sought out and made use of the resources provided by Black and white activists. Over time, definite networks developed in the region, such as one that stretched east across Will County and into Indiana, as well as other paths connecting white activists across the region with white and Black families in Chicago.

This book endeavors to present journeys, people, and locations for which we have strong documentation. Every freedom seeker account and each instance identifying a place or person of assistance falls in a range of certainty and documentation. This range reaches from a general comment about activity in a place to very specific, firsthand evidence reinforced by multiple sources. These pages reflect stories with levels of documentation that make them verifiable and probable. In some of the accounts, reference to local traditions indicates that there may have been connections there, though currently there is no evidence to support claims about the presence of or assistance for freedom seekers.[17]

Freedom Seekers in Northeastern Illinois

Freedom seekers came to the Chicago region along many different routes. Most came by traveling up the Illinois River valley, overland from the Mississippi River valley, and near and through the towns of Cairo, Chester, Alton, Quincy, Galena, and innumerable smaller places. Some came north overland through Indiana, some by foot, horseback, and stagecoach from Iowa and Wisconsin, and some, starting in the mid-1850s, by train. Throughout, the vast majority came from Missouri, Kentucky, and Tennessee. A limited number came up the Mississippi River valley from Louisiana, Mississippi, Alabama, and Arkansas. Some records mention travelers who were originally enslaved in Virginia and the Carolinas, and there are a few stories of freedom seekers

Map I.1. Many freedom seekers traveled up the Mississippi and Illinois
River valleys, coming to settle in northeastern Illinois and Chicago
or onward to Detroit and Canada. A small number traveled overland
from Iowa and the more northern parts of the Mississippi River, and
some came directly north overland from the Ohio River valley.

traveling across the South from southeastern states. The broad sweep of movement from the "Slave States" into Illinois in 1850 (see Map I.1) followed patterns of movement established by freedom seekers traveling into northeastern Illinois in the 1820s, 1830s, and 1840s. Starting in 1852, some traveled on to Detroit by train and after 1854 some were on trains coming to Chicago.

In the decades before the Civil War, around 3,000 to 4,500 freedom seekers came through northeastern Illinois. This estimate has been developed over the past twenty years based on stories and journeys identified in research and the figure is congruent with references in accounts about abolitionist activists. This figure accounts for freedom seekers traveling through Chicago and northeastern Illinois; nationally, 35,000 to 50,000 persons found freedom through the Underground Railroad, with most of these freedom seekers traveling to Canada. In May of 1851, the Canadian-based newspaper *Voice of the Fugitive* estimated that before the passage of the Fugitive Slave Act, "there was about 30,000 colored persons in Canada more or less, at least 20,000 of whom were fugitives from slavery," with an additional 4,000 to 5,000 in the months since the law's passage. In 1864, the federal government issued *The Refugees from Slavery in Canada West, Report of the Freedmen's Inquiry Commission*, which looked closely at conditions in Canada and suggested that "according to the most careful estimates," there were between 30,000 and 40,000 what the report identified as "exiles," that is, freedom seekers, in Canada. Some current historians suggest movement in a range from one thousand to several thousand migrants per year from 1830 through 1860–61, roughly 30,000 to 50,000 in total. All these estimates, of course, do not reflect the unknown, tragic number of freedom seekers who struck north, only to be captured, returned and reenslaved.[18]

Over time, a significant number of freedom seekers in Illinois saw themselves as refugees, remaining in Chicago due to a relatively open and safe environment. For others, temporary safety in the Chicago region served as the base for then heading to Canada. From northeastern Illinois, the major goal for many was Detroit, where movement to Canada was relatively easy. There were significant bases for support both in Detroit and in settlements across the Detroit River in Ontario, Canada. Most freedom seekers traveled overland from northeastern Illinois through northwest Indiana and southern Michigan to reach Detroit. Starting in the late 1830s, some left Chicago and other Lake Michigan towns for passage on vessels going to Detroit. After the mid-1850s, travel by train was of growing importance to freedom seekers,

Map I.2. Freedom seekers traveled in two streams of movement through
northeastern Illinois: by roads paralleling and in the I&M Canal corridor
to and through Chicago and by following the Sauk Trail corridor
across Will and southern Cook Counties.

especially for those traveling to Chicago from Cairo, other Illinois towns, and
Iowa, and those going on from Chicago to Detroit (see Map I.2).

From the early 1830s, Black residents of Chicago were providing aid to
freedom seekers. Young white families joined in these efforts by 1838. Communications across northeastern Illinois grew rapidly in the early 1840s, and
by this time, they were self-identified as the Underground Railroad. In Chicago, starting in the mid-1840s, the work of receiving, assisting, and sending
freedom seekers on their way or settling them in the city was led in large measure by leaders in the African American community. After 1845, the work of
white and Black activists in Illinois was at times parallel and at other times,
integrally related. From the late 1840s into 1861 and the Civil War years, because of their common work, there were growing biracial collaborations and
enduring friendships across racial lines, especially in Chicago.

In examining the movement of freedom seekers and the evolution of the networks of the Underground Railroad, it is useful to see some broad distinctions as to who was involved. By the 1850s, a significant number, probably a majority, of people living in northern Illinois were broadly "antislavery." They did not want to deal with slavery; it was an aspect of Southern life some distance from them, and there was a growing sense of the immorality of it all. Within that number, some who pushed to respond through political and church-based organizing became "abolitionists," that is, they were ready to publicly oppose the basic immorality and worked to "abolish slavery." Among those who were motivated by political and religious purposes, a very small number chose to challenge the system and were willing to break the law. This small number were the activists of the Underground Railroad. Across Illinois, a number of abolitionist leaders were assumed to be directly involved but were not. Everyone fully understood the illegality of providing aid. Some, when confronted with critical needs related to specific freedom seekers, provided direct assistance, but overwhelmingly, those in the abolitionist movement were supporting changes in the laws and were not themselves breaking them. However, particularly after the Civil War, those with abolitionist sentiments were often identified as activists based on very thin evidence.

As stories of the Underground Railroad grew in the latter part of the nineteenth century and have continued to the present day, the work was often characterized as being conducted in great secrecy and this perspective was applied to activity in the Chicago region. Yet, across northern Illinois, the Underground Railroad was a relatively public process. Perhaps the stories of secret hiding places, tunnels, and collaborations kept deeply hidden were experienced in other parts of Illinois and in other states. However, in Chicago and northern Illinois, in large part because of broad-based abolitionist sentiments by the 1850s, activists needed to be discrete but not totally secretive. Stories in the Chicago region are compelling enough and it is a distraction to force romanticized images of the situation.

At the national level, the railroad imagery, and the language of "conductors," "lines," and "stations" imposed a kind of order and organization where it rarely existed. From the late 1830s, writing about the Underground Railroad used this railroad language but also usually noted that it was never really so formal. Those involved with and reacting to the movement of freedom seekers picked up on the most compelling new language of the day, the new technologies and terms associated with the coming of the railroads.[19]

Although it is helpful to leave behind the notions of specific routes and regular schedules, it is also important to note that by the 1850s in Illinois, collaboration among those assisting freedom seekers was well-developed. These networks were in place because of common interests and communication of white activists through antislavery societies and Congregational churches and because of connections between Black activists through African Methodist Episcopal and Baptist churches and occasional "colored conventions." Looking back on the accounts of these networks and the descriptions of journeys taken, clearly some stage and coach roads and rail lines can be accepted as "routes." However, these are best seen as corridors of passage that, in differing ways over time, connected farms and settlements where freedom seekers found assistance.

Along with the concentration on routes and regularity, popular perceptions traditionally reinforced assertions that the Underground Railroad was almost totally the work of courageous antislavery men, with a clear implication that this meant "white" men. The crucial activities of people of African descent, in Chicago and other communities across the state, were simply not reported. As an example, *Waller's History of Illinois*—used by thousands of Illinois school children in the first two decades of the twentieth century—briefly explained the Underground Railroad and some of its routes, and it added, "The engineers, conductors, brakemen and station agents upon these lines were God-fearing men, who had the courage of their convictions." Several years earlier, Rufus Blanchard, a prolific writer on Illinois and Midwest history, reflected this image of the power and "righteousness" of the workers of the Underground Railroad. He wrote about the leading white activists, noting that their work was "subtle and determined" and they labored "under the palladium of justice." Frederick Francis Cook noted in 1910 that he looked carefully at the work of the Underground Railroad in Chicago and identified twelve white men as those who ran it.[20]

Particularly after 1845, crucial, central leadership was provided by people of African descent in Chicago. This leadership was a continuation of the aid provided by Black residents from the very beginnings of Chicago and across the state. In addition, wives, daughters, and other women, in both white and Black families and communities, were deeply involved with the work of the Underground Railroad. It is obvious that the work of men needed practical collaboration with their wives and families. They were often opening their homes to visitors, changing work and family schedules, and providing food and clothing. The research presented here also includes examples of women directly engaging with slave catchers and providing direct assistance to freedom seekers. This is particularly true of the work of African American women and the traditions of the "Big Four" women based at Quinn Chapel in Chicago. Along with identifying women who provided aid, the present work gives, whenever it is known, the names of the enslaved men and women involved in the decisions and journeys to freedom and of the husbands and wives involved in providing aid.[21]

Along with understanding the role of both women and men in providing aid, it is highly important to recognize the now profoundly outdated "celebration" of the work of white abolitionists in the 1870s, which focuses on the roles of those assisting and casts freedom seekers as passive passengers. Again and again, the actual details of events in Illinois and elsewhere tell of freedom seekers arriving on their own, moving on after some assistance, and otherwise managing their own passages to freedom.

In examining the Illinois stories, we know more and more about individual journeys to freedom. Thus, research and storytelling about the Underground Railroad can center more fully on the decisions and actions of freedom seekers coming to, settling in, moving through, and leaving areas outside of the slave states. By moving beyond details about the "conductors," it is possible to recover many of these stories and enrich our understanding of the deeply human dimensions of this part of our national American history.

In addition, the movement of freedom seekers and the networks of the Underground Railroad have often been seen in static images. Frequently, one particular story and its unique dynamics in movement and forms of assistance are seen as a kind of example that lasted over time. Yet, engagement with the Underground Railroad had great fluidity. Activity in Illinois took different forms over time. It may also be useful to see that experiences in Illinois were roughly paralleled by activities in Indiana, Michigan, and Wisconsin. Similar patterns emerged in Iowa and Kansas. However, in Ohio and in places further east, the movement of freedom seekers and the growth of the networks of the Underground Railroad were different and began significantly earlier.

As this book explores the movement of freedom seekers and the networks of the Underground Railroad, it reveals significant changes in journeys and encounters over time. The following chapters explore:

Chapter 1, "Slavery and Freedom in Illinois, 1800–1838," covers a period of state formation and the emergence of early communities, during which freedom seekers acted on their own and received spontaneous assistance from individuals and settlements. Black settlements like Rocky Ford, Brooklyn, and New Philadelphia developed and provided direct assistance. Encountering freedom seekers in predominantly white farming regions and small towns encouraged those holding antislavery opinions to organize, provide aid, and form antislavery societies. The small Black community in Chicago provided assistance to freedom seekers. Young white families connected with each other organizing networks of response.

Chapter 2, "The Underground is Underway, 1839–1844," examines how networks of assistance developed among white abolitionists with the independent movement of freedom seekers and activity in Black communities. Statewide antislavery societies emerged across the Midwest, with a multitude of local groups in Illinois. A very small number of antislavery people were activists in what they were now calling the Underground Railroad. Records from the time began to identify specific freedom seekers and related their journeys and encounters. Chicago had clearly emerged as a "point of refuge" for freedom seekers. The small group of relatively young white abolitionist activists in the city were well organized under the leadership of Dr. Charles and Lousia Dyer and were in regular contact with their counterparts across the region. Working before and congruently with them were individuals in Chicago's initially small Black community.

Chapter 3, "Leaders and Travelers, 1845–1854," looks at how, across the region, the independent movement of freedom seekers led to increasingly organized assistance. The completion of the I&M (Illinois and Michigan) Canal in 1848 expanded the options for movement through the Illinois River valley. In Chicago, there was clear and visible leadership provided by people of color. The work of John and Mary Richardson Jones, the Isbells, the Wagoners, parishioners at Quinn Chapel, and others in the Chicago region connected with the work of other African Americans across Illinois and with white activists. Railroads were completed from Detroit to Chicago and became an option for far more rapid movement toward Canada.

Chapter 4 "Open Secrets and Railroads, 1855–1861," describes a time when support networks across northern Illinois and among Black communities and churches across the state were well established. Along with the membership at Quinn Chapel, families at Zoar Baptist Church were deeply involved. Although independent travel continued, increasing numbers of freedom seekers were moving across the region using rail lines in operation in the late

Map I.3. More than forty locations were places of assistance for freedom seekers traveling through northeastern Illinois.

1850s, coming into Chicago and on to Detroit. Although the activity of slave catchers had always impacted freedom seekers and the work of the Underground Railroad, by the late 1850s, organized kidnapping bands were working out of St. Louis and in southern Illinois. These activities, at times, brought national attention to the movement of freedom seekers to Chicago.

The epilogue summarizes the later life of some of the key freedom seekers introduced through the earlier chapters. The first appendix provides data on population patterns in northeastern Illinois. The second appendix presents an overview of sites related to freedom seekers and the Underground Railroad.

Northeastern Illinois reaches from LaSalle County and Boone County on the western border to the Indiana state line on the east. Livingstone County and part of Iroquois County are its southern section and the Wisconsin border is its northern edge. In the decades before the Civil War, the population of the region was overwhelmingly white, with a noticeable Black population in only a few districts by 1860.

In northeastern Illinois, at least forty communities and locations have verifiable and probable sites reflecting the movement of freedom seekers and the activities of Illinois residents providing aid (see Map 1.3). Several traditional sources suggest close to ninety additional sites across the rest of the state. To date, only a handful of sites are fully researched and publicized. The National Park Service Network to Freedom program has Underground Railroad site reports on activity in around twenty-five Illinois communities.[22]

Historical research has come a long way since the ground-breaking work in Larry Gara's *The Liberty Line: The Legend of the Underground Railroad*, published in 1961, along with his criticisms of research on the Underground Railroad in Illinois. His warnings about the ways in which stories of assistance were romanticized and enlarged continue to be important. However, these pages use a range of source materials for a much fuller picture of the stories and journeys of freedom seekers and the white and Black individuals and families who aided them. Building on the work of so many others, this book is an effort to explore the northeastern Illinois and Chicago chapters of this American story.[23]

CHAPTER ONE

Slavery and Freedom in Illinois, 1800–1838

Claiborn and Charity

IN 1822, A MARRIED couple, Claiborn and Charity, were living just outside Florence, Alabama, enslaved by the Jackson family. As was the case for many enslaved people across the South, this young couple chose their own liberation. When leaving their place of bondage and heading north, they had the advantage of a nearby river.

The Tennessee River played a unique role in the movement of freedom seekers to Illinois. From its origins in the mountains of eastern Tennessee, it flowed southwest to a place that became Florence, Alabama, then turned north through Tennessee and Kentucky to join the Ohio at the southern edge of Illinois. For freedom seekers with access to the Tennessee River, as with the Cumberland River, it was possible to go "down river" and thus be moving "up north!" The uniqueness of these waterways meant that from the earliest days of settlement in northwest Alabama and western Tennessee, there were runaways heading north toward Illinois. This path is reflected in "fugitive slave notices" published in the newspapers of southern Illinois during the 1820s and after.

By 1820, James Jackson, with his wife and young children, had settled in northwest Alabama. By 1840, this white family was prosperous, with significant land holdings and eighty-six slaves. They obviously attended to their financial interests, as is reflected in an 1822 attempt to recover lost property. An advertisement in the *Illinois Gazette*, published in Shawneetown in southern Illinois, demonstrates their sense that freedom seekers would head north into Illinois and eventually move through the Chicago region. In November of 1822, the *Gazette* published Jackson's announcement that these two slaves ran away:

Claiborn is a very likely negro man, about 5 feet 10 or 11 inches high, re-markably well made, his features formed more like those of a white man than a negro, has a rather down look and is slow spoken, he is an intelligent cunning fellow; ...

Charity is a small yellow wench, very well formed, about 26 or 28 years of age, very light complexion, long Black hair and teeth; ... I am inclined to think they will push for those free states, and probably descend the Ten-nessee River.

Jackson reported that the two had stolen horses, which returned, most likely after Claiborn and Charity reached the river and let them loose. He also offered a reward of $200 plus expenses for their capture and return.[1]

Early Freedom Seekers in Illinois

As indicated in the story of Claiborn and Charity, newspaper notices seeking fugitives, along with sheriffs' notices about persons captured and held, were common in the early newspapers of Illinois. Hundreds were published in the 1820s and 1830s.

Ran away from the subscriber, at the town of Illinois [East St. Louis], op-posite St. Louis, about the 1st of August last, a mulatto woman, known by the name of Harriet Hewlett, between 40 and 45 years of age, marked by the small pox, and has the appearance of an Indian.
—Kaskaskia, IL, *Western Intelligencer*, October 7, 1820[2]

Ran away from the subscriber, living in Overton County, Tennessee, ... a mulatto slave named Elijah, about 30 years of age, near 6 feet high, low forehead, crooked nose and well made, a house carpenter by trade.... It is expected he will make for Illinois somewhere.
—Shawneetown *Illinois Gazette*, November 17, 1821[3]

A negro man, who calls himself Wilson Thomas. He seems to be about 30 years old, of a sour aspect, about 5 feet 6 or 8 inches high, has a large scar on his forehead, of a dark mulatto complexion, has on a tolerable good fashionable fur hat, a linsey roundabout coat and vest, a blue pair of cloth pantaloons. He has with him various papers, which are no doubt spurious; one of them contains directions from Florence, Alabama, to Detroit.
—Shawneetown *Illinois Gazette*, March 13, 1830[4]

Fig. 1.1 "A Slave Hunt." So captioned in Johnson, *From Dixie to Canada*.

Other advertisements include one from November of 1829 concerning a "Black man named Mingo," running from Tuscaloosa, Alabama, who crossed into Illinois at the mouth of the Tennessee several months earlier.[5] Another ran from St. Louis, a man who worked at the "confectionery business and may pass for a pastry cook," with forged papers heading for Canada in September 1831.[6]

Freedom seekers like these moved northward into Illinois after crossing the Mississippi or Ohio River. For those coming from Kentucky, Tennessee, Mississippi, and Alabama, downriver passage on the Tennessee or Cumberland River was a strong option. As with the Tennessee, the Cumberland flowed from eastern Kentucky southwest into Tennessee, and, beyond Nashville, it turned north through Kentucky to meet the Ohio across from the southern edge of Illinois. The northward flow of each of these rivers was a useful conduit for freedom seekers heading in that direction (see Figure 1.1).

As it was used in the journey of Claiborn and Charity, the Tennessee River was used in 1828 by a young couple, Orange and Russey. He was twenty-two, escaping with his wife aged eighteen or nineteen. Their owner, living south of Florence, Alabama, described her as "a dark mullato; round full face; rather inclined to be fleshy; she never had a child; of a middle size, she left home dressed in a white cotton homespun frock." The advertisement has an almost reluctant quality. Benjamin Harris wrote that he had personally raised these two, always thought of them as his confidential servants, and, thus, he treated them "more like children than slaves." He wrote "there has been no difference or threats of any kind, therefore, they must have meditated the plan of leaving me some time before they started, and I suppose their intention must be to get to some of the free states, and if so, their most easy mode of travelling will be, by water down the Tennessee River to the Ohio."[7]

The fugitive slave notices and reports from sheriffs in Illinois about runaways held in their custody provide a remarkable glimpse into this movement of people seeking to escape their enslavement. These notices and reports from the early decades of the nineteenth century reflect the fact that from the earliest days, freedom seekers were on the road in Illinois.

Slavery and Resistance in Illinois

From the beginning of European settlement in North America, most people of African descent and some Native Americans were enslaved, living as the

Fig. 1.2 "Fugitive Slave as Advertised for Capture." Schomburg Center for Research in Black Culture, Photographs and Prints Division, New York Public Library.

property of others. Outside the original English colonies, French and Spanish explorers and settlers also held Africans and Native peoples in bondage. Enslavement occurred in European settlements along the Mississippi including in what became Illinois. A French missionary visiting Illinois Country (southwestern Illinois along the Mississippi) wrote in 1750, "We have here Whites, Negroes, and Indians, to say nothing of cross-breeds ... perhaps eleven hundred whites, three hundred Blacks, and some sixty red slaves or savages." The French were counted as "souls" and Black people and Native Americans were counted as slaves. In the 1760s, close to three thousand people, of whom 30 percent were enslaved, were stretched along this region in the bottomlands of the Mississippi River. However, by the conclusion of the French and Indian War in 1763, rather than live with English rule, many free persons migrated with their enslaved people to New Orleans and other locales. By the beginning of the nineteenth century, as Americans were looking west toward the Mississippi River valley, there were only around 1,600 non-Native residents in what would become Illinois, with 600 of these enslaved.[8]

Even in these early days, there were reports of individual freedom seekers in Illinois. In the early interaction with these self-liberating travelers, assistance generally grew out of spontaneous reactions to being confronted by men, women, and families escaping oppression.

These early encounters were affected by the controversies and legislation that established the United States. Along with other crucial matters, the Founding Fathers fiercely debated the range of issues concerning the ownership of some human beings by others. The new national Constitution, adopted in 1787 and ratified by the states in 1789, muted the dilemma of slavery in America. Through the 1790s and into the nineteenth century, the issue was set to the side; a union of the states would not have been possible without so doing. Slavery was shrinking in the northern states; the far southern states found it essential; and the middle states struggled, marked especially by deep debates in Virginia. An extension of the American commitment that "all men were created equal" did not happen; the commitment did not extend to women, nor to the original inhabitants of the land, and certainly not to people of color.[9]

After extensive negotiations, the Constitution had mandated the end of the external slave trade (without calling it that) by 1807 and created that peculiar compromise that for purposes of enumeration for public life and office, "those bound in service" counted as three-fifths of a person. In addition, anyone "held to service" in one state could not be "discharged from such service" if they reached another state, but rather, "shall be delivered up." Beyond this indirect language—indirect but understood by all—the document was silent, and the question of slavery would be left to following generations. Into the 1830s, the resolution of "Negro servitude" would be a constant yet unresolved, and to a large extent unspoken, paradox.[10]

Parallel to the adoption for the Constitution was the creation of legislation related to the Northwest Territory. This region was the huge tract to the northwest of the Ohio River, and included what became Illinois, Ohio, Indiana, Michigan, Wisconsin, and part of Minnesota. The Congress of the Confederation passed legislation in 1787 organizing this land as the Northwest Territory; it was confirmed under the new Constitution and fully adopted in 1789. The territory, north of the Ohio River and west to the Mississippi, included claims to land control by various eastern states; all these claims were ceded to the central government.

The Ordinance for the Northwest Territory prohibited slavery. Article VI stated that there would be "neither slavery nor involuntary servitude" in this vast territory. However, led by representatives of Virginia, the ceding of state claims came with the recognition that existing residents could retain existing rights and possessions. Along the Mississippi River, in Illinois Country, "existing possessions" included maintaining the ownership of slaves. In fact, the governor of the Northwest Territory held that Article VI was intended to halt the introduction of slaves into the territory, not to eliminate or free those already held in bondage.[11]

The reality and practice of slavery in Illinois Country was reenforced by this founding document as it held that any persons who escaped to the territory from one of the original states could be "lawfully reclaimed." As with the Constitution, this national legislation supported the notion of "fugitive recovery," that is, that "runaway slaves" were to be returned (see Figure 1.2).[12]

Several years later, the Fugitive Slave Act of 1793 helped make the national compromise official. Using specific language, the Law directed that fugitives could be apprehended and returned to their home states and local police officials were to assist in the process. Providing some sense of balance with the Fugitive Slave Act, the next major piece of national legislation regarding slavery moved in the other direction. In January of 1808, following the directive of the Constitution, Congress voted to officially ban the slave trade coming to the United States.[13]

As the Illinois population grew, so did the controversies over slavery. The economic value of slaves continued to be protected under the language and varying conditions related to "indentured servants." In the early years of the nineteenth century, the Indiana Territory adopted a series of laws for what would become Indiana and Illinois that defined the relations of "masters" and "servants" and severely limiting and denying a range of rights for people of color. These became the basis for the enduring "Black Laws" or "Black Codes" of Illinois.[14]

However, as the movement for statehood gained momentum in 1816–17, leaders realized the need for some compromise to protect the status quo yet gain approval for statehood by Congress. It was clear that Illinois could not be admitted to the Union as a slave state. Ohio rejected slavery when admitted in 1814, and Indiana provided for the freeing of slaves when admitted in 1816. The Illinois compromise was reflected in the state's Constitution of 1818.

In Article VI, the new state Constitution held in the first section that "Neither slavery nor involuntary servitude shall hereafter be introduced, otherwise than for the punishment of crimes. . . ." In the second section it stated that "slaves bound in other States shall not be hired for service in Illinois, except (until the year 1825) within the district of the salt works near Shawneetown." The third section provided that indentures established before 1818 were protected for their full terms. Thus, the "Black Laws" of territorial days were maintained and the compromise was sufficient to allow Congress to act for admission of Illinois in late 1818. [15]

However, proslavery interests led in the next year to further "refinements." Persons identified as "negro or mulatto" could only reside in the state if they had a certificate of freedom attested to and filed with their county of residence. Selling or transferring a contract of ownership was permitted. If an owner wished to free a person, they had to post a bond of $1000. It was a felony to assist a runaway or to block the actions of an owner seeking to regain their property. Any person of color without the right certificate could be arrested, detained, and publicly sold. In addition, there were a variety of details related to causes for whipping, and it was against the laws of Illinois to bring a person of color into the state with the intent of freeing them. Thus, although Illinois was a "free" state, conditions were still brutal for people of color.[16]

It is probable that, in the days before statehood, some persons held in slavery in the Illinois Country sought their freedom by choosing to live with

Native American peoples. Around 1819–20, the first mention of freedom seekers receiving aid was noted in Bond County in southern Illinois, where a group of antislavery families, mostly Quakers, had moved to, coming from Brown County in Ohio.[17]

In the spring of 1819, Edward Coles journeyed with a contingent of seventeen enslaved people from his family's home in Virginia to new land outside Edwardsville in Illinois. These enslaved people were Ralph and Kate Crawford, with four children; Robert Crawford and his sister Polly; Thomas Cobb and Nancy Gaines; and Manuel and Sukey, with five children. While traveling by flat boat down the Ohio River, in April 1819, Coles granted freedom to all with the hope that they would continue with him to this new land, where he intended also to give them individual land parcels. Accounts indicate that they accepted and, with proper documentation from Coles, settled into Illinois as "free people of color." Their land was near his, east of Edwardsville. These families made a total of seventeen free Black people living in Madison County in 1820. They formed the community known as Pin Oak. It is very likely that they provided support for the movement of freedom seekers through that part of the state. Coles became Governor of Illinois in 1822 and thereafter played a key role in maintaining the antislavery momentum in Illinois.[18]

The issues over slavery came to a head in a bitterly fought contest to call a state constitutional convention in 1824. Proslavery interests wanted to change the state's constitution so that Illinois would permanently allow slave ownership. This possibility grew with the national conversation about allowing the admittance of Missouri into the Union as a slave state, as Illinois shared a long boundary with that state. In Illinois at the time, essentially all the settled population was in the southern part of the state. Many came west from southern states and settled in the southern counties. Settlers from northern states and European countries were further north along the Mississippi and in the eastern counties.

In reaction to the call for the convention, some of the earliest organizations opposing slavery in Illinois emerged. The St. Clair (County) Society for the Prevention of Slavery in Illinois was organized in 1823 by a minister from Connecticut. Some distance to the north, in 1824, the Morganian Society formed in Morgan County. It proudly published its intent "to promote the public good, by using all honorable means to prevent the introduction of slavery into this state." Both societies were, in effect, preabolitionist, seeking more to keep slavery out of Illinois than to see its demise.[19]

In 1824, a significant part of southern Illinois was made up of counties where slavery already existed or where slave owning would be tolerated. However, the final vote was 4,072 for and 6,640 against holding the convention (see Figure 1.3). The question of "legalizing" slavery in Illinois dropped from the public agenda following this vote. Even though far-southern Illinois would retain its "Southern" orientation, it was clear that the state's future was as a free state. In the struggle to defeat the call for the convention, Governor Coles played an essential role. Two of his strongest public supporters were Warren Hooper, editor of the *Spectator*, Illinois' first antislavery newspaper, and William Hubbard Brown, a journalist in the state. Both Hooper and Brown eventually moved to Chicago and became part of the networks of the Underground Railroad as it emerged in northeastern Illinois in the late 1830s.[20]

The controversies over the question of slavery reflected a north-south tension in Illinois. Just as the counties in the "northern" part of southern Illinois were settled by families predominantly from New England and New York, the actual northern part of the state would be settled by the "Yankees" from these states. As the issues around slavery intensified over the decades, so did the animosity.

Following the controversies of 1824, the first clearly antislavery group formed in Lofton's Prairie (now the small community of Dow) in Jersey County, northwest of Alton and several miles from the Mississippi. At meeting of this group, which was created in 1830, Owen Lovejoy gave one of his first antislavery speeches. Lovejoy went on to play a public role in the 1840s and into the Civil War years as a congressman and radical abolitionist in Princeton, Illinois. By 1836, the Lofton's Prairie group expanded to become the Jersey County Anti-Slavery Society. Citizens of Adams County, mostly within the Mississippi river town of Quincy, created their society in 1836.[21]

Elijah Parrish Lovejoy (Owen's brother) was a Presbyterian minister and newspaper editor. In 1834, he began writing editorials in the St. Louis *Observer*, taking increasingly strong positions against slavery. Through his experiences in Missouri, with efforts related to legislation, court cases, and interactions with other Presbyterian leaders, he became decidedly abolitionist in his writing, speaking, and preaching. After three printing presses were destroyed by proslavery mobs, he moved across the Mississippi. He started the Alton *Observer* as an abolitionist paper, and in July 1837, he published a call for a gathering of antislavery advocates from across Illinois. This led to the Illinois

The Black Counties went for Slavery, while the White Counties were for Freedom. Johnson County was a tie.

(Map shows counties as they were in 1824.)

Fig. 1.3 For and Against Slavery in Illinois. Smith, *Student's History of Illinois*.

Anti-Slavery Congress meeting at the end of October of that year. Most of the delegates were from central and southern Illinois and included only six delegates from the northern part of Illinois, two from LaSalle County and four from Will County. Tragically, less than two weeks after this first state-wide meeting, on November 7, 1837, Elijah Lovejoy was killed in a mob that was seeking to again destroy his press.[22]

Spurred in part by the work of Elijah Lovejoy, in 1837, societies were founded in Putnam County, on the Illinois River, and in Madison County, with Alton on the Mississippi River. Earlier in that year, in February, the Will County Anti-Slavery Society organized as the first formal society in north-eastern Illinois.[23]

By the end of 1837, these and other antislavery groups grew across northern Illinois and other parts of the state. Especially in northern Illinois, most who had recently settled had come from New England and New York and a good number of these settlers held some level of commitment to antislavery ideas. In those years, this generally meant opinions, opposed to the expansion of slavery beyond the South into new territories. Over time, a growing number also became abolitionists, that is, opposed to the existence of slavery itself. These groups, formed by white farmers and townspeople, were in part shaped by their encounters with freedom seekers journeying through and, on occasion, seeking help. Their antislavery opinions were challenged and strengthened by direct engagement with the protection and movement of these self-liberated travelers. Across the state and in northeastern Illinois, much of this activity focused within and among white congregations. Most of these were Congregationalists, but there were also folks involved from Methodist, Presbyterian, and Baptist churches.[24]

Early Black Communities

From the 1820s onward, people escaping from chattel slavery moved north into and through Illinois, and European Americans and African Americans who were "free people of color" provided information and direct assistance for these people of courage. Northern Illinois was seen as a hotbed of abolitionist sentiments, with a small number of people who not only sought the end to slavery but also provided aid for fugitives. By the 1830s, in slave states close to the Mississippi River, there was a developing awareness for both slave owners and enslaved people that , the Chicago region was a destination and a gateway to freedom for those in bondage. Related to the growing notion of Chicago as a goal for travelers, small Black settlements emerged in southern Illinois at Brooklyn, Miller Grove, New Philadelphia, in and near Alton, and in Gallatin County.

In 1829, a group of free and enslaved persons moved from St. Louis across the Mississippi to start the community of Brooklyn, Illinois. Eleven families came with Priscilla Baltimore and her husband, John. Born enslaved, Priscilla Baltimore was purchased by a Methodist missionary and eventually paid for her own freedom. She carried a lifelong commitment to church work and with that commitment, developed and maintained a series of relationships across the Mississippi. She was deeply immersed, as were the other settlers of Brooklyn, in connections with both enslaved and free people of color in the St. Louis region. The initial small community that had gathered as "Mother Baltimore's Freedom Village" evolved into the town of Brooklyn, a Black community initiated and sustained by Black leadership. Their community served as a stimulant and passageway for the movement of freedom seekers out of Missouri and into Illinois. "Mother Baltimore" has been referred to the "Moses of the West" in recognition of the parallel with Harriet Tubman regarding her success with supporting fugitives.[25]

In her work, Mother Baltimore was sustained, in part, by ongoing contact with Rev. William Paul Quinn. He was the remarkable missionary traveler for the African Methodist Episcopal (AME) Church across the Midwest. Working with Baltimore, Quinn organized in Brooklyn the first African Methodist Episcopal Church in Illinois in the late 1830s. Over time, through the creation of congregations by the AME Church, Brooklyn was linked to other Black settlements in Illinois leading to Chicago. Quinn's work developing and connecting AME congregations was so significant that not only was the Brooklyn church named to honor him, but also the historic Chicago congregation adopted the name "Quinn Chapel".[26]

Roughly forty miles to the north of Brooklyn, Black families settled both north and south of Alton, which was a major gateway into Illinois. In 1839, Quinn worked with families to create the Lower Alton African Methodist Episcopal Church and formed a congregation in Rocky Ford, several miles north of Alton. There may have been freedom seekers in the area of Rocky Ford from 1816 forward. In addition, by 1836 there were Black Baptist congregations in Alton and Upper Alton. Through these congregations and mutual interests, the families and individuals settling in these communities were well-known to one another; these connections were invaluable as they responded to the needs of freedom seekers passing through. Records related to these communities reinforce the understanding that freedom seekers were assisted and directed toward Chicago through the 1830s. Key leaders in Chicago's Black community in the late 1840s included the families of John and Mary Jones, Henry and Ailey Bradford, and Lewis and Margaret Isbell. The three women were sisters and earlier lived in Alton in the family of Elijah and Diza Richardson.[27]

Located near the Ohio River and some thirty miles north of Paducah, Kentucky, the community of Miller Grove grew with the arrival of Black families in the 1840s. Cheryl LaRoche has carefully argued to see this place, as with Brooklyn, Alton, and Rocky Ford, as a location of support for freedom seekers. The connections of these Black communities, particularly through families, churches, and lived experience with enslavement, supports their engagement as initial networks of the Underground Railroad.[28]

In 1830, Frank and Lucy McWorter, with four of their children, left Kentucky and moved to Illinois. "Free Frank," as he was known, established a farm in Pike County in western Illinois and, in 1836, created the community of New Philadelphia. Their oldest son, Frank, Jr., had escaped to Canada years earlier and returned to join his parents in Pike County. Their community was located on a main road from the Mississippi River at a point across from Hannibal, Missouri, going east toward Jacksonville and Springfield. One of the remarkable examples of a set of towns founded across the country in the nineteenth century by African Americans, New Philadelphia grew as a biracial community, becoming predominantly Black in the 1860s. From here, freedom seekers were regularly directed north toward Chicago and, on occasion, were accompanied by members of the family.[29]

Along with his entrepreneurial endeavors in farming, stock raising, and land speculation, Frank was systematic in establishing all the legal details as to the free status of his family. Over a period of forty years, he purchased freedom for himself and fifteen members of his family. They had success in this frontier environment but took great care to protect their personal papers, particularly to guard against the dangers of their being kidnapped by slavecatchers.[30]

According to family tradition, Frank and Lucy also were deliberate about preparing to assist others and created a place to conceal fugitives in even their first cabin. Building on his own experience of fleeing to Canada, Frank, Jr., along with his three brothers occasionally assisted freedom seekers on their journeys. From western Illinois, their overland travel brought them north through the Illinois River valley. This took them to the Sauk Trail, an ancient path from the Mississippi River near Rock Island that reached eastward across Illinois, northwest Indiana, and southern Michigan to Detroit. From Will County, travelers could head northeast to Chicago or continue east into Indiana.

In addition to providing shelter and food support for freedom seekers on their way north, there is a strong family tradition that New Philadelphia residents also provided shoes for the journey. With the guidance of Frank and Lucy, New Philadelphia continued as part of the network of assistance reaching to Chicago. Frank died in 1854, but Lucy and their children persisted. Lucy lived there until 1870.[31]

In addition to these small communities engaging in assisting freedom seekers, Gallatin County, adjacent to the Ohio River, engaged in similar actions. The salt works on the Saline River were specifically identified in the constitution for Illinois that was adopted in 1818 as an area where slavery could continue. However, those enslaved were accompanied by a number of free Black persons in the County. In 1820, there were 267 enslaved persons and 32 free persons; in 1830, 160 and 306; and in 1840, 24 and 671. Given evidence from other parts of Illinois, it is highly likely that the large number of free Black persons meant there was a significant amount of activity in support of freedom seekers traveling through Gallatin County. South of Gallatin, Pope County, also across the Ohio River from Kentucky, had African American permanent residents likely to be helpful. The potential that there was assistance being given by these Black communities is supported by the large number of fugitive slave notices published in Shawneetown's *Illinois Gazette* in the 1820s and 1830s, some of which were seen earlier in this chapter. Years later, Bejamin Bond, a delegate to the state constitutional convention in 1847, complained about these small colonies of "free negroes" particularly in Gallatin County who help "slaves from the south to escape their masters."[32]

The existence of the community of Quakers in Bond County; the small group of ex-slaves freed by Edward Coles gathered at Pin Oak; the communities of Brooklyn, Rocky Ford, and Miller Grove' the work of the McWorters in New Philadelphia; and Black individuals and families in Alton and in Gallatin and Pope Counties, along with others scattered across the state, marked the beginnings in Illinois of organized efforts to assist freedom seekers traveling into and through the state.

Bordering the slave states of Missouri and Kentucky, the free state of Illinois served increasingly as a beacon for freedom. The southern portion of the state is somewhat like an arrow pointing into the western part of the South, and it is, in fact, further south than most of the state of Virginia. Among those seeking direct access to this free state in 1833 was an enslaved man named William who escaped from St. Louis (just across the Mississippi River from Illinois) with his mother. He wrote later that they traveled close to 150 miles into Illinois basically on their own, with no contacts at all. They ended up going in a giant circle and then, when finally in contact with farmers, they were urged to simply follow the roads north toward Chicago. Soon they were captured.[33]

Upon their return, his mother was sold, placed with a large group of other enslaved people on a steamboat, and carried down river to be sold for work on plantations. Within a year, William again sought escape while he worked on a steamboat on the Ohio River, which led to a friendship with a Quaker in Ohio who helped him travel north to Canada. He was so grateful for the assistance, he adopted the man's name, becoming William Wells Brown. He spent time in the region around Buffalo assisting freedom seekers into Canada and writing his autobiography, which was published in 1847 and soon well-known in abolitionist circles. A profile writer throughout his life, in 1852, he published an account of his three years traveling in Europe, and in 1853 wrote the first known and widely published novel by an African American.

In the 1850s, William Wells Brown was one of several successful Black lecturers in Great Britain seeking funds in support of abolitionists in the United States. Along with similar efforts by Henry "Box" Brown and J. C. A. Smith, Wells Brown created and carried large-scale, dramatic, full-color "panoramas," described as "illustrated presentations containing a series of scenes portraying slave life. Panoramas used by the two Browns were particularly effective because they included scenes of their own escapes."[34] In 1850, Wells Brown had artists in London create a lengthy canvas: a full-color rolling diorama with twenty-four scenes. This panorama included dramatic images of the horrors of slavery, with four of the scenes reflecting incidents in his life, all of which were unrolled behind him on stage as he told his story. He wrote a forty-eight-page pamphlet describing the scenes, and the sales of these pamphlets added to the income generated from his tours.

In the images accompanying his speeches, two scenes reflected dramatic moments in his efforts at escape through Illinois. The seventeenth picture in the panorama was a view of St. Louis from across the Mississippi River, with a dramatic image of a riverboat on fire and two figures in a small boat—William and his mother seeking their escape.[35] Two scenes later was a greatly enlarged copy of a drawing used in his *Narrative of William W. Brown, a Fugitive Slave, Written by Himself*.[36] In this scene, he is with his mother being captured well into Illinois, demonstrating that no fugitive could find security, "until he shall succeed in escaping to Canada."[37]

Across Northeastern Illinois

In the 1820s and 1830s, there were some refugees from slavery living with Native peoples in northern Illinois before they were forced out by the actions of the national government. An extraordinary example is in the story of Black Bob, a well-settled, married member of a LaSalle County Potawatomi community who worked with Rev. Jesse Walker. From northeast of Ottawa to Plainfield, in western Will County, Rev. Walker operated as in itinerant minister with the Potawatomi and encouraged white settlement. Local counties record his work and identify him as the first permanent non-Native settler in the late 1820s. However, he managed because Black Bob, identified as a fugitive slave from Kentucky, was his interpreter and defender and already well placed in the community. Thus, in the region southwest of Chicago, the first "white settler," that is, the first non-Native resident, was a Black man.[38]

A handful of Black people lived across northeastern Illinois in the 1830s. In 1834, two Black women came to Kendall County as "servants" for white families from South Carolina. They were probably enslaved, but in Illinois, they were identified as servants, and they both lived in the county into the 1870s. Parallel to this is the story of a Black man named "Dick" who was well-known across Will County. He was the first permanent Black resident of the county, having lived there as a free person since the mid-1830s.[39]

In 1834, Amos Bennett and his family settled in Lake County, between Chicago and Wisconsin. He was a free person of color who had grown up in Connecticut and then lived in New York State. By 1840 he was married with two children and engaged in farming. Bennett has been clearly recognized as the first original, non-Native settler, and, distinguishing himself from the Native peoples, he asserted that he was "the first white man that ever planted corn" in Lake County.[40]

At the same time, some freedom seekers traveled through the region in the 1830s. They were in contact with Quakers in Putnam County as early as 1831.

This was just to the west of LaSalle County, and these travelers were directed onward to the Chicago region. Another early source notes that one of these Quaker families moved from the abolitionist community in Bond County in 1830, and with them was a freedom seeker as part of their household. In December 1835, two young women from St. Louis, who had escaped earlier in the year, were kidnapped by slave catchers in southwest Wisconsin. Seeking to return them to enslavement in Missouri, the catchers, with their captives, sought lodging with the family of Elijah Smith in Bureau County. Local abolitionists managed to free the women from the slave catchers, and they were taken east, most likely to Chicago and then on to Canada. Soon after establishing their farms in 1835–36, families scattered across Will County, south of Cook County, were in contact with each other as antislavery advocates and were responding to assist travelers. They formed one of the first antislavery societies in Illinois in February of 1837.[41]

Black settlers were part of the small community of Chicago from its beginnings in 1833. In that year, Chicago undertook the first city census, listing 317 white and 33 Black inhabitants. In 1837, a census noted 4,066 residents and identified 77 as "Colored," including 41 males and 36 females. Most had originally lived in Missouri and Kentucky. These earliest Black residents were roughly half families and half single men and women who were often servants connected to a white family. How many were refugees and how many were always free people of color is not certain. Active in this small community was John Johnson, who arrived in 1837 to become Chicago's first Black barber. In 1838, Lewis Isbell, at age twenty, came to Chicago and went to work for Johnson. Isbell was born enslaved in Kentucky in 1818 but came to southern Illinois in 1823 with his master. Upon their arrival, the master gave freedom papers to Isbell and, as Isbell recalled, about three hundred other persons he held in bondage. He carried clear memories of growing up in Paris, Illinois, on the farm of his former enslaver and may have been his son. Isbell was a successful barber and was well acquainted with many in the young city, both Black and white. He helped provide leadership for the Black community for many years (see Figure 1.4). Along with Johnson and Isbell, it is highly likely that most, if not all, of these early Black residents were directly involved with freedom seekers coming on their own into and through Chicago.[42]

The total number of freedom seekers traveling through in these early years is uncertain, but some forms of assistance were underway in Chicago in the 1830s. Although traditionally the first account of aiding a fugitive occurs

Fig. 1.4 Lewis Isbell. Chicago History Museum,
ICHi-022359; Johnson, photographer.

in 1839, runaway slave notices were placed in the Chicago *Democrat* in 1834 and 1835 by St. Louis slave owners, suggesting they knew that although Chicago was gaining a reputation as a place of refuge, it was also a place with others willing to capture and return those seeking to escape. One slave owner in Missouri felt it prudent to advertise in the *Chicago American* in May of 1836, seeking a runaway named Martin who was close to six feet tall and about fifty-three years old. He was described as having "a Black complexion, stout build, uncommon large arms, high forehead, rather hard features; he had had one foot badly burnt, which left a scar." The notice, which carried a $100 reward for Martin, also sought the return of a young companion named Titus, about twenty-five years old, described as "being of a yellow complexion, rather forward, feminine voice." An announcement in the *Chicago Democrat* in 1836 came from an owner in Tennessee who thought the fugitive would head for Missouri or a free state or to "the Indians in Arkansas, to some of the other negroes." Another ad had been placed by the sheriff in Putman County, on the Illinois River, for a "runaway negro man who calls himself William Russell," whom the sheriff had in jail and who claimed to be a free man. This notice first appeared in the *Democrat* in March of 1836 and ran in twelve issues. In October of 1836, a resident of Springfield, Missouri, posted a notice with a reward of fifty dollar for a nineteen-year-old runaway named Telmon, "a tolerable good Blacksmith." Reflecting some lack of success, the same notice was posted the following year, in August 1837, noting this also was carried in the *State Register* in Vandalia; the *Journal* in Springfield; the *Democrat* in Chicago; and the *Salt River Journal.*[43]

In the 1830s, white residents in Chicago and the region were not only seeing fugitive slaves notices in their papers, but very likely, they were coming face-to-face with actual people who had seized their own freedom. These white settlers, most from New England and New York, had perhaps already been antislavery, but now, they began to act on their opinions to oppose slavery. Some in Will County organized their antislavery society in 1837, and late in that year, in Chicago, a group of young white men called a meeting wanting to respond to the shocking death of Elijah Lovejoy. However, in a real sense, this was a kind of "preabolitionist" gathering. Their outrage had more to do with the attack on the freedom of the press and the need to defend this crucial element of public life. Of course, at its heart, the attacks on Lovejoy came from his commitment to challenge the evils of slavery. These young men wanted to take a stand publicly but were uncertain as to the reception for antislavery views in their new home. Years later, a friend of these young men wrote about that first meeting: "It was called to be held in the Saloon building, a small public hall on the corner of Clark and Lake Streets, on the third floor, and the meeting was held not without fears that it would be broken up by a mob. There was an abundance of caution used in the calling and holding of the meeting, to avoid any collision 'with the fellows of a baser sort.' "[44]

This gathering was a step in Chicago becoming a central point for abolition and safety for freedom seekers. Calvin DeWolf recalled years later that it was in these early years that enough new residents from New England and New York had arrived to see the onset of new ideas in business, religion, and politics, including fresh ideas about abolition. However, it appears that at the onset, their new ideas did not include engaging with the small Black community that was directly involved with aid for freedom seekers.[45]

These key men who gathered, with the support and engagement of their wives, would grow old together as central to the white leadership in the fight for the freedom, support for those traveling to and through Chicago, and eventual collaboration with Black leaders. Philo Carpenter, from Massachusetts, arrived in 1832 to find a village with a population of "only about 200."[46] Rev. Flavel Bascom came from Connecticut for the American Missionary Society with his wife Ruth in the summer of 1833. Dr. Charles Volney Dyer and his wife Louisa journeyed from Vermont in 1835, and he was soon serving as a doctor for the military post and investing in local real estate. Calvin DeWolf was in Chicago by October 1837, traveling from Pennsylvania and starting out in teaching and office work as he prepared to work as a lawyer. These four, with a small handful of others, gathered in Chicago to protest the death of Lovejoy and would soon become the base for the initial white networks of the Underground Railroad in Chicago. Carpenter was thirty-two, Bascom was thirty-three, Dyer was twenty-nine, and DeWolf was twenty-two. Although not recorded, it is likely that James H. Collins, J. Young Scammon, and Isaac Arnold attended the meeting and were part of this core of young activists. Collins, thirty-seven, settled in Chicago in 1834; Scammon, twenty-three, in 1835; and Arnold, twenty-four, arrived in 1836.

The Movement of Freedom Seekers

Going beyond Chicago in the 1830s, freedom seekers traveled south through the Calumet region to get around the bottom of Lake Michigan and then moved eastward. The Calumet region, in both Illinois and Indiana at the southern edge of the Lake, includes the watersheds of Lake Calumet and the Little Calumet River. The region was crossed by the major road connecting Chicago to Detroit, and a significant stretch of it followed early Native American trails along the shoreline or inland.

The Detroit-Chicago Road crossed the Little Calumet River about fifteen miles directly south of Chicago, which was then roughly the size of the current city's downtown. It is likely that freedom seekers had contact with three families who had settled on the banks of the Little Calumet: the Matthews, the Osterhoudts, and the Doltons. In 1836, Dolton and Matthews opened a ferry service over the Little Calumet, and the main road from Chicago to Detroit shifted from a lake front route along the beaches to a more inland route crossing the Little Calumet. Within a few years, this was replaced by a toll bridge. Freedom seekers traveled this road as they went toward Chicago from the south or from Chicago to the east, heading for Detroit and Canada. Although these first settlers have not been identified as abolitionists, as with the young activists in Chicago, they came from parts of the country where such sentiment was supported, and they no doubt were approached by freedom seekers at the ferry and bridge.[47]

Freedom seekers moving through northeastern Illinois in these early years shaped the responses that became the Underground Railroad in Illinois. For the most part they traveled on foot, with some assistance from time to time. By 1834, regular steamboat transportation was underway along the southern coast of Lake Michigan, between Chicago and St. Joseph, Michigan, "making only 175 miles land carriage between Chicago and Detroit." It is possible that some freedom seekers obtained passage on these steamboats.[48]

Emerging Networks

In the early years of Illinois's statehood, hundreds of people were enslaved in Illinois, and brutal "Black Laws" limited options for free people of color in the state. These years, however, also saw the evolution in Illinois of arguments about slavery, the rise of abolitionism, and continuing differences in opinion between southern and northern Illinois around such issues and arguments.[49] Integral to all these differing elements was the growth of an antislavery movement in the latter part of the 1830s. White settlers, particularly in northern Illinois, found common commitments, building connections with one another regarding their willingness to aid fugitives. Parallel to this was the emergence of small Black communities and the connections developing between them, particularly through congregations of the African Methodist Episcopal Church and the Wood River Baptist Association. Black activists in Chicago and around the state directly aided freedom seekers. Beyond the possible connections with the families freed by Edward Coles and with the persons living with Quaker families in Bond and Putnam Counties, little evidence exists of any significant ongoing contact or mutual work between Black and white people in the assistance given freedom seekers.

The death of Elijah Lovejoy while defending his press in Alton in 1837 drew a rallying cry for action and response among white abolitionists and their sympathizers across the country. The impact was especially felt throughout Illinois given that many in the state were personally aware of his struggles in St. Louis and then Alton, and they were aware of his call, only a few months before his death, for the formation of the Illinois Anti-Slavery Society. The statewide society held its first formal meeting in Farmington, west of Decatur, in 1838, with ninety-nine delegates. A formal organization did not emerge in Chicago until late in 1839. However, along with these organizational developments, the networks of response that would become the Underground Railroad were emerging within Black communities and, increasingly, among white activists.[50]

CHAPTER TWO

The Underground is Underway, 1839–1844

꙰

John and Eliza Little

EARLY IN 1841, ELIZA and John Little arrived in Queen's Bush, a rural area of southern Ontario about two hundred miles east-northeast of Detroit. They traveled for months after escaping enslavement in western Tennessee (see Map 2.1). In Queen's Bush, they settled in, created a prosperous farm, and, over time, provided leadership for their community and assistance for other freedom seekers arriving from the United States. However, the journey to Queen's Bush had not been easy.

Born in North Carolina, throughout his life, John Little actively resisted his enslavement. On several occasions, he ran away, was captured, sold, and resold. All his life, he carried scars and remnants of a bullet in his body from these early confrontations. His rebellious attitudes and behavior eventually led to his sale to a farmer in western Tennessee, near Jackson. There, he met and fell in love with Eliza, who was working on a nearby farm. Eliza had been born enslaved in Virginia.

In 1840, John and Eliza resolved to seek their freedom and when the timing appeared right, headed north. They followed the northward flow of the Tennessee River, eventually reaching the Ohio River. There, they discovered that dealing with the terrain could be as terrifying as the fear of capture and return. John remembered tying their small traveling parcels on his wife's back, putting her on a log in the water and then pushing her through a swampy area next to the Ohio River. He knew that "Had the log turned right or left, she would have slipped off, and the packs would have sunk her." The whole ordeal was overwhelming for Eliza—she feared drowning, but both she and John deeply understood it was their only option. They would not return to being enslaved.

Map 2.1 The journeys of the Littles and Caroline Quarlls exemplify
the thousands of similar journeys undertaken by freedom seekers
from southern states and especially from Missouri.

After finally crossing the Ohio River, they found themselves just east of
the river town of Cairo. Camped near the riverbank, they were almost discovered by people who were traveling on a riverboat up the Ohio. John and
Eliza were determined to avoid capture and convinced that heading north on
their own was the best option. John remembered: "From Jackson to the Ohio
River was called one hundred and forty miles, – crossed the river to Cairo;

then we footed through Illinois to Chicago; all the way we lay by days and traveled nights."[1]

Traveling up the Illinois River valley and overland west of Springfield, for weeks, they moved by night. When they were north of Springfield, they felt safe enough to travel in daylight, finally reaching Chicago after walking the entire distance—370 miles. There they made contact, most likely with members of Chicago's small Black community, who provided funds to ensure their passage to Detroit. They set out for Detroit, most likely by lake steamer, and then across the river to freedom in Canada.

The Underground Railroad Takes Shape

By 1839, most freedom seekers were coming to northeastern Illinois and Chicago up along the Mississippi River valley, traveling on the river or overland close by. Many were crossing over the Mississippi from Missouri with a few traveling north into Iowa and then east. Still other freedom seekers were coming north across the Ohio River from Kentucky, Tennessee, and the northern parts of Alabama and Mississippi. The towns of Cairo, Chester, Alton, and Quincy, all on the Mississippi, were becoming recognized as destinations and stopping points. Developing networks led through Galesburg and many of the small communities of western Illinois. In some of these places on and near the Mississippi, specific houses and individuals were becoming known as places of safety with people willing to help.[2]

From such places and people, a variety of routes headed north and northeast formed, with many in and near the Illinois River valley. By the end of the 1830s, steamboat travel was well-established on the Illinois River, with regular service from the Mississippi up to Peoria and on to the river towns of La-Salle and Peru. Over the next twenty-five years, this steamboat route would become an increasingly useful option for the movement of freedom seekers.[3]

From early on, Chicago was a significant destination for freedom seekers coming into Illinois. It was in the far north, the point of access to the Great Lakes and beyond to Canada, and had always had a Black community. Slave owners were advertising for runaways in Chicago newspapers throughout the 1830s, and those in Missouri were convinced that "a regular system has been adopted by the abolitionists in Canada," running through Chicago.[4]

Although Chicago was gaining a reputation as a destination and a way station for those heading to Canada, there were also drawbacks for freedom

Table 2.1   The Early Population of Chicago

Year	Total	White	Black
1833	350	317	33
1837	4,066	3,989	77
1840	4,470	4,417	53
1843	7,580	7,515	65

From Census reports and Pierce, *History of Chicago*, 44.

seekers. Of greatest impact was the sheer distance, the need to travel over 350 miles from the southern end of the state. The population of that southern part of the state was predominantly proslavery. They would not assist travelers and would often inform authorities about their presence. Accounts from freedom seekers indicate they did not feel safe about traveling in the daylight until they reached the northern part of the state. In addition, although residents of Chicago became increasingly abolitionist, there continued to be some who supported southern traditions of enslavement and several newspapers in Chicago and the region opposed abolition. Thus, there was not total support from residents favoring the presence of freedom seekers, and there was almost always some share of slave catchers watching for new arrivals and seeking to track down specific persons who escaped their enslavement.

From its first settlement by Du Sable in 1790, the community included people of African descent. Incorporated as a village in 1833, Chicago's population of 350 included 33 residents identified as Black (see Table 2.1). Within ten years, the city has increased to over 7,000 while the recorded Black population was 65. Throughout its history, Chicago included both settled refugees who fled the South and free people of color from the eastern states.

For freedom seekers coming to, settling in, and moving on from Chicago, the emerging Black community was crucial. The traditional record has focused only on the engagement with white residents in the city, but it is crucial to recognize that there were Black residents in Chicago from its earliest days and they were of real assistance to travelers, even if there is scant documentation. There were connections between Black Chicagoans and early Black settlements in Illinois like New Philadelphia, Brooklyn, and those in and near Alton and Gallatin Counties. Members of Chicago's small Black community likely assisted John and Eliza Little as they came through in 1840–41.

The Traditional Chicago Story of 1839

Although freedom seekers were moving through northeast Illinois and Chicago in earlier years, nineteenth- and twentieth-century Chicago historians traditionally began with the claim that the first organized effort to assist a fugitive slave was in 1839. The key player reporting this encounter was Zebina Eastman, who later lived in Chicago.

Eastman played a powerful role among abolitionists and activists throughout the 1840s and 1850s and was for many years the editor of various papers in Chicago that articulated abolitionist positions and reported regularly on activities of the Underground Railroad, especially through his work as editor of the *Western Citizen*. In 1839, Eastman was living in the small town of Lowell in LaSalle County, about ninety miles southwest of Chicago. He had gone there to work with the great abolitionist editor Benjamin Lundy.

The traditional story holds that neighbors brought a "strange, famished, terrified negro, clad in rags and skins" to Eastman who in turn arranged for the man to get to Chicago, passing through Ottawa and Plainfield. In Chicago, he was placed in the hands of Dr. Charles V. Dyer, who was already well-known as a strong abolitionist. After some time, the fugitive was secretly taken to a lake steamer, the *Illinois*, under the command of Capt. Blake, for passage to Canada. Of course, the captain was aware of this, yet also knew he carried several white Southerners on the vessel. A few days into the trip, he made a public show of discovering the fugitive on board and then declared that he would be removed at the first possibility. After reaching the Detroit River, he headed for a port on the Canadian side, had the fugitive dragged from below decks and "kicked him off to freedom."[5]

This is the traditional beginning of a cycle of parallel stories, all with that resonance of the frightened fugitive being delivered to his or her freedom by the courageous white person who stands up to the task. These stories appear, for the most part, to be based on real events, but they have contributed to obscuring the activities of others who assisted and have helped create the images of passive and at times helpless fugitives. All too often, the persons seeking their freedom are framed as simple objects or used as occasions to tell romantic stories of the courage of those giving aid.

Beginnings in Chicago

As explored earlier, freedom seekers were moving to and through Chicago throughout the 1830s, and from the beginning, there was active awareness and assistance from early Black settlers. A small group of African Americans, probably less than 80, were in the Chicago area in the 1830s. The regular 1840 Census noted 53 Black residents in the community of close to 4,500 residents. The drop may reflect the movement of persons on to Canada or other locations, or it suggests that some refugees were prudent in being absent during the count for the local and national census. There are documented stories of other freedom seekers arriving near the time of Zebina Eastman's encounter.

In October 1839, Polly Berry Walsh settled in Chicago after escaping from her enslavement in St. Louis. It is likely that Black residents helped her find a home. Unfortunately, her master, working with slavecatchers, found her there and returned her to St. Louis. Following a series of complex legal battles, Walsh won her freedom in 1843 and moved with her daughter, Lucy, to Quincy, Illinois, in 1845. In response to the efforts to capture Walsh and others, in 1845, the *St. Louis Republican* noted appreciation for the help of Chicago citizens in capturing runaways—it was clear that fanatics in Chicago were willing to "interfere with the property" of Southerners—but the paper's editor lamented that Chicago, like Cincinnati, was becoming a haven for Black people. Such newspaper reports reflected the awareness that an increasing number of fugitives were finding their way to Chicago in the 1830s. These reports add to the evidence of the presence of freedom seekers coming to and through Chicago as seen in the 1830s advertisements in Chicago papers seeking the capture and return of fugitive slaves.[6]

Also in late 1839, a young couple escaped from St. Louis, crossed the Mississippi, and took a stagecoach into Chicago. Their owner was in pursuit and reached them as they sought to board a steam ship in Chicago. He dragged them off the ship and deposited them in the Cook County jail. A young white man named Calvin DeWolf, a lawyer in the city, managed to get the man before the court and acquitted of charges that he stole a horse as part of his escape effort. Following DeWolf's advice, the young man headed for Canada. Meanwhile, the owner tried to remove the woman from the jail. DeWolf tried to intervene, but the sheriff pulled a gun and forced the young woman back into the jail. With that, DeWolf filed charges against the sheriff that he had engaged in kidnapping by forcefully rejailing the woman. The sheriff was himself jailed on the charge of false imprisonment and then taken to court. The judge found him guilty as charged but noted that this was more a situation of basically bad judgment and released him on condition that he in turn would release the young woman fugitive. The great irony (and difficulty for DeWolf because he could not defend her) was that upon the release of the woman, she was immediately delivered to her master. They returned to St. Louis and she, to bondage.[7]

Not every freedom seeker was who they seemed to be. In the summer of 1840, Madison Henderson visited Chicago, ready with the claim that he was a fugitive escaping to Canada. He knew it was well established by that year that Chicago was a regular stopping point for freedom seekers. However, he had robbery in mind. He had traveled up and down the Mississippi with a gang of friends, stealing from individuals, banks, and stores and committing other "acts of rascality." Technically, he was the slave of a man in New Orleans, but he traveled across the country, periodically sharing his "winnings" with his master. After a few days in Galena looking for places of opportunity for robbery, he left and went on to Chicago to visit with an old friend named Morris, who was a barber in the city. He ran into several other people he knew and, when challenged, easily used the excuse that he was a fugitive heading for freedom. He saw no real opportunities in Chicago and returned to Galena, "resolved to rob the bank." A year later, following a major robbery, fire, and death of several residents, Henderson and three of his friends were hanged in St. Louis.[8]

The stories of Polly Berry Walsh, the young couple from St. Louis, and Madison Henderson suggest the range of experiences freedom seekers had when coming to Chicago in the 1830s and 1840s. For years earlier than these recorded encounters, the barbers John Johnson and Lewis Isbell and other Black residents helped freedom seekers traveling through.

With the engagement of Black residents and cluster of young white families, forms of response to freedom seekers continued to develop in Chicago. These (illegal) activities were paralleled by the beginnings of social and political movements against slavery itself. After the formation of the Illinois Anti-Slavery Society in 1837, a key decision led to hiring Rev. Chauncy Cook to work as a traveling agent for the society developing organizations in each county. His and others' efforts led to some success, including in parts of northeastern Illinois. Within a few years, the abolition movement in Illinois would be led by Chicago-based voices and activists.

This activity in Chicago was first formalized in late 1839 at a meeting at the home of Joseph Meeker, one of the founders of the first Presbyterian Church in the city. The Chicago Anti-Slavery Society adopted the ideas espoused by state and national antislavery groups. The meeting included those who opposed slavery, and, among them, those activists willing to challenge and break the laws to assist freedom seekers. Rev. Flavel Bascom was elected president, George Manierre was elected treasurer, Calvin DeWolf was elected secretary, and Philo Carpenter participated. Bascom, DeWolf, and Carpenter had attended the meeting in 1837 protesting the death of Elijah Lovejoy, and all four men would continue to be part of the networks of the Underground Railroad. [9]

Also in 1839, other white Chicago residents expressed sentiments against slavery by forming the Chicago Colonization Society. As part of a larger national movement, this action reflected the view that the "solution" to slavery was to send enslaved persons back to Africa. The Colonization Society included several Chicago leaders sympathetic to abolition but looking for less drastic alternatives. The efforts to advance colonization in Africa had little impact and, over the next several years, the white leadership central to the Underground Railroad in Chicago came out of activities of the Anti-Slavery Society and not the Colonization Society. [10]

Although the number of residents in Chicago who supported the movements for the abolition of slavery grew dramatically during the years leading to the Civil War, in these early organizing days, support was limited and controversial. Along the way, those white residents actively engaged with freedom seekers remained a small, passionate few within the ranks of antislavery folks. Those involved knew each other well and were collectively supportive of their antislavery comments and actions, and soon, they themselves talked about their work as the "Underground Railroad."

Records from the time period almost always refer only to men having public roles in the struggles. However, it is obvious that the often personal work of having strangers in one's home would engage the entire family. Little about the roles of women in these activities was recorded. However, Ann Carpenter, Louisa Dyer, Ruth Bascom, Mary DeWolf, Esther Freer, and other white women married to white public abolitionists and activists in Chicago were deeply involved in this work and were supportive of emerging women's groups opposed to slavery. In 1844, women in the city founded the Chicago Female Anti-Slavery Society. [11]

White Activists in Chicago's Underground Railroad

At the center of the early work were Dr. Charles V. Dyer and his wife, Louisa (see Figure 2.1). They arrived in the city in 1835 and established his work as a physician and their engagement in real estate and other enterprises. He was a director of the North Chicago (Street) Railway Company and one of the founders of Rosehill Cemetery, and he had connections with the Chicago, Burlington and Quincy Railroad. (For the latter, however, he did not serve as president as is often suggested.) Charles and Louisa provided direct support for freedom seekers, both at their home and his offices. Their children remembered this involvement and their engagement with the major abolitionists of the day. Louisa's brother James Gifford was one of the founders of Elgin and a key activist in assisting freedom seekers in Kane County, which is to the west of Chicago. Louisa and Charles were close friends of J. Y. and Mary Ann Scammon and with them started the Swedenborgian Church in Chicago. After the death of Dr. Dyer in 1878, the announcement in the *Chicago Tribune* noted that Dyer had helped more than one thousand fugitives to escape to freedom.[12]

A ship's captain based in Chicago in the early 1840s remembered Dyer's engagement in the Underground Railroad and that his connections with people of color caused him to be "bitterly denounced" by many on the streets of Chicago. The captain remembered deeply offensive racial epithets used in reference to Dyer. He vividly recalled seeing Dyer in conversations with Black barbers and other members of the Black community in Chicago and knew the stories of his work with travelers. He was pointing to connections that lasted. This biracial collaboration was remembered at the funerals of both Charles and Louisa Dyer. More than thirty years later, Rev. Abram T. Hall and John Jones, longtime central leaders in the Black community, participated in the couple's funerals, and Hall was a pallbearer for both.[13]

The visible collaborations of white and Black activists started with the Dyers. Key to this collaboration was the work of the Black barbers John Johnson and Lewis Isbell. Although there is no direct evidence of Johnson's involvement with white activists, Isbell's name surfaces again and again in reports by white activists about their work with the Underground Railroad.[14]

The white activists throughout northeastern Illinois knew the Dyers and would often reference them as the central participants in the work of the Underground Railroad. The Dyers worked closely with a dedicated group

Fig. 2.1 Dr. Charles V. Dyer. Blanchard,
Discovery and Conquests of the Northwest

of other early Chicago settlers, mostly young families, including Philo and
Ann Carpenter; L. C. Paine and Esther Freer; Rev. Flavel and Ruth Bascom;
attorneys Calvin DeWolf, James Collins, George Manierre, J. Young Scammon, and Isaac Arnold; newspaper men Zebina Eastman, Warren Hooper,
and James McClellan; the hotel keepers Charles and Amanda Cook; and the
lake steamer captains Augustus Walker an Chesley Blake.[15]

Philo and Ann Carpenter were remarkably involved church members and
community leaders. Philo arrived from Massachusetts in 1832 and opened

the first drug store in Chicago (see Figure 2.2). He married Ann Thompson Carpenter after his first wife died and Ann came to Chicago in 1834. As charter members of the Presbyterian Church, in 1852, they led a group out of that congregation to form the First Congregational Church, which rapidly became a center for Underground Railroad actions. Their friends called it the "Black Abolition Church," their adversaries called it "Carpenter's N——r Church."[16] Both his drug store and their home were places of refuge. Philo also was deeply involved with Freemasonry and with temperance movements. Several sources note that the couple assisted at least two hundred freedom seekers to find their way to Canada. Rufus Blanchard, a later nineteenth-century historian who knew most of the white activists, wrote about Carpenter: "His home was ever a free hiding place for fugitives, whence he piloted them by night to Canada-bound vessels." Ann was deeply involved in assisting freedom seekers, and several accounts of freedom seekers include her involvement and decision-making when Philo was not available.[17]

L. C. Paine Freer and his wife, Esther, arrived in Chicago in 1836 from New York. He was an attorney (see Figure 2.3), and while involved in a variety of activities with abolitionism and assisting freedom seekers, he came to be a close friend of John Jones, one of the key leaders of Chicago's Black community. During Jones's first years in Chicago, Freer helped him write letters and eventually assisted him learning to read and write. The Freers and Dyers were close friends of the Joneses for many years. Esther Freer was "always in full sympathy with his acts in the 'great cause,' and assisted him to the extent of her opportunities." Freer was centrally involved with the Great Chicago Exodus, with the key organizing taking place at his law offices. An obelisk marker for the Freer family rises in Graceland Cemetery in Chicago just a short stroll from the more modest marker for John and Mary Jones. Their engagement with the Underground Railroad was substantial and included an honest reach across racial lines through friendship. In the romanticized language of the late nineteenth century, it was noted that "his home was open not only to colored speakers, but also to the humble fugitive from slavery. He encountered personal danger on more than one occasion, as he was forced to oppose armed court officials and slave owners, the former with legal warrants. There was a standing reward in one slave state for his head." This source continues with several of the heroic white men stories common to Underground Railroad accounts. In one, Freer and others on horseback chased slave catchers across northern Illinois, never quite reaching them. A

Fig. 2.2 Philo Carpenter. Blanchard,
Discovery and Conquests of the Northwest.

second, and more colorful, story had Freer teamed up with Dr. Dyer and
Calvin DeWolf to disguise themselves as ruffians to rescue a "light colored
woman" who had lived for many years in Chicago.[18]

Rev. Flavel Bascom and his wife Ruth arrived in Chicago in July 1833 due to
his appointment as missionary in the West for the Home Missionary Society.
A native of Connecticut, he graduated from the Divinity School at Yale in
1828 as part of the "Yale Band" of young preachers who came west to organize
churches. Through his mission work, he was connected to the early growth of

Fig. 2.3 L. C. Paine Freer. Blanchard,
Discovery and Conquests of the Northwest.

the First Presbyterian Church in Chicago and served as pastor from 1839 into 1849. He was a leader in the abolitionist and activist work that was underway in that congregation, and, in 1840, he began holding antislavery prayer services. Due to these services, and with his public commitments to abolition, he found himself presiding over the controversies in the congregation that led, in 1842, to the creation of the Second Presbyterian Church, which was formed by members of First Presbyterian Church seeking a less politicized congregation. These ongoing controversies led, in 1852, to another split at

First Presbyterian Church. Because of their desire to clearly support abolition, Philo Carpenter and others left to create Chicago's First Congregational
Church as an abolitionist and activist congregation. Over the years, Bascom
was a leading voice among Presbyterians and Congregationalists in support
of abolition. He helped organize the Ivanhoe and Millburn Congregational
Churches in Lake County. In 1864, he became pastor of the Congregational
Church in Princeton that had been the pulpit of Owen Lovejoy.[19]

Calvin DeWolf arrived from Pennsylvania in 1837 and spent most of his
career as an attorney (see Figure 2.4). He was one of the key young men who
gathered for the initial public meeting in response to the death of Elijah Lovejoy and soon after spent the winter of 1837–38 as a schoolteacher in Hadley
in Will County. There, he taught the children of a group of families directly
involved with assisting freedom seekers. No doubt, this position helped push
him toward a full commitment to abolition and support for freedom seekers
coming though Chicago. In 1841, he married Mary Francis Kimball of Connecticut. With Philo Carpenter and others, he helped organize the Chicago
Anti-Slavery Society, serving as its first secretary. Then, in the early 1840s, he
helped establish the *Western Citizen*. Throughout the 1850s, he engaged in
legal controversies involving freedom seekers, and in the late 1850s, the voters of Cook County elected him as a justice of the peace. He continued to
serve in public offices with the courts and was active in Republican politics
after 1860.[20]

DeWolf was a close friend and colleague of James H. Collins. Collins was
one of the most aggressive and articulate of the Chicago activists, and many
regarded him as second only to Dr. Dyer in his willingness to support freedom seekers traveling through. A contemporary wrote that Collins was "a
good lawyer, a man of perseverance, pluck and resolution, and as combative
as an English bulldog." He came from New York with his wife Olive and three
children in 1833. After a few months in Kendall County, they opted to settle
permanently in Chicago. In New York, James studied with Gerritt Smith, the
famed abolitionist, and he brought Smith's convictions with him to Illinois.
L. C. Paine Freer worked in Collins's law office when he first arrived in Chicago. A key figure in abolitionist circles and among the activists working with
freedom seekers, Collins died of cholera in 1854 at age fifty-four.[21]

Collins came to prominence in abolitionist circles through his work on
behalf of several fugitives caught up in Chicago courts and his defense of
activists, especially Owen Lovejoy. In 1843, Lovejoy was accused of helping

Fig. 2.4 Calvin DeWolf. Blanchard,
Discovery and Conquests of the Northwest.

two women escape. The case involving Agnes and Nancy unfolded before a
courtroom packed with partisans on both sides. Both slaveholders (and their
sympathizers) and the abolitionists saw it as a crucial point in the ongoing
argument about the right of return when runaways were captured. Newspaper accounts say that Collins spoke for seven hours without notes and overwhelmed the jury with arguments on the power of a "higher law" that superseded the human laws about slavery and those seeking to escape. It was also
clear that the prosecution could not definitively establish the claim that they
were slaves. After successfully defending Lovejoy in Bureau County, Collins

traveled on to Will County to assist with the defense of two men jailed for assisting freedom seekers.[22]

After coming to Chicago in 1835, George Manierre married Ann Hamilton Ried in 1842. He served as the first treasurer of the Chicago Anti-Slavery Society in 1840 and on two resolution committees that were formed in response the Fugitive Slave Act. Later in life, he served as a judge with the circuit court in Chicago and recruited a unit for battle in late 1861 known as the "Manierre Rifles." His portrait was included with a group of notable Chicagoans honored on the walls of the Second Presbyterian Church. In a family memoir, his son noted that freedom seekers were coming through Chicago very regularly "between 1846 and 1854," and he remembered his father, on one occasion, "taking a suit of his clothes and dressing a runaway slave" in the rear of their house located at Michigan and Jackson.[23]

Another committed abolitionist, Johnathan Young "J. Y." Scammon, became one of the wealthiest men in Chicago. Born in Maine, he came to Chicago on his own in 1835 at age twenty-three. In 1837, he married Mary Ann Dearborn of New York. Over time he was a lawyer, banker, politician, and engaged citizen. He helped establish the first railroad in Chicago, the Chicago and Galena Union and founded the *Chicago Inter Ocean* newspaper. He established the congregation of the Swedenborgian Church, with the Dyers as charter members.[24]

It appears Scammon supported, but kept some distance from, the direct work of the Underground Railroad. With his wife, he left Chicago in 1857 and traveled for three years throughout Europe. Because of this trip, he was not part of the increasing abolitionist and Underground Railroad activities happening in those years. On one occasion, he was accused of assisting with the escape of a fugitive from some police officers. Brought to court, he was challenged as to what he would do if called to help apprehend a fugitive. He replied, "I would certainly obey the summons, but I should probably stub my toe and fall down before I reached him."[25]

Politician Isaac Newton Arnold came from New York in 1836. He and his wife, Harriet Dorrance Arnold, had nine children. He engaged with the abolitionists in Chicago from the early days and served in a variety of volunteer capacities. In 1837, he was elected clerk for the newly formed City of Chicago. An increasing political role took him to the national Free Soil Convention in 1848; he served in the state legislature, and he was elected to Congress as a Republican in 1860. Arnold wrote a biography of his close friend Abraham

Lincoln, introduced the first resolution to abolish slavery in the House of Representatives, and, in his later years, served as president of the Chicago Historical Society. Evidently, he was careful to not be too engaged in direct aid to freedom seekers, but was a close colleague of Owen Lovejoy, and was prominent in legal matters, including service as one of the six attorneys defending John Hossack.[26]

Staunch abolitionist Willliam Hubbard Brown worked closely with J. Y. Scammon and Isaac Arnold. The three were early and strong supporters of the emergence of the Republican Party and the candidacy of Abraham Lincoln. Both Scammon and Brown were elected to the state legislature in 1860 as firm Republicans. Born in Connecticut, in 1818, he came to southern Illinois, where he played a crucial role, along with Illinois governor Edward Coles, in defeating the efforts for the proslavery convention in 1824. Within a decade, he lived in Chicago. Because of his advocacy for abolition, he was later identified as one who worked on the Underground Railroad. Nineteenth-century records, however, have no mention of his direct involvement.[27]

Zebina Eastman played his most crucial role in the abolitionist movement as a dogged editor (see Figure 2.5). He first worked with activist and editor Benjamin Lundy on the newspaper the *Genius of Universal Emancipation* in 1838–39. After Lundy's death, Eastman sought to continue it as the *Genius of Liberty* while still seeking to work out of his base in Lowell, Illinois. While there, he was involved in (or possibly even the author of) the traditional first story of the Underground Railroad in Chicago, which was about bringing a fugitive from Lowell to Chicago in 1839. In 1842, he was invited by Dyer, Collins, and others to come to Chicago to edit the *Western Citizen*. Not only did he serve as the lead journalist for the abolitionists in Chicago and work closely with the activists assisting freedom seekers throughout the 1840s and 1850s, but he also was the central figure in organizing the great abolitionist reunion of 1874.

Warren Hooper was one of the early public abolitionists in Illinois, and one of the first newspaper men in the state. He started the *Spectator*, Illinois' first antislavery newspaper, in Edwardsville in 1819 and worked on antislavery activities in the 1820s with Governor Coles. Hooper, along with Coles, not only was antislavery in the sense of keeping slavery out of Illinois but also shared the emerging abolitionist position, that is, that the institutions of slavery should be abolished everywhere. Later, Hooper moved to Lowell, Illinois, joining Zebina Eastman on the *Genius of Universal Emancipation* and

Fig. 2.5 Zebina Eastman. Blanchard,
Discovery and Conquests of the Northwest.

helped start the *Genius of Liberty*. He came with Eastman in 1842 to develop
the *Western Citizen*.[28]

James McClellan was active in abolitionist politics and assisting freedom
seekers from his home in Joliet, in Will County, and in Chicago. He was a
close colleague and longtime business partner of Zebina Eastman in managing the *Western Citizen* and related efforts. In 1848, he was one of nine delegates from Illinois to the national Liberty Party convention, along with Dyer

and Collins and several others in the state who were directly involved with freedom seekers.[29]

Also arriving in the early years, Charles and Amanda Cook opened one of the first hotels in 1836, the Mansion House on Michigan Avenue. Although they were not public abolitionists, they were deeply committed to antislavery and temperance movements. A few years later, they managed the American Temperance Hotel, the first hotel built in Chicago without a bar and drinking areas. Their hotels served as meeting places for those involved with assisting freedom seekers, and the latter were regularly housed there on their way to Canada.[30]

Capt. Augustus Walker and Capt. Chesley Blake served for years as steamboat captains who took freedom seekers to Detroit or directly to Canada. Capt. Blake had played the key role in transporting Eastman's "first fugitive" safely to Canada. Both captains often allowed freedom seekers on board, and they paid their way by working as firemen with the boilers. Some other captains and ships were involved, but the most well-known were Walker on the "Great Western" and Blake on the "Illinois."[31]

A later history of Chicago noted that Walker and Blake were recognized as men of "generosity and courage" and trusted to safely carry fugitives to Canada. "In the saloons of these steamers there might be the slave masters from one of the southern states, with wives and daughters, reveling in the luxury of a northern summer trip, while one or more of their runaway slaves were firing up the boat in the hold below. The masters were happy in the plenitude of their power, but the slaves were happier in their assurance of freedom."[32]

As was the case with settlement across northeastern Illinois, these early white antislavery activists and their families came from New England and New York and settled permanently in Chicago. They worked together in the region and knew each other well, some through church connections. For decades they played a critical role in the movement of hundreds of freedom seekers. Other white activists would arrive in Chicago later, and after 1845, Black leadership was crucial to the work of the Underground Railroad.

Activism in the 1840s

From the spontaneous encounters with travelers in the 1830s and the beginnings of systems of response by Black activists in Chicago and young white activists across the region, the early 1840s saw the growth of both abolitionist organizations and the networks of the Underground Railroad. In 1842, formal political activities were initiated through the formation of the Liberty Party. 1842 was also the year of the infamous "twenty-five-cent sale."

As related in many Chicago histories, the twenty-five-cent sale was the only slave sale (or, at least, the only one really remembered) in Chicago. Edwin Heathcock, a Chicago resident, free person of color, and member of the Methodist Church, was arrested after being accused of not having his free papers. After a trial and conviction, he was put up for auction. S. J. Lowe, the sheriff of Cook County, duly published an announcement that Heathcock was determined by court order to be a fugitive slave and was being held.[33] Zebina Eastman printed up a flier with the title "Man for Sale" and with friends, plastered it all over town. So, a considerable crowd showed up. The sheriff sought bids, surrounded by a sullen and silent crowd. After a period of no response and the increasing desperation on the part of Sheriff Lowe, Mahlon D. Ogden stepped forward offering twenty-five cents. Ogden was the younger brother of Chicago's first mayor. The sheriff was stunned, but after no other offers, the sale was complete. Upon producing the twenty-five cents, Ogden told Heathcock: "Edwin, I have bought you; I have given a quarter for you; you are my man—my slave! Now, you go where you please."[34]

In May of 1842, the first state "Liberty Convention" gathered, responding to a call from February of 1841, when a number of white activists had gathered in Lowell and concluded that they needed a more political response in Illinois to the issues of slavery. At the May gathering, with a hundred delegates, resolutions passed to adopt the national Liberty Party platform, to oppose the state's infamous "Black Laws," and to create an abolitionist paper based in Chicago. The young men from Chicago—Dyer, DeWolf, Collins, Carpenter, and others—played key roles in this convention, reinforcing that Illinois leadership for abolitionist ideas and actions were shifting to a Chicago base. Reporting on this meeting, the *National Anti-Slavery Standard* newspaper asserted that the people of Chicago, and most of Illinois, were "generally, nay, almost wholly" opposed to slavery.[35]

Dr. Dyer, James Collins, and Philo Carpenter invited Zebina Eastman, in 1842, to come to Chicago to become editor of the new *Western Citizen*. With the support of initial stockholders Carpenter, Freer, Bascom, Dyer, DeWolf, and a few others from Chicago, along with Peter Stewart, Allen Denny, the Cushings from Will County, and Rev. John Cross, Eastman rapidly turned the *Western Citizen* into the major voice out of Chicago for abolitionists and the direct activists. The newspaper began with the subscription list of the *Genius of Liberty*, around four hundred names, and by the end of its first year, its circulation had grown to about one thousand.[36]

In August 1842, the Illinois Anti-Slavery Society met in Chicago for the first time. As with the financial backing for the *Western Citizen*, many of the abolitionists participating in this gathering were directly engaged with assisting freedom seekers. They passed a resolution urging residents in Illinois "to extend the hand of kindness and hospitality in all things necessary for his escape, to every panting fugitive from the Southern Prison House, who may come within the reach of their benevolence."[37]

Since attendance at the 1842 meeting included many of the activists involved with the Underground Railroad, the gathering likely provided an informal occasion to strengthen friendships and connections in the work. Examining the attendance list of the approximately 150 delegates, at least twenty-eight activists from northeastern Illinois were there. Will Country representatives included Samuel Cushing, Moses Cook, Allen Denny, and Peter Stewart. Nathan Gould came from LaSalle County and Zebina Eastman listed himself with that county. From Cook County came James Collins, Charles V. Dyer, Philo Carpenter, L. C. Paine Freer, Flavel Bascom, and Calvin DeWolf, along with many others. The officers for the coming year included Freer as one of the vice presidents, DeWolf as recording secretary, Dyer as corresponding secretary, and James Collins and Samuel Cushing among the board of managers. In this meeting, as in others in the early 1840s, the participants were white activists and there was apparently no formal connection with leaders in the Black community in Chicago or other Illinois towns. Rev. Owen Lovejoy chaired the meeting, and the secretaries were Collins and Freer.[38]

Initially somewhat ineffective as a statewide operation, the Illinois Anti-Slavery Society grew in strength, and by the end of 1843, hundreds of new members had been recruited. New local antislavery societies were formed in Kane, DeKalb, Lake, and DuPage Counties. These new societies joined with the local efforts of societies in Will and LaSalle Counties and in Chicago. In addition, along with the emerging Liberty Party, they adopted the *Western Citizen* as their official organ, and by the end of 1843, it was well-established and supported as the voice of the Illinois Anti-Slavery Society.[39]

However, although the Anti-Slavery Society was actively developing local societies, by late 1843 and into 1844, organizational energies shifted into support for local chapters of the state Liberty Party. In October of 1843, the first of these local chapters organized in Chicago and thereafter the role of antislavery societies began to diminish as the more political approach grew and the Liberty Party was increasingly seen as the avenue for abolitionists to move forward. The state Liberty Party convention met in January of 1844 in Aurora, identifying candidates for offices across the state, and campaigning began.

One component in campaign activities was the use of occasional freedom seekers to particularize the terrors of slavery. In 1844, the great spokesman for abolition, Ichabod Codding, spoke at rallies around Lake County with the company of William Jones. Jones was a free man of color who told the gatherings about how he was kidnapped and robbed while on a trip to Chicago. Such appearances helped humanize the struggle and reinforce the power of the resolutions passed decrying slavery and seeking political solutions. Being together also provided the context for activists to compare experiences and options for responding to contact with freedom seekers.[40]

Churches across northeastern Illinois were taking public positions in opposition to slavery, but the first declaration in Chicago came in 1844 from Second Baptist Church (also known as the Tabernacle Baptist Church). In May of 1844, as it sought formal recognition within the Baptist Fox River Association, the church declared: "Resolved, That slavery is a great sin in the sight of God, and while we view it as such we will not invite to our pulpit or communion those who advocate or justify, from civil policy of the Bible, the principle of the practice of slavery."[41]

At about this same time, the predominantly white Clark Street Methodist congregation included two persons of color in its membership and had taken no positions regarding slavery and support for freedom seekers. At one point, on a Sunday morning, the minister, Rev. James Mitchell, gave separate invitations for communion (as was the custom), with the Black members invited after the white members. Some of the latter held back, and when he announced, "now, let our colored friends come forward," about a dozen of the white members joined the two Black members at the communion railing. Mitchell graciously offered communion to all and later guaranteed that this would not happen again. The final resolution of the matter is unclear.[42]

Alongside the evolution of local antislavery efforts, the emergence of the Liberty Party and abolitionist politics, and the declarations by churches and actions within congregations, the activity through the Underground Railroad continued to grow. Across northeastern Illinois, there was increasing contact with freedom seekers and growing assistance for them on their journeys to and through Chicago or directly toward Detroit.

Organizing across Northeastern Illinois

Following the removal of Native peoples from the region, and in some instances contemporaneously with their removal, northeastern Illinois outside Chicago was rapidly settled, predominantly by pioneers from New York and New England. Many of the present communities of the region trace their beginnings from the mid- to late 1830s. These settlers tended to be sympathetic to antislavery ideas in contrast to many of the settlers in southern Illinois who often came from Virginia, the Carolinas, and other southern states.

One remarkable indicator of this orientation was the arrival in 1838 of the veteran abolitionist Benjamin Lundy in the small emerging settlement of Lowell. Lundy was a lifelong Quaker with relatives among the Quakers who settled in Putman and western LaSalle Counties starting in 1836. Located in west central LaSalle County, Lowell was near the old state road from Springfield to Chicago. Considered by many as the father of American abolitionism, Lundy reestablished his venerable newspaper, the *Genius of Universal Emancipation*, in this small Illinois town. He played a remarkable (and today, almost unknown) role in the abolition of American slavery.[43]

Born in New Jersey, he lived as a young man in Wheeling, West Virginia, and there encountered the terrors of slavery with coffle gangs heading down the Ohio River. Of those early years, Lundy wrote: "I heard the wail of the captive; I felt his pang of distress; and the iron entered my soul." He organized the first abolition society west of the Alleghenies in Ohio and in 1821, he began publishing his monthly newspaper, the *Genius of Universal Emancipation*. He lived and worked for a time in Ohio, Tennessee, Washington, Baltimore, Philadelphia, and finally in Lowell. He also made two trips to Haiti investigating options for Black colonization and explored slavery in Texas and colonization in Mexico and Canada. A young William Lloyd Garrison became a crusader learning from Lundy, and a young Zebina Eastman came to help with his printing activities in Lowell. Abolitionist friends and admirers encouraged him to settle in Illinois, and he felt an obligation to be there to help carry the challenges laid out by Elijah Lovejoy, who died a year before Lundy's arrival.[44]

After settling in Lowell in the summer of 1838, Lundy only managed to publish twelve issues of the *Genius of Universal Emancipation*. At the initial meeting of the Illinois Anti-Slavery Society in October of 1838, the delegates designated the *Genius* as the official paper for the society. In the spring of 1839, Zebina Eastman arrived and provided much needed help in the basic logistics of printing the paper. He oversaw the last issue in August of that year, due to Lundy's unexpected death from a sudden illness. He is buried on a quiet, green hillside above Clear Creek in a Quaker cemetery near Lowell.[45]

Parallel to the settlement of the young, white, activist families in Chicago, some families arriving across northeastern Illinois shared the sentiments of Benjamin Lundy and developed the wider networks of the Underground Railroad. They came to LaSalle County as early as 1834, across Will and southern Cook Counties from 1834 to 1838, and into Kane and DuPage Counties by 1837. By 1844, all of these young white families across the region were deeply connected with the activists in Chicago.

By 1840, in the region south-southwest of Chicago, LaSalle, Will, and southern Cook Counties each had around ten thousand new settlers. Some who established farms and small communities in LaSalle, Livingston, and Kendall Counties had direct contact with freedom seekers and organized both to be of assistance and to support antislavery causes. Grundy County had a relatively small, settled population and few public abolitionists. Immediately east were settled areas in Will County that became significant sources of support and, in 1837, these first settlers organized the first antislavery society in northeastern Illinois. Settlers in Will County developed networks of support with like-minded abolitionists in south Cook County, north into Chicago, and east into Indiana. In addition to the freedom seekers who traveled through those networks, a small number came overland from directly south in Illinois and Indiana, traveling into Will County after passing through Iroquois and Kankakee Counties on the Vincennes Trace (Hubbard's Trail).[46]

Families settling in the western part of LaSalle County in 1833–34 collaborated with their friends and relatives just west in Putnam County. In the town of Magnolia and other communities in that county, Quaker families assisted freedom seekers on their way through LaSalle County and on to Chicago and were active in the Putnam County Anti-Slavery Society. Amos Ebersol arrived in 1834 and when he married Calista Whittlesey in 1844, they traveled to Princeton to have Rev. Owen Lovejoy conduct the ceremony. Their involvement with assisting freedom seekers was reflected in a remarkably detailed journal kept by John, which included a number of specific references to helping individuals and families traveling through.[47]

Samuel and Ann Lewis were Quakers whose parents came to Putnam County in 1833. They moved to Fall River Township in LaSalle County in 1843, and over the years shared vivid memories of their work with freedom seekers. Later, Samuel helped form the Republican Party, was very actively politically, and served as a state senator. The Ebersols, Lewises, and other neighbors supported a resolution by the Putnam County Anti-Slavery Society in 1843 affirming "the members of this society will obey God rather than man by 'feeding the hungry, clothing the naked and protecting the fugitive who has escaped from his master to us.'"[48]

In the early 1840s, one of the few Black persons living outside Chicago was a resident of LaSalle County and recorded simply as "Freeman." He traveled back and forth to Missouri from LaSalle County to rescue his family and then carried them safely on to Canada. This may be the Mr. Freeman encountered by Caroline Quarlls and Lyman Goodnow southwest of Chicago in their travels from Wisconsin to Canada.[49]

From Ottawa in LaSalle County, one of the main roads passed into Kendall County, through Newark, to present-day Yorkville. From Yorkville, travelers went due east to Plainfield or northeast to the Naper Settlement (now Naperville) and then on into Chicago. A little to the south of Yorkville, in Big Grove Township, lived the family of Jonathan Raymond. They settled there in 1834, and their daughter, Sarah, remembered their involvement: "With my young, girlish eyes I looked on and listened to the strange stories told by these dark brothers in my father's house."[50]

Key families settled from 1834 to 1838 across Will County and came to know each other very well, collaborate on abolitionist issues, and work together assisting travelers. All stayed on their farms through the Civil War and longer. Hale and Sabrina Mason, a leading antislavery family, lived in Lockport, on the I&M (Illinois and Michigan) Canal. They came from Massachusetts in 1834 with three young sons and Sabrina's mother, Sally Codding. Sally was the sister of Ichabod Codding, the great abolitionist orator (see Figure 2.6). Born in New York in 1810, by the age of twenty-six, Ichabod Codding was an agent of the American Anti-Slavery Society and already well-known as a spellbinding orator, lecturing across New England. He was invited to become pastor of the Congregational Church in Waukesha, Wisconsin, in 1846. For many years thereafter, he preached in churches and gave abolitionist lectures across Wisconsin and Illinois. Lockport became his home base and he stayed for extended periods in the Mason home with his sister and mother.[51]

Earlier, during his travels around Illinois and Wisconsin, Codding had an occasional direct hand in assisting freedom seekers. In the early 1840s, while John and Martha Hossack, who later were very active in Ottawa, were living in Gooding's Grove, Codding arrived with three freedom seekers and asked the Hassocks to get them on their way to Canada. In response, Hossack harnessed his team to his farm wagon and took them to Chicago. Along the way, the road paralleled the construction underway on the new I&M Canal. At several points, Irish workers yelled at them and threw stones, but they escaped injury and Hossack delivered them to Dr. Dyer in Chicago.[52]

Ichabod Codding and the Masons were related to the Lockport Congregational Church, formed in 1838 and a significant base for antislavery activity. In 1844, antislavery resolutions were passed by the congregation and several of the pastors were known as strong advocates for abolition. Codding was a close friend of Owen Lovejoy in Princeton and eventually corresponded with Abraham Lincoln. He worked closely with both men in the emerging Republican Party during the 1850s. He is buried with the Mason family in the pioneer cemetery in Lockport with a monument bearing these words: "A fearless apostle for freedom for the slave and in religion."[53]

A few miles south of Lockport, the historic Sauk Trail passes through Joliet. For hundreds of years, the trail was a major route for travel by Native Americans from the Mississippi River to Detroit. This became a major wagon and coach road, and part of it was absorbed by the Detroit to Chicago Road. East of Joliet, the Sauk Trail passed through the Hickory Settlements, which became New Lenox and Mokena. Active here were the families of Samuel and Hephzibah Denny Haven and Allen and Polly Denny.[54]

North of New Lenox and Mokena, abolitionists in Homer Township assisted freedom seekers traveling north and northeast from Joliet and those following the Sauk Trail corridor. From Joliet, an important post road angled to the northeast to Chicago through the small hamlet of Hadley. On the edge of Hadley was the farm of the family of Deacon Levi and Melinda

Fig. 2.6 Ichabod Codding, Olin, *Record of the Olin Family*.

Savage, who helped start the Hadley Congregational Church in 1834. This was another early church associated with strong abolitionist ideas. The first schoolteacher in Hadley was the young Calvin De Wolf, who came west from his home in Pennsylvania. Isaac and Betsy Preston arrived in 1836 from New York. They were early advocates of abolition in New York and were active in Hadley in providing aid to freedom seekers.[55]

Originally from Scotland, Peter and Elizabeth Stewart settled in Wilmington, in the southwestern corner of Will County, in 1836. He served for many years as an engineer with the I&M Canal, and later as superintendent. Peter, who in later years referred to himself as "President" of the Underground Railroad, in 1846, built the Stewart House Hotel in the middle of the river town of Wilmington with its back on the riverside. Both their home and the hotel welcomed freedom seekers over the years. Will County historian George Woodruff referred to Peter Stewart as "an Abolitionist of the most ultra kind." The author of several books about Will County, Woodruff was in the middle of it all, and knew his fellow abolitionists very well. He happily referred to his activist friends as "fanatics."[56]

Along with the Stewarts, other residents in Wilmington and on nearby farms assisted in providing a network of stopover points. Freedom seekers coming east from the Illinois River valley were directed onward to Joliet and Lockport and east across Will County. The Stewarts knew the Havens and Dennys, the Masons in Lockport, and the cluster of activists near Crete on the eastern edge of the County.

Following the coach and wagon roads north from Wilmington through the Midewin prairies, travelers came to the long-established river and later canal town of Joliet. Its role in the Underground Railroad includes one the earliest stories involving a Black person in the region. This is the story of Henry Belt, a free person of color with papers issued in Pennsylvania "certifying to his freedom." However, in 1840, he became the object of professional slave hunters who went to great lengths to have him labeled as a runaway slave from Missouri.[57]

Henry worked as a barber in the Exchange Hotel in the middle of Joliet and was well liked in the community. Slave catchers noticed him and sent one of their number back to St. Louis to obtain a bogus warrant for his capture as a runaway with a detailed description to match their claim for him. With this warrant, he was arrested and, unfortunately, taken before a lower court justice well-known to be a "negro-hater." However, good friends of Henry demanded a writ of habeas corpus, and he was brought before the circuit court judge. A large crowd came to the courthouse to see what would happen. Unfortunately, "the judge was of the same stripe as the justice" and thus ruled in favor of the slave catchers. While everyone focused on the court proceedings, Henry's friends quietly grabbed him from the sheriff and managed to slip him out of the courthouse. The place was chaos, the slave catchers were furious—and, for some reason, most of the folks in the courthouse were pretty much in the way as they had struggled to get out and pursue Henry. Henry Belt simply disappeared. "Henry was nowhere to be found—never was found." After staying in Joliet for a few more days, the slave hunters gave up, recognizing that "he had escaped by that mysterious means, the 'underground railroad.'"[58]

Some freedom seekers traveled north from Joliet to Plainfield. In the Plainfield area, several families provided aid, in part through the Plymouth Congregational Church. Louisa Ashley Hammond, whose family settled two miles north of Plainfield in the early 1840s "on the direct stage route from Chicago to Ottawa," recalled a time her father was approached to help a young woman. Louisa went with her father, carrying the young woman all through the night to reach Chicago, going to "Dr. Dyer's Depot."[59]

Ezra and Martha Goodhue lived in Plainfield and many reports by activists in LaSalle and Kendall Counties mention their home as the next stop for freedom seekers. Goodhue is one of six "Conductors" listed by Wilber Siebert in Will County. The others were Deacon Beach, Deacon Cushing, Allen Denny, Samuel Haven, and Col. Peter Stewart.[60]

George Randolph Dyer settled near Plainfield in 1841 and was elected sheriff of Will County in 1856. He married Elizabeth Kimball, the daughter of one of the founding families of Aurora. Dyer was the brother of Dr. Charles Dyer. Who married Louisa Gifford, daughter of the other founding family in Aurora. At their home northeast of Plainfield, George and Elizabeth regularly assisted freedom seekers before sending them on to his brother in Chicago, Dr. Dyer.[61]

Continuing northeast toward Chicago, the old wagon and stage road from Plainfield passed through what is now Indian Head Park. Here, the Lyonsville Congregational Church was established in 1843 as an antislavery congregation. Local and church traditions hold that the Rufus Brown home was a place of refuge. The possibility of direct contact is supported by the accounts of freedom seekers coming through both Plainfield and Joliet on their way to Chicago.[62]

Although some traveled toward Chicago through Plainfield, many of the freedom seekers passing through Joliet continued east along the Sauk Trail, some connecting with the Havens, others with the families just north in

Mokena and Homer Township. East of New Lenox and Frankfort, the Sauk Trail passes into the far southern part of Cook County and through what are now Richton Park and Park Forest. On the north side of the trail, just east of where it crosses Thorn Creek, the McCoy farm was a safe house. John and Sabra McCoy, born in New Hampshire and Vermont respectively, were well-known and well-respected early residents on the trail. Descendants of the McCoys carried family stories connected to the Underground Railroad. The McCoys had the occasional help of other families living nearby on the Sauk Trail.[63]

Freedom seekers on the Sauk Trail continued east into Indiana, or they followed an old post road that veered to the southeast into Will County. Northeast of the present-day village of Crete, this road came to the settlement known as Beebe's Grove. The settlement included families active in the Beebe's Grove Congregational Society (eventually the Crete Church), which was started in 1839 with a reputation across the region as a nest of abolitionists willing to help fugitives (see Figure 2.7). In January of 1841, they supported a resolution taking a strong position against slavery: "Believing American slavery to be oppressive and sinful and contrary to the teaching of the Bible, resolved that we recommend to our members to do all they consistently can as citizens and Christians to bring about its speedy and peaceful overthrow."[64]

This was one of the earliest such resolutions adopted by churches in Illinois. By 1843, the networks of the Underground Railroad across Will County coming to Beebe's Grove were well-known among Illinois activists and one of the stops on the journey of Caroline Quarlls.

As with many abolitionists active in the network of the Underground Railroad, Samuel and Elizabeth Cushing came to Beebe's Grove from New England and New York. Samuel was born in New Hampshire and Elizabeth, in Massachusetts. After some time living in New York, where their two oldest children were born, the Cushings moved to Illinois. In late 1838, they purchased eighty acres across the road from the Beebe family.[65]

Deacon Cushing was well-known across Will County as one who assisted freedom seekers. In October of 1843 he was indicted for "harboring Slaves." At the same time, Peter Stewart of Wilmington and Samuel Haven of the Hickory Settlement were arrested.[66] The indictment of Cushing indicated that on three occasions, he had provided direct assistance to fugitive slaves from Missouri: the first instance with four fugitives; the second, involving a

Fig. 2.7 Crete Congregational Church. Author's photo.

man and a woman; and the third, with "two coloured persons." The grand jurors issuing the indictment included George Woodruff, the author of the county history; Dwight Haven, son of the Havens family in New Lenox; and other known abolitionists. Cushing and Stewart were arrested and taken to jail in Joliet for several days. Dwight's father, Samuel Haven, never went to trial and was released.

Before the trial commenced, several attorneys volunteered to serve as Cushing's lawyer, including the Chicago abolitionist, James H. Collins, who was returning from the similar task of defending Owen Lovejoy in Princeton, Illinois. The original accusers of Cushing reconsidered their complaints, and the prosecutor had no arguments to present to the court. Therefore, they were released and thus freed to continue "aiding and harboring slaves."[67]

Nearby were the farms of Moses and Hannah Cook and Joseph and Dyantha Safford. Both families supported the work of the Cushings. On occasion, Cook took freedom seekers by wagon "to Indiana, with a load of vegetables." The 1850 Census notes that living with the Cooks was a Black laborer named Victor Slain, one of a handful of Black residents in Will County. It is most likely that he was working on the Cook's farm for some time and thus was visible in the community. The Safford's daughter, Mary Jane, was a hero of American nursing due to remarkable service throughout the Civil War. Late in her life, Mary Jane was interviewed and remembered her parents sent freedom seekers on their way with "well-filled knapsacks and explicit directions."[68]

Caroline Quarlls

On the Fourth of July in 1843, a young woman named Caroline Quarlls decided to seek her independence and ran away from her owners in St. Louis (see Figure 2.8). She was sixteen years old, the child of an enslaved woman and her first master's son. Caroline's remarkable journey took her up the Mississippi, across northern Illinois, into southern Wisconsin to Milwaukee, and, from there, south and east in an arc around Chicago, to Detroit and freedom (see Map 2.2).[69]

Gathering up about one hundred dollars and a few clothes when she escaped, she traveled on her own up the Mississippi by steamboat to Galena, Illinois. A free man of color living there saw her and immediately urged her to get away, helping her to take the next stage out of town. She traveled northeastward, eventually ending up in Milwaukee. Caroline became the first fugitive slave recorded as seeking refuge in Wisconsin. Initially, the local white abolitionists were not sure how to best help her and Caroline spent several weeks staying with families in small communities west and south of Milwaukee. Finally, the abolitionist leaders asked Lyman Goodnow, a leader of the Congregational Church in Prairieville, Wisconsin, to travel with Caroline to Canada.

They headed for the most well-known route to freedom: the Underground Railroad network established in Will County in Illinois (see Map 2.2). A whole cast of acquaintances assisted Caroline and Goodnow as they traveled across northeastern Illinois. Coming south from Wisconsin, they came into McHenry County and were assisted by the family of a Rev. Fitch, a minister of the Disciples of Christ. Years later, Mrs. Fitch wrote about the visit by this "beautiful young lady" and that she learned that once Caroline knew she was safe, Caroline spit into her hands and rubbing them together had declared "with a thankful heart, 'Master ain't got my best days.'"

From McHenry County, Caroline and Goodnow traveled in a severe rainstorm to the home of a Methodist layman named Russell. He was not known to be an abolitionist; however, when they arrived at his door, he welcomed them and let them know "he was more than willing to assist any human being to freedom. If that was being an Abolitionist, he was one." Russell went

Map 2.2 Caroline Quarlls's travel through northeastern Illinois was exceptionally well documented. This map illustrates many of the specific stopovers she made during her journey to Canada.

with the travelers to the home of Dr. Anson Root in Dundee, about forty miles northwest of Chicago. Root was a well-known abolitionist and activist in Kane County.

After stopping at Root's home in Dundee, Caroline and Goodnow rode south on the coach road along the Fox River and Goodnow realized they were now comfortable traveling in broad daylight. They kept well west of Chicago and potential encounters with slavecatchers. They stopped with Deacon Alvah Fowler in Naperville and further south, they "fell in with a Mr. Freeman," who gave them specific directions for finding assistance in Will County. It is most likely that this "Mr. Freeman" was an African American living near Ottawa in LaSalle County. Freeman was active in assisting freedom seekers and knew the area into which they were moving.[70]

A few miles north of Joliet, they took a road east crossing over the developing route of the I&M Canal at Lockport. The canal and adjoining roads

Fig. 2.8 Caroline Quarlls. Olin, *Record of the Olin Family.*

were a major corridor for the movement of freedom seekers out of the Illinois River valley and on to Chicago. They rode in the open and Goodnow added that since it was midday in Lockport, "the people were eating dinner, and of course so occupied that they did not notice us."[71]

They moved through Lockport and east into Homer Township and the small settlement of Hadley. They stopped at the home of Deacon Beach and continued on to Hickory Grove, where they hit the Sauk Trail. Traveling east, they came to Beebe's Grove, on the eastern side of the village of Crete. They stayed with the Beebe family for two days and met many of the local folks. From there, Caroline and Goodnow continued through northwest Indiana and on across Michigan to Canada. She settled in western Ontario, fell in love, and raised a family; today, there are a host of her descendants in the Detroit region. Years later, Caroline wrote to Goodnow expressing her great appreciation for his assistance and sharing details about her life and new family in Canada. Using this information and his own recollections, Goodnow wrote about their experiences.[72]

Activism West of Chicago

Parallel to families south and southwest of Chicago, to the west of Chicago, some abolitionist families settling from the mid-1830s into the early 1840s became activists. In both Kane and DuPage Counties, as they responded to the needs of freedom seekers, these families connected with the band of activists in Chicago. In her journey, Caroline Quarlls traveled through the region, crossing areas northwest and west of Chicago and then across Will County and the southern edge of Cook County on her way to Detroit and Canada.

The initial settlers and founders of Elgin included families from New York and New Hampshire. One of the founders, James Talcott Gifford, from New York, saw his sister, Louisa, marry Dr. Charles Dyer in 1837. Over the years, this relationship nourished the connections between the activists in the Elgin area and Dr. Dyer as the key operator on Chicago's Underground Railroad. Around 1840, Sheldon Peck, an artist and activist with the Underground Railroad, painted a portrait of James Gifford and his wife, Laura. Theirs was one of many portraits he painted of abolitionists involved with the Underground Railroad.[73]

In 1834, the early settlers of what became St. Charles included families from New Brunswick in Canada. With them was a young man, James Wheeler, who built a small cabin on the west side of the Fox River. Years later, his son remembered that their "little cabin" received travelers and there were "nights when we heard strange stories from the lips of fleeing slaves." Joel, the youngest son of the Moody family remembered an encounter from when he was ten years old. The first Black person he had ever seen arrived at his home late at night concealed in a wagon. The man stayed for several days until he was taken into Chicago and assisted to obtain passage on a lake steamer. He told young Joel that he would never be taken back into slavery alive.[74]

In Aurora, an abolitionist-leaning congregation built their first church in 1841, organized as a Presbyterian, then becoming a Congregational Church. Among the first families were the Elliotts and Strongs, both known for "assisting slaves to get to Canada." Deacon William J. Strong led the activists in Aurora, and his wife, Caroline Blodgett, was related to the Blodgetts in Downers Grove.[75]

Also in the congregation were John and Laura Wagner, who settled early in Aurora and responded to travelers as they came through. About 1844, Sheldon Peck painted their family portrait and, to highlight their abolitionist commitments, portrayed John Wagner with a copy of the *Western Citizen* in his hand. Their daughter remembered being up in the night to cook meals for those her family referred to as "gentlemen of color." When morning came, her father took them on to the next "station." A neighbor growing up near the Wagner farm remembered as a young boy seeing "many colored people of both sexes stopping at this farmhouse [the Wagners'].... It was well understood that these guests were fugitives from the south."[76]

To the west of Aurora, on the main road from Ottawa, the family of Ezekiel and Lucinda Mighell directed freedom seekers on to the Wagners' home. Just east of Aurora, in the small settlement of Eola, the family of Thompson Paxton, originally residents of Virginia, was strongly opposed to slavery and their home was often a stopping point for freedom seekers.[77]

Across the northern part of Kane County, Scottish immigrants helped establish small settlements with familiar names: Inverness, Elgin, Huntley, and Dundee. It was said that these were "sturdy, hardheaded Presbyterians, who took as naturally to Abolitionism, when they struck the soil of the land of freedom, as they did to the principles of John Knox."[78]

In the summer of 1842, these leaders gathered with other friends to form the Kane County Anti-Slavery Society. Over the first several years, the society had 177 members including forty women. Reflecting the county population, they had come mostly from New York (43 percent of members) and from New England (24 percent of members). In addition, 11 percent of the members were Scottish. Meeting on July 14, 1842, congruent with county-level societies across northern Illinois, they formed as an auxiliary of the state organization, declaring: "We believe we owe it to the oppressed, to our fellow citizens who hold slaves, to our whole county, to posterity, and to God, to do all that is lawfully in our power to bring about the extinction of slavery."[79]

As elsewhere in Illinois, the gathering of abolitionists had within it a few committed to direct action in assisting freedom seekers. Thus, in the minutes of the society, we find the names of Allan Pinkerton, Dr. Anson Root, William and Charlotte Kimball, five members of the Moody family, five Youngs, and James T. Wheeler. Also listed in membership is Dr. Flavel Bascom, who was in the thick of activity for years in northeastern Illinois, and Rueben Beach, related to the Beaches in Will County who aided travelers.[80]

Adding to this number, in 1843, came a newly married young Scottish couple, Allan and Joan Pinkerton. They sailed from Scotland the year before, lived briefly in Chicago, and then moved to Dundee where Allan set up his own barrel-making shop. They moved back to Chicago in 1847. From the beginning, the barrel factory in Dundee and their homes in Dundee and Chicago served as locations of assistance. Some freedom seekers stayed in Dundee for relatively short periods to work in the barrel factory learning cooperage and carpentry skills. While still in Dundee, Allan Pinkerton became well-acquainted with the Dyers and Carpenters and other white abolitionists active in Chicago.[81]

The work of the activists in the Kane County is reflected in a letter in 1844 from the treasurer of the Kane County Anti-Slavery Society who resigned because he was moving into DuPage County. He ends his letter by writing: "Hoping that you will consider Me as ever ready to furnish all the assistance in my power to aid and sustain the underground railroad in all Lawful undertakings to obtain passengers and their Safe Deposit; . . . I remain yours. George W. Waite" He was, of course, in pointing to "all Lawful undertakings," pointing to the laws of God, the great natural laws that stood above the human laws that supported slavery and the return of human beings as property to owners.[82]

In DuPage County, Joseph Naper started the Naper Settlement in 1831, bringing twelve families from New England. A congregation was established in 1833 with connections to the Presbyterians and Congregationalists, and, in 1843, it became the First Congregational Church of Naperville. It was to this congregation and to Deacon Alvah Fowler that Caroline Quarlls traveled in her 1843 journey. Among the organizing members of the church were Israel and Avis (Avice) Blodgett who came with Naper from Massachusetts.[83]

The Blodgetts bought property in 1836 in what became Downers Grove, built a small cabin, and, by 1849, completed a frame house. They were among the "active spirits" in the Underground Railroad: "From Aurora to Downer's Grove [sic] was one night's run, thence to Chicago another night's run." Their daughter recorded her memories of their experiences, that they "were always helping groups of three to fourteen to get to Chicago." Once in Chicago, they went to the home of Philo and Ann Carpenter, often hidden in a load of hay or corn. She noted that Carpenter's home, on Morgan Street between Randolph and Washington, was surrounded by shade trees that provided "great protection" for arriving fugitives.[84]

On one occasion, in 1842, Israel Blodgett went to see his son, who was studying law with James Collins in Chicago. He left Downers Grove around midnight with a strong team of horses on his wagon. He first called on his old friend Philo Carpenter and knocked quite early in the morning. He said to his friend: "O! Mr. Carpenter; want any beef?" After Carpenter got dressed, he came out to find the "beef"—that is, four fugitives—hidden in the wagon, and within a few hours, he arranged to have them on a boat to Canada.[85]

One family story told of a time when a rider stopped at the house and requested food for himself and his horse. Avis Blodgett was happy to respond and after the rider rested for a few hours he continued to Chicago. However, a few days later, the same rider came back and proved to be a slave catcher who had successfully done some business in Chicago, as he had a fugitive, tied by the wrist to the horse bridle. The mounted man rode up to the house, and pleasantly requested if once again he could receive some "refreshment." She came forward with bread and water, handing these to the exhausted slave and responding to the rider: "Not a mouthful for you, Sir, but for this man, such as I have, I gladly give." Israel Blodgett realized it would be a good idea to also provide something for the rider and his horse and arranged for that. Also, in response to an inquiry about lodging, he directed the rider to a home down the road where he was confident that the folks would help the slave to escape from his abductor. Later, they learned that, in fact, the slave disappeared, the family was "surprised and indignant" over the escape, and they proceeded to lead the slave catcher on fruitless efforts to find him.

Their son, I. P. Blodgett, related how the family regularly received fugitive slaves and "passed them along" to people in Chicago. He also told a story of one particularly effective form of assistance involving a government official working for the courts in Chicago. This official would be approached by people looking for a particular fugitive. Being well-placed in the community, he would find the person being sought and announce to that person: "'Look here, Jack, I want you. Be sure to be on hand tomorrow morning at nine o'clock. Someone has come after you, and you must go back with him.' By nine o'clock the next morning Jack would be a lot nearer Canada than Chicago."[86]

Sheldon and Harriet Peck settled with their family in Lombard, just north of Downers Grove, in 1837 (see Figure 2.9). Peck was both an artist, doing mostly portraits, and a committed abolitionist. Many of the existing portraits done by Peck were of abolitionist husbands and wives in DuPage and Kane Counties. Peck was active in assisting freedom seekers, regularly transporting them into Chicago. His youngest son, Frank Peck, wrote, "Our home was used as headquarters for all opponents of slavery in this part of the county." Along with harboring fugitives, the Pecks hosted antislavery meetings and speeches from leading abolitionists from Chicago like John Jones and H. Ford Douglas. In Frank Peck's memoir is specific mention of a freedom seeker known only as "Old Charley" who stayed with the Pecks for an extended period. The current house museum includes a portrait of Old Charley, believed to have been painted by Peck's daughter Susan. Local collaborators with the Pecks were the brothers, Thomas and J. Walter Filer. Both were delegates to the 1842 Chicago meeting of the Illinois Anti-Slavery Society.[87]

On the road from Lombard to Chicago, in what is now the village of Maywood, the old Ten Mile House sat on a confluence of trails and roads at the place where they crossed the Des Plaines River. Built in the 1840s, this combination tavern and hotel served as a stopover point for farmers and livestock dealers taking their wares into Chicago. Local traditions hold that this was an occasional stopping point for travelers on the Underground Railroad.[88]

Ogden Avenue cuts diagonally through DuPage County, following the old coach and wagon road from Ottawa to Chicago. Near York Road, in present-day Hinsdale, was the small settlement of Fullersburg, an area originally settled by the Grant, Fuller, and Coe families. Local traditions connect them with the Underground Railroad. Descendants of John and Harriet Coe remember that they regularly provided shelter. The home of the Fullers still stands, and there are strong local traditions that this was a place of assistance. It is now relocated close to the Graue Mill, a well-known local historic structure. Although the educational exhibits and programs at the Mill are useful

Fig. 2.9 Sheldon and Harriet Peck Homestead. Author's photo.

introductions to the Underground Railroad, at present, there are only local traditions supporting claims of contact or support for freedom seekers.[89]

The northern part of the region, including Boone, McHenry, and Lake Counties, did not experience the same levels of early settlement as south and west of Chicago. By 1840, more than thirty thousand people had settled south and southwest and roughly twelve thousand had settled west of the small town of Chicago. To the north and northwest, there were only around seven thousand permanent residents. In addition, most freedom seekers came to the region from the south, southwest, and west, seeking to reach Chicago and move on to Michigan and Canada. Thus, the areas north of Chicago were out of the way. As settlement north and northwest of Chicago increased in the late 1840s and through the 1850s, farmers in these areas began to have some contact with freedom seekers, as is reflected in the next chapter.

From the mid-1830s until 1844, the networks of the Underground Railroad fully developed both in Chicago and in the region south and to the west of the city. Along with the ongoing support provided by Black residents in Chicago, newly arrived white settlers connected with one another as they responded to the arrival of freedom seekers on their doorsteps. Some of these latter efforts were organized through the unique work of Rev. John Cross and tied to the emergence of local congregations.

An agent working in Ohio, Indiana, Michigan, and Illinois for the American Anti-Slavery Society starting in 1836, Rev. John Cross received instructions in 1839 to focus his work in Illinois. Based near Galesburg and for a time in Bureau County, Cross traveled around the state giving antislavery lectures and meeting with groups, families, and individuals encouraging them to put their antislavery sentiments into action. They could act by providing direct assistance to freedom seekers and being aware of others doing the same. Activists in southwestern Michigan and northwestern Indiana were aware of his activities and had some contact as he sought to develop networks of aid from Illinois through to Detroit. When Cross found receptive folks, most likely many of whom were already assisting freedom seekers, he formalized these connections by following up with a letter reaffirming their willingness to be "ready to receive visitors at any hour of the night."[90]

By 1844, he was well-known across the state, and involved in several well-publicized controversies with freedom seekers. For his activism, he was informally recognized as the "Superintendent" of the Illinois Underground Railroad. One activist remembered: "Mr. Cross had hand bills and large posters circulated through the country advertising his business and calling on abolitionists everywhere for assistance in carrying out his plans."[91]

In the recollections of several old-time abolitionists is a—perhaps apocryphal—story of Cross being arrested by a sheriff (in one account, in DeKalb County) for assisting fugitives. However, the sheriff was afraid that abolitionist agitators in a certain town would be incensed to see Cross under arrest. So, the good reverend suggested that they drive through that town with Cross managing the horses and the sheriff hidden in the wagon. The ruse succeeded and on the other side of town, the sheriff resumed command and took Cross in. However, evidence was insufficient, and Cross was released by the court.[92]

Cross was also responsible for the now-iconic advertisement for the Underground Railroad published by the *Western Citizen* in 1844 (see Figure 2.10). In this image, a train is seen going into a mountain, that is, underground, with an invitation to travel on the "Liberty Line." It is signed: "*J. Cross, Proprietor*" (see Figure 2.10). Several years later, Cross collaborated with other clergy, most abolitionists, in the founding of the Illinois Institute, which later became Wheaton College. He served as the first president for the institution, established in 1853. After that, he continued to be active as a minister with Congregational churches in northern Illinois.[93]

LIBERTY LINE.
NEW ARRANGEMENT—NIGHT AND DAY.

The improved and splendid Locomotives, Clarkson and Lundy, with their trains fitted up in the best style of accommodation for passengers, will run their regular trips during the present season, between the borders of the Patriarchal Dominion and Libertyville, Upper Canada. Gentlemen and Ladies, who may wish to improve their health or circumstances, by a northern tour, are respectfully invited to give us their patronage.

SEATS FREE, *irrespective of color.*

Necessary Clothing furnished gratuitously to such as have *"fallen among thieves."*

"Hide the outcasts—let the oppressed go free."—*Bible.*

☞For seats apply at any of the trap doors, or to the conductor of the train.

J. CROSS, *Proprietor.*

N. B. For the special benefit of Pro-Slavery Police Officers, an extra heavy wagon for Texas, will be furnished, whenever it may be necessary, in which they will be forwarded as dead freight, to the "Valley of Rascals," always at the risk of the owners.

☞Extra Overcoats provided for such of them as are afflicted with protracted *chilly-phobia.*

Fig. 2.10 From *Western Citizen*, July 13, 1844. Reproduced
in Harris, *History of Negro Servitude.*

As an increasing number of New England families came into Illinois in the 1830s and 1840s, early efforts were made to establish Congregational churches, fostered in part by the activities of John Cross. Even though there was a national Plan of Union through which the Congregationalists and Presbyterians agreed that the first churches in Illinois would be Presbyterian, by 1836, there were already six small Congregational churches across the state. In that year, they formed the initial Illinois Congregational Association. Parallel to the formation of the first antislavery societies in the state (and often helping to lead them), members of the association passed resolutions condemning slavery, called for it to be abolished, and indicated support for all those seeking full emancipation. In their initial meeting they also resolved that no slaveholder should have access to "our Pulpits and communion tables."[94]

Several years later, the Illinois Association of Congregational Churches organized at the church in Princeton where Owen Lovejoy was pastor. This led to representatives of over eighty congregations in Illinois meeting in Farmington, in the central part of the state, in 1844. For their first constitution, the representatives passed resolutions declaring that no minister could be in the fellowship but those who saw slaveholding as among the most "heinous sins" and that placing persons in jail for assisting fugitives was "a wicked interference with the rights of conscience."[95]

By 1844, five of the congregations passed specific resolutions condemning slavery and refusing membership to lay people and ministers who were slavery sympathizers. In the stories of assistance recounted in this book, again and again, the key white activists are often connected with Congregational churches. Such was the case in LaSalle, Kendall, and Kane Counties; in the movement across Will County; in the journeys noted to the west, northwest, and north of Chicago; and in Chicago. As the Illinois Anti-Slavery Society was forming in 1837 and 1838, more than half of its initial 245 members were from Congregational churches. Many of the key leaders in the society were Congregational clergy men.[96]

By 1844, across Illinois, abolitionists had created a variety of formal organizations, and the antislavery societies were transitioning to become elements within the new Liberty Party. Years later, Zebina Eastman reflected on this transition indicating that in Illinois, as was true across the country, the original antislavery impulses came out of "religious sentiment." It was compelling to say to other people of faith in the country, and particularly in the South, that it was now necessary to abandon the practices of slavery. As this had little impact on Southerners, in much of the North, deep controversies arose as to how to move from religious demands to political demands and develop the laws to end slavery. However, Eastman felt that, in Illinois, there was a near unanimous sense of movement from the antislavery organizations to the formation of the Liberty Party and other political avenues. With this, of course, were the ongoing commitments and increasingly well-organized networks to assist freedom seekers.[97]

One interesting reflection of these networks is found in the "mail books" of the *Western Citizen*. The mail books were the subscription lists, and the radical abolitionists who created the networks of the Underground Railroad are almost all found on these lists.[98]

The *Western Citizen* provided extensive reporting on the activities of the antislavery societies and the emerging energies in the Liberty Party; the paper also offered two series of articles with dramatic stories of freedom seekers. The author of these was Mary Brown Davis, a remarkable abolitionist based in Peoria and active in the work of the Illinois Women's Anti-Slavery Society. Davis and her husband moved to Peoria in 1837; they were publishers of the *Peoria Register and North-Western Gazetteer* and worked closely with abolitionists and activists in northeastern Illinois.[99]

A broad range of white women were directly involved with their husbands and brothers in the work of abolition and in assisting freedom seekers. This included the emergence of women's groups opposed to slavery. The first of these were the Female Anti-slavery Societies in Putnam and Bureau Counties, both west of LaSalle County. A statewide Female Anti-Slavery Society formed in 1844 and met for several years at the same time as the Illinois Liberty Party. In this way, abolitionist husbands could attend the Liberty Party meetings, with many of their wives gathering just before or after to meet as the Illinois Female Anti-Slavery Society. Following the formation of the Chicago Anti-Slavery Society in 1840, by 1844, a Chicago Female Anti-Slavery Society was in place, which was, as with the others, organized by white women.[100]

Although the public purposes of the societies focused on abolition and the elimination of the "Black Laws" in Illinois, the meetings of such groups no doubt provided occasions for women to discuss ongoing strategies of assistance. The Female Anti-Slavery Society in Putnam was the most obvious in declaring in 1843 that whatever the consequences of their work, they would "obey the laws of God rather than the laws of men," and support "the 'star-led' pilgrim in his struggle after freedom." The Putnam County women resolved to also provide a clothing depository so that a freedom seeker traveling through could "replenish his scanty wardrobe." In 1844, at the Peoria meeting of the Illinois Female Anti-Slavery Society, a freedom seeker noted that a Mrs. Wiltslow appealed to the assembled women for funds to enable her to purchase her daughter who was still held in slavery in Louisiana. The group responded to her plea and passed a resolution that declared their sympathy and support for "our colored sisters in bonds."[101]

In the small settlement of Bristol, in Kendall County on the route from Ottawa to Chicago, women in the Wheeler family responded to the practical needs of freedom seekers. A woman in the town remembered that as a young girl, she saw clothing and other supplies collected and held in readiness for distribution to those in transit on the Underground Railroad.[102]

The Underground is Underway

From 1839 into 1844 and beyond, freedom seekers continued to travel independently across northeastern Illinois, with many finding places of support. An existing frame of wagon and coach roads, mostly coming up from the Illinois River valley, provided the routes for travel. As these corridors of travel were becoming more regular, so were the points of dependable assistance where some travelers found help when needed. White activists across the region connected with one another over shared commitments, and the networks of the Underground Railroad were well in place by 1844. These networks, through personal and church connections, tied activists along the routes to those operating in Chicago. The work of white activists continued in parallel with the ongoing support given by the small Black community in Chicago, led by the barbers John Johnson and Lewis Isbell, and with connections through small Black communities in Illinois and their activist African Methodist Episcopal and Wood River Baptist Association congregations.[103]

Available evidence indicates that by 1844, six hundred to one thousand freedom seekers came to and through northeastern Illinois. The Black activists in Chicago and almost all the white families providing aid in Chicago and across the region remained on their farms and in their communities and continued to be deeply engaged with travelers until the beginnings of the Civil War. The fundamental networks of the Underground Railroad were in place by 1844 and soon, their use would grow dramatically. Word of Chicago as a place of refuge and a place of assistance for reaching Canada continued to spread among freedom seekers, especially in Missouri. The number of travelers and the deepening networks of support would soon be affected by the emergence of a whole new group of young leaders in the Black community in Chicago and by the compelling impact of the 1850 Fugitive Slave Act.

CHAPTER THREE

Leaders and Travelers, 1845–1854

Henry Stevenson

THE ILLINOIS AND MICHIGAN Canal, the "I&M," stretched ninety-six miles from Peru and La Salle to Chicago, coming up through the region southwest of Chicago. Following the Illinois River and then the Des Plaines River, the canal paralleled older trails and the rivers that had been used for passage from the Great Lakes to the Mississippi River watershed and waterways. It was finished in 1848, after decades of planning and twelve years of labor. Northeast of the upper reaches of the Illinois River, it was a natural alternative for freedom seekers on their way to the Chicago region. A vivid example is in the escape of Henry Stevenson, born into slavery in Audrain County, northwest of St. Louis, in Missouri. His journey to freedom came in 1850 (see Figure 3.1 and Map 3.1).[1]

Stevenson was directed by his master to help track down two runaways, Anthony and Margaret, a married couple. The two lived on nearby farms in Audrain County when they decided to seek their freedom. Immediately upon their escape, Margaret's owner, John Wilfeley, was ready to pursue them and hired a slave catcher named Uriah Hinch. He asked Henry's owner if he could use Henry in the search. They included Stevenson because they knew they would need to get information from any free Black people they ran into. In an interview years later, Henry remembered that they were hesitant "to go poking 'round for runaway slaves" on their own. Hinch learned that Anthony and Margaret headed for Chicago, and they immediately set off in pursuit.[2]

Stevenson was a good friend of the couple who escaped, and seeing some possibilities for his own liberation, he both assisted and frustrated the efforts to find them. The small group followed the movements of the two fugitives out of Missouri and after reaching Quincy, Illinois, traveled by horseback to

Map 3.1 Henry Stevenson traveled with slave catchers by horseback, river steamer, and canal boat to Chicago. He later traveled on his own by lake steamer and railroad in his journey to Detroit and freedom in Canada.

the Illinois River and then took a steamboat to Peoria. The trackers stopped at many places including Peoria, where Stevenson said, "I tole master I would go, and stay with my own color—that was the way to hunt."[3]

Further up the Illinois River, they switched over to the tow boats on the I&M Canal and traveled on to Chicago. For pulling the boats, horses were changed every ten miles. Every time they did so, Stevenson went on deck to watch, and every time while the horse changing was underway, workers called to him, "You are free now, don't go back." But each time he declared that he needed to serve his master. That is, until he reached the end of the canal.[4]

Upon arrival in Chicago, a crowd of around three hundred greeted the boat, as the new canal was a great attraction. Stevenson, supposedly looking for the runaways, jumped on a wagon with a Black driver. The driver immediately asked him if he was seeking his freedom and when Stevenson said yes, the driver responded, "You're free right now." He was then taken to a barber shop, possibly that of Lewis Isbell. After making the necessary arrangements, Stevenson went back to see Hinch and after getting money for expenses, told him that he would find the runaways that very night. Instead, he boarded the *Sam Ward*, a small lake steamer that stopped along the coast around Lake Michigan. The boat took Henry to New Buffalo. There, he received help from a Black resident who directed him to the train to Detroit where he was to look for a barber named Gordon. The barber saw Stevenson arrive and immediately assisted him to get over to Windsor in Canada.[5]

Meanwhile, many people in Chicago were very much aware of the presence of this slave catching party that included Henry. One paper noted that Hinch was in town with a Black servant. When his intentions became known, a few of the local white citizens reminded Hinch that his was a risky business. Meanwhile, the paper also reported that the servant, this of course was Henry, boarded a lake steamer and was on his way to "the Queen's dominions." Hinch soon learned that Stevenson escaped and that a possible coat of tar and feathers was being prepared for him. Seeking some protection from a judge, an antislavery lawyer approached him and suggested "immediate flight as the safest course." Hinch took off on the next stagecoach out of town.[6]

This all happened just a few weeks after the passage of the Fugitive Slave Act on September 18, 1850, and many of the residents of Chicago were alarmed at the potential consequences for both freedom seekers and the settled Black population. In response to the passage of the Fugitive Slave Act and the practical encounters with Uriah Hinch, the Chicago-based *Western Citizen* noted: "It is proper to add that our colored population are fully prepared for any emergencies. While they do not propose to commit any violence unless driven to the wall, they will not suffer the new law to be executed upon their persons." Frederick Douglass, in the *North Star*, called Henry's escape "The First Slave Hunt" following the passage of the Fugitive Slave Act and called it an example of that law's failure.[7]

Fig. 3.1 A group of refugee settlers. Standing from left:
Anne Mary Jane Hunt, Mansfield Smith, Lucinda Seymour; seated from left:
Henry Stevenson, and Bush Johnson. Stevenson's journey to freedom came in 1850.
Taken in Windsor, Ontario, in 1895. Schomburg Center for Research in Black
Culture, New York Public Library Digital Collections.

The Black Community in Chicago

By 1845, the population of Chicago almost tripled, from 4,500 in 1840 to over 12,000. By 1850, it exploded to 30,000. The small Black community experienced a similar pattern, growing from just 53 Black residents recorded in the federal Census of 1840 to 140 in 1845 and over 320 in 1850. The full size of the community, of course, is not exact, given that some number of persons of African descent in Chicago no doubt felt it prudent to *not* be recorded in any official way. Freedom seekers traveling through the city and those who decided to stay for an extended period or make Chicago their home could be reluctant to affirm their presence to persons representing the government given their illegal status and the potentials for becoming known to slave catchers.

Whatever the full number, a substantial Black community emerged with a set of remarkable activists in Chicago in the latter half of the 1840s. There was a sense that Chicago and other parts of Illinois and "the West" were places of possibility for Black families and entrepreneurs. Henry Wagoner, a few years after his arrival, wrote to the *Frederick Douglass Paper*, published in Rochester, New York, that if Black people chose to stay in the United States, coming to Chicago was a good option: "Permit me to again admonish our colored brethren of the East, and especially those of capital and enterprise, to come to the western states (Indiana excepted), where a little cash money can be laid out to good advantage. Now is the time to get a hold of a sale and establish ourselves among this hardy race of Northern Europeans."[8]

The increasing number of Black families along with a sizable group of individuals, many living as servants in white households, spread across the small city. White and Black residents lived next to each other, and in practical terms, the economy and living space was integrated. In this context, a few Black institutions and businesses began to emerge.[9]

As Chicago's African American community grew, its leadership continued the long engagement with assisting freedom seekers, both parallel to and at times in collaboration with white activists. Two churches were crucial in these efforts. Quinn Chapel started as a prayer group in 1844 and Zoar Baptist Church began its congregational life in 1847 and formally organized in 1850.[10] By 1847, Chicago's religious communities also included the white First Methodist, First Presbyterian, Tabernacle Baptist, and St. Mary's Catholic churches.

In 1844, several recently settled African Americans met for prayer in the home of John Day, who lived just off State Street, between Lake and Randolph. Fairly soon, a larger meeting space was needed, and the prayer group moved nearby to the home of Maria Parker. Soon the emerging congregation gathered in a local school and then in the home of Madison Patterson, known as an "eloquent exhorter." In 1847, the congregation decided to become part of the African Methodist Episcopal (AME) Church. Rev. William Paul Quinn, a remarkable bishop of the AME Church, along with missionary Rev. George Johnson, came to Chicago to assist in organizing the church.

Quinn worked with Black communities across the Midwest in the 1830s and 1840s and eventually was recognized as one of the early great leaders in the AME tradition. He was called the "Pioneer," in recognition of his work across what was at the time the great "western" part of the country, the frontier states of Kentucky, Indiana, Illinois, and Missouri. He traveled extensively through the region, meeting with potential church members in slave and free communities. In the late 1830s, he worked with Priscilla "Mother Baltimore" Baltimore in Brooklyn, Illinois, across the river from St. Louis, to establish was came to be called Quinn Chapel in that community. A man constantly on the move, his work helped create networks of communication among Black communities that assisted freedom seekers. He established a base of operations in Richmond, Indiana, and worked closely with Quakers engaged with the Underground Railroad. On occasion, he personally assisted individuals on their journeys, most of whom were heading for Chicago.[11]

To honor his energy and dedication, the newly formed church in Chicago took the name of Quinn Chapel. Significant leadership at Quinn Chapel in those early years came from Rev. Abram T. Hall, who started out as part of the original prayer group and worked as an assistant to the barber Oliver Henderson. As with all the early AME churches, the members at Quinn Chapel were integrally involved with freedom seekers. Over time, they engaged with the network of AME Church congregations across Illinois providing secure contacts for travelers.[12]

In 1850, the editors of the *Chicago Daily Journal* were very much aware of the growth of Quinn Chapel. In several articles, the newspaper mentioned the strength of the congregation and noted, "They have a plain, but neat church edifice, which is thronged whenever opened for services, with a congregation, that in point of decorum and personal appearance, will by no means suffer in comparison with other congregations, of greater pretensions in greater houses."[13]

The Wood River Baptist Association of Black churches in Illinois noted in 1846 that they had fourteen churches across the state with a total of 242 members and a presence in Chicago. There was not a formal congregation, but several residents had connections with the Baptists, and this led in 1850 to the creation of Xenia Baptist Church, starting with three members.[14]

In 1853, Xenia became Zoar Baptist and, parallel to the emergence of Quinn Chapel, its members were key to the work of assisting freedom seekers. Over the next few years, its members and leaders included John and Mary Jones, William and Amanda Johnson, Henry and Susan Wagoner, and Henry and Ailey Bradford. In 1854, William Johnson submitted the application for recognition to the Wood River Association as a congregation with nineteen members.[15] Within a few years and with the help of sister congregations, Zoar Baptist erected a small building at the intersection of Buffalo and Taylor. After several years of growth, the congregation split over differing opinions on slave marriage and foot washing rituals, and in 1860, a small group left to form Mt. Zion Baptist. The groups reconciled in 1862 to become Olivet Baptist Church, which eventually became one of the largest Protestant congregations in the world.[16]

As was the situation with Quinn Chapel, the participation of Zoar Baptist in a statewide organization certainly helped facilitate communications among Black communities about the details of support for freedom seekers coming through Illinois. At the time of the Great Chicago Exodus in April of 1861, because of the leadership connected with the congregation, the final church service before the refugees departed was held at Zoar. As both congregations developed, they added to the stability of Chicago's Black community and provided environments in which free people of color, settled refugees, and travelers found connections and safety.

In 1846, Henry Bibb, living in Canada and editing *The Voice of The Fugitive*, wrote a letter to the *Signal of Liberty*, the abolitionist newspaper of Guy Buckley in Ann Arbor, Michigan. Bibb wrote of attending the Western Antislavery Convention in Chicago at the end of June. There, he heard inspiring speeches by Owen Lovejoy, Ichabod Codding, Dr. Charles Dyer, and others. He also noted the warm reception he had received from the Black community in the city and observed, "Our colored friends in Chicago seemed to be doing well and are awake to the great subject of Liberty. I rejoice to hear there is very little prejudice existing in Chicago against the colored citizens."[17]

By 1850, the Black population in Chicago had grown to an official 323 persons, including 181 men and 142 women. However, a good number who arrived from 1845 did not show up in official records, and therefore, the Black community was likely larger and more fluid than reflected in the Census numbers. The individuals and families leading these free people of color and refugees were directly involved with the arrival of freedom seekers and the efforts to provide support.[18]

Beginning in the 1840s, the leadership in the tight Black community of Chicago was also deeply involved at state and national levels in public opposition to slavery and the well-established "Black Codes" and in support of community-building endeavors. Because of connections through churches, especially the African Methodist Episcopal churches and the Wood River Baptist churches, and through networks related to "colored persons' conventions," these leaders knew their state and national counterparts well.[19]

Black community leaders were consistently objecting to the Black Laws (also called the Black Codes) of Illinois. Laws created in the territorial days that were directed specifically against Black persons had been codified immediately following statehood in 1819. The limits on Black persons continued to be defined in state laws through the 1820s and 1830s. The "Revised Statutes of 1845" superseded and codified a detailed range of limits and denials. It was necessary for Black persons entering Illinois to obtain a certificate of freedom and post a bond of $1000 attesting that one would not become a burden to the state. Anyone who helped avoid these requirements could be fined $500. Black men could not vote or serve in the militia. Persons held in bondage could not be brought into Illinois and freed. The statue continued with a detailed range of additional limits and obligations in regard to people of color, both within and outside forms of bondage.[20]

In 1847, the debates for a new constitution for Illinois included significant conflict between those expecting the Black Laws to be clarified and tightened and those seeking to abolish the laws. The elements in the Black Laws remained in place in the "Revised Statues" and the new constitution directed the state legislature to develop further laws specifically to "prohibit free persons of color from immigrating to and settling in this state" and to "prohibit the owners of slaves from bringing them into this state, for the purpose of

Fig. 3.2 John Jones. Blanchard,
Discovery and Conquests of the Northwest.

freeing them." This section of the new constitution was presented separately
to the voters of Illinois and approved by an overwhelming vote. The statues
had direct impact on all Black residents in the state and on those who assisted
with the movement of freedom seekers. Although less and less enforceable
in northeastern Illinois due to abolitionist sentiments, these statutes were
the law. [21]

Particularly through the writings of John Jones (see Figure 3.2), Chicago
leadership connected with Black leaders across the state and appealed to
white voters to repeal the Black Laws. As the debates in the constitutional
convention were underway, in 1847, Jones published detailed arguments

against the Black Laws in the *Western Citizen* and the *Chicago Tribune,* and in the . following year, with the support of others he formed a public committee in Chicago to publicly oppose them . He continued these public appeals for years, culminating in his 1864 pamphlet, "The Black Laws of Illinois and a Few Reasons Why They Should be Repealed," and action by the state legislature in 1865 to finally repeal them.[22]

Opposition to the Black Laws was one of several Illinois struggles shared with people of color across the country. From 1848 forward, John Jones and others were corresponding with Black publications and organizations with a national audience.[23]

In the same year that activists were challenging the Black Laws, Jones and Rev. Abram T. Hall, connected with Quinn Chapel, were delegates to the Colored National Convention meeting in Cleveland. One of a series of national conventions throughout the antebellum period, the Cleveland meeting raised the full range of concerns for Black Americans, including opposition to slavery, Black Laws, and the colonialization movement, and affirmation of community efforts for education, temperance, land owning, and a range of other interests. At the convention, Frederick Douglass (see Figure 3.3) was elected president and John Jones was elected vice president. In a series of resolutions, the convention affirmed a full range of commitments including opposition to any source that is "derogatory to the universal equality of man" and a commitment to using "all justifiable means in aiding our enslaved brethren in escaping from the Southern Prison House of Bondage." Given the growing intensity of violent encounters with slave catchers in places like Chicago, the convention resolutions included a clear statement on the need to acquire the skills of the "military sciences," to be able to "measure arms with assailants without and invaders within," and to form in each state "Vigilant Committees."[24]

On September 11, 1848, Jones and Rev. Hall met with Black residents in Chicago to recap the activities and resolutions from the national convention. Rev. Hall served as secretary for the gathering, which passed several resolutions calling for meetings in the state to petition the state legislature to repeal the state's oppressive "Black Laws."[25]

Leaders in Chicago's Black Community

At the center of these activities and directly involved with assisting freedom seekers coming into Chicago were John and Mary Jones, Henry and Ailey

Fig. 3.3 Frederick Douglass. Schomburg Center for Research in Black
Culture, Jean Blackwell Hutson Research and Reference Division,
New York Public Library Digital Collections.

Bradford, Lewis and Margaret Isbell, Henry and Susan Wagoner, Barney and
Julia Ford, William and Amanda Johnson, Rev. Abram and Joanna Hall, Isaac
and Emma Jane Atkinson, James Bonner, Joseph and Anna Hudlin, Joseph
and Maria Barquet, H. Ford and Sattira Douglas, and Rev. Byrd and Jane
Parker. Their involvement continued the efforts to assist travelers that was

started by Chicago's first Black settlers through the work of Lewis Isbell, John Johnson, and others. [26]

John and Mary Richardson Jones arrived in Chicago in 1845 (see Figure 3.4). John came from North Carolina; his father was German and his mother was a free biracial woman. Born a free person, he was apprenticed to a tailor who moved to Tennessee and John went with him. There, he met and fell in love with Mary Richardson, a free woman whose family was in Tennessee where her father was a blacksmith. The Richardson family moved to Alton, Illinois, and John soon followed, marrying Mary in 1844. While in Alton, they obtained their free papers and came to Chicago in 1845 with their young daughter, Lavinia. From an initial small apartment at what is now the corner of Madison and Wells, and later a home at 119 Dearborn Street, John started a tailoring business. Over time, he became a successful businessman in the city and emerged as one of the key leaders for the Black community. Within a few years of their arrival, John developed friendships with Dr. Charles Dyer and L. C. Paine Freer that lasted throughout their lives. Starting in 1847, he worked actively for years to resist Illinois's Black Laws and often represented his community at state and national conventions convened to oppose slavery and lift up "colored" communities. Throughout the late 1840s and into the years of the Civil War, both John and Mary were deeply involved with their community, provided active support for freedom seekers, and were active in the creation and life of Zoar Baptist Church. Their daughter remembered their home was "a haven for escaped slaves" and that they had been involved with "sending hundreds of fugitives" on to safety in Canada. They were hosts for John Brown, the militant supporter of Black emancipation, whenever the radical was in town. [27]

Mary Jones was interviewed late in her life and recalled details about their encounters with John Brown and the white and Black activists assisting freedom seekers in Chicago. Their personal involvement began soon after they had arrived in Chicago in the fall of 1845, when they became unexpected hosts for three girls who had been enslaved in Missouri. The three arrived late in the year, hidden under straw in a wagon, and stayed with the Joneses through the winter before continuing to Canada. [28]

Henry and Ailey Bradford came to Chicago to join family, as Ailey was the older sister of Mary Jones. Well established by 1850 with Henry working as a barber, they likely arrived in 1847, several years after John and Mary Jones had settled. They were all involved with church life at Zoar Baptist and Henry

Fig. 3.4 John and Mary Jones. Courtesy of Dr. Bruce Purnell, Washington, DC.

was active with John Jones in wider community leadership. This included his work as a representative from Chicago with the state "Convention of Colored Citizens" held in Alton in 1856, serving on the executive committee, and his participation in the Chicago committee formed to investigate claims related to immigration to Haiti in 1857. He was part of the leadership for a Chicago mass meeting convened in late 1857 to invite Stephen Douglas to come to Illinois to debate Fredrick Douglass.[29] While there is little available documentation on the Bradfords' direct engagement with freedom seekers, their involvement is sensible given their community leadership and the family connection with John and Mary Jones.[30]

From the time of his arrival in Chicago in 1838, Lewis Isbell was at the center of activity for assisting freedom seekers. He collaborated regularly with white activists conveying travelers into Chicago, and later, among both white and Black activists, he was seen as a central leader. Isbell developed a lasting friendship with Allan Pinkerton after his arrival in Chicago, and they worked together at the heart of the Underground Railroad networks across northeastern Illinois. One observer noted that over the many years, Isbell may have helped as many as one thousand freedom seekers on their way to Canada. Isbell was proud of the fact that, over time, at his barber shop in the Sherman House, he provided services for all the mayors of Chicago and a wide range of others, including Abraham Lincoln, Ulysses Grant, and Stephen Douglas. He installed the first reclining barber chairs to be found in Chicago and owned one of Chicago's first bathhouses. He attended the 1853 state Convention of Colored Citizens held in Chicago and was one of four delegates from Cook County to the 1856 Convention in Alton, Illinois. Living until 1905, he outlived all his contemporaries, and at "old-timers" reunion in Chicago, he often shared stories of his work on the Underground Railroad.[31]

Mary Richardson Jones settled in Chicago in 1845, and her sister Ailey Richardson Bradford joined her in 1847. Soon afterward, their youngest sister Margaret visited. She met Lewis Isbell and in 1849, they returned to the family home in Alton, Illinois, to be married. Thus, these families—the Joneses, Bradfords, and Isbells—were tied together through the three sisters. In their work assisting freedom seekers, they collaborated with family members in Alton. Alfred Richardson, brother to the three sisters, settled in Alton in the 1830s and helped establish the Union Baptist Church of Alton in 1836. Several years later, the entire family relocated from Tennessee to be with Alfred. The family remained in Alton for many years and their close connections with the three families in Chicago was helpful in many ways. In addition, these family connections came into play in the 1850s when Jones, Bradford, and Isbell, with several others, initiated the secret society that became in Chicago the North Star Lodge of the Prince Hall Freemasons.[32]

Henry and Susan Wagoner settled in Chicago in 1846, moving from Chatham, Ontario, where he worked for the *Chatham Journal*. He was born in Maryland, his mother a freed slave and his father a German American merchant (see Figure 3.5). Henry benefited from an early education and, as a free

Fig. 3.5 Henry O. Wagoner. Simmons, *Men of Mark*.

Black person, traveled to western Virginia and then settled for a year in Ohio, where he taught school. After this, he spent some time in New Orleans and St. Louis before settling for a while in Galena, Illinois, where he worked several years for the *Northwestern Gazette and Galena Advertiser*. The newspaper work led to his employment in Chatham, in southwestern Ontario, east of Detroit, an area then called Canada West. Susan was born a free person in Indiana and moved to Canada, where she married Henry in 1844. When they arrived in Chicago, he convinced Zebina Eastman to hire him to work for the *Western Citizen*. Along the way, he met Frederick Douglass, and after Douglass began publication of the *North Star*, his fiercely antislavery newspaper in 1847 in Rochester, New York, Wagoner occasionally wrote articles for Douglass. Over time, the Wagoners acquired property and operated a small grain mill in Chicago, becoming an integral part of Chicago's small Black community. He advertised regularly in newspapers for "Wagoner's Manufactory of Hominy, Sarup, Grits, Cracked Wheat, Hominy Meal, Graham Flour, Feed, &c."[33]

Born enslaved in Virginia, Barney Ford eventually ended up working on a Mississippi steamboat. In 1848, he seized his freedom by walking away from his master in the Illinois port of Quincy and found assistance to travel overland to Chicago. He walked much of the way, going near Champaign and Kankakee on his travels east and north. He met Henry and Susan Wagoner and Julia Lyons, Susan's sister who was living with them. In 1849 he and Julia married. Ford worked with Wagoner in the mill, and together, they were active in assisting freedom seekers coming to Chicago and in giving leadership in the Black community.[34]

In 1851, the Fords decided to head for the gold mines of California. When their ship stopped at Greytown in Nicaragua, they recognized that it might be more profitable to stay there and opened a small hotel to serve the large numbers of Americans coming through on their way to the gold country. The United States Hotel proved to be a profitable venture, but unrest in Nicaragua led them back to Chicago and to the Wagoners in 1855.[35]

During the 1850s, both Henry Wagoner and Barney Ford were deeply involved in Chicago's Black community. When meetings were held, both men often served in leadership capacities. They were collaborators with John and Mary Jones, and other Black activists, in providing leadership in the Black community and assistance for freedom seekers.[36]

The names of Jones, Wagoner, and Ford appear together on various committees and in attendance at meetings over the years. In January 1852, Jones chaired a "meeting of colored citizens" in Chicago, organized in response to the tragedies of the raid in Christiana, Pennsylvania, and Wagoner sat on the key resolutions committee. In December 1853, a "mass meeting of colored citizens" passed resolutions in support of the work of Frederick Douglass; the meeting was called to order by Jones and again, Wagoner headed the resolutions committee. An 1857 meeting opposing the statements of Senator Stephen Douglas was chaired by Barney Ford with Wagoner in charge of resolutions. An 1858 gathering at Quinn Chapel about emigration to Haiti was chaired by a Rev. Smith, from North Carolina, with Wagoner and Ford serving as secretaries. A year later, a similar public meeting also saw Wagoner and Ford appointed as secretaries. In 1860, Wagoner and Jones provided leadership to establish a free library for their community and made an appeal to the residents of Chicago to contribute books.[37]

Henry Wagoner developed a friendship with John Brown, starting in 1857. When Brown came to Chicago with his group of liberated Missouri slaves in March of 1859, the Wagoners and the Fords provided shelter and food for the fugitives for three days, and John and Mary Jones hosted the white men. However, the whole situation with John Brown, his cohorts, and the liberated slaves was dangerous for Wagoner, who was well-known throughout the city because of his business activities. The interaction of Black and white leadership in Chicago came into play as Allan Pinkerton stepped in to assist the Wagoner and Jones families by arranging for funds and transport to move the freedom seekers with John Brown and his men on to Detroit."[38]

One of the best-known barbers in Chicago and an eloquent speaker, William Johnson arrived in 1846 and became closely involved with John Jones and Henry Wagoner in leadership roles. Their names often appeared together with various meetings and committees. William and his wife Amanda came from Kentucky with a young daughter and William's mother. They arrived when William was twenty-eight and Amanda was twenty-four, and they lived three houses from the DeWolf family. Eventually they ended up at the core of the first Baptist congregation, which became Zoar Baptist and then Olivet Baptist Church. William was the first clerk (lay leader) for the congregation, serving for five years in the 1850s.[39]

The other significant congregation, Quinn Chapel, was organized in 1847 with the help of Rev. Abram T. Hall and his wife, Joanna. They both arrived in 1845 and married in 1846. Hall, a free man aged twenty-three, came from a free family in Pennsylvania and worked as a barber and as an itinerant minister (see Figure 3.6). Joanna came from North Carolina through the networks of the Underground Railroad, arriving in Chicago at age sixteen. Early in his life, Hall organized churches in Pennsylvania, and after settling in Chicago, he assisted with the development of other congregations in northeastern Illinois, Iowa, and Wisconsin. These connections with African Methodist Episcopal churches in various communities were useful in assisting freedom seekers. Rev. Abram not only emerged as a key leader for the Black community, but also had sustained contact and developed friendships with white

Fig. 3.6 Rev. Abram T. Hall. Chicago History Museum, ICHi-022352.

abolitionist activists. He was a lifelong friend of Dr. Charles Dyer and upon
Dyer's death in 1878 joined Isaac Arnold and Zebina Eastman among the
pallbearers. By 1850, the Halls acquired their own home. John Jones and Rev.
Hall were selected in 1848 to be representatives from Chicago to the National
Colored Convention in Cleveland.[40]

The active membership of Quinn Chapel included Isaac and Emma Jane
Atkinson (see Figures 3.7 and 3.8). They arrived in 1853, moving from New
York with two children. Born in Virginia, Isaac was about thirty-three and
Emma, from Connecticut, was twenty. Family traditions and records indicate
that both of them had mixed racial backgrounds that included African and
Cherokee ancestors. In their work as part of Quinn Chapel, Emma was one
of the "Big Four," a remarkable set of women who organized assistance for
freedom seekers through Quinn Chapel.[41]

James Bonner was a close friend and business associate of John Jones and
came to Chicago in 1848 with his wife and four children. In the early 1850s,
Jones and Bonner managed what they called the General Intelligence Office as an employment and real estate business. This business served as a
means for finding temporary work for local Black residents and for those
traveling through. In addition, they were involved in 1854–55, with Frederick Douglass, in developing a national "Manual Labor School" on behalf of
the National Council for Colored People, an outgrowth of the national "colored" conventions movement. The Bonner family was involved with others
through Quinn Chapel and James assisted with fundraising for a new building for the congregation. He unexpectedly died in late 1855 and both Henry
Wagoner and Frederick Douglass wrote brief but eloquent memorial statements that were published in *Frederick Douglass' Paper*. Douglass wrote: "His
heart and his purse were ever open to the weary wanderer from the prison
house of slavery."[42]

These longtime established residents took on leadership roles and were
involved with the work of the Underground Railroad soon after their arrival.
Coming a few years later, there were several others publicly involved with assisting freedom seekers. James and Mariah Green escaped from Kentucky and
came through Chicago on the Underground Railroad in 1848 and settled in
Michigan. After her death and that of two of his three children, James came
back to Chicago in 1857 to live and help.[43]

Joseph and Anna Hudlin both moved to Chicago in 1854 and married in
1855 (see Figures 3.9 and 3.10). Born in 1840, Anna came from a Pennsylvania

Fig. 3.7 Isaac Atkinson. Chicago History Museum, ICHi-021952.

Fig. 3.8 Emma Atkinson. Chicago History Museum, ICHi-021943.

Fig. 3.9 Elizabeth Anna Hudlin. Chicago History Museum, ICHi-022356;
Chicago Photographic Studios, photographer.

Fig. 3.10 Joseph Hudlin. Chicago History Museum, ICHi-022357;
Worthington, photographer.

family given their freedom by Quaker owners. Joseph was born enslaved in 1830 in Virginia. They were the first African American family to build their own house in Chicago and there, they had nine children. Their home was near the intersection of Taylor and State, and family members remember stories of assistance they gave to freedom seekers. Joseph was an early member of the North Star Lodge and, most likely, collaborated with Jones, Isbell, and Bradford on providing aid. They joined Quinn Chapel and were active members until their deaths. Later reports say that through the years, they were beloved members of the Black community and Joseph had a remarkable career with the Chicago Board of Trade.[44]

Joseph and Maria Barquet were active in Chicago for a few years in the 1850s, working with John and Mary Jones. Joseph Barquet attended the 1853 Convention of Colored Citizens and joined Johnson, Isbell, and others in sending the invitation throughout Illinois for the 1856 convention. By 1860, the Barquet family moved to Galesburg and Joseph was one of the first Black residents of Illinois to enlist in the famous 54th Massachusetts Infantry.[45]

As was the case with some of the other Black leaders in Chicago, H. Ford Douglas, born in Virginia in 1831, was the son of an enslaved woman and free white man. By age twenty, he was a well-known orator and advocate for abolition and emigration. Throughout the 1850s, he traveled in midwestern states and Canada lecturing and was a writer-editor for the *Provincial Freeman*, a Black-owned newspaper based in Canada. Starting in 1855, Chicago became home base for him and his wife, Sattira. By all accounts, he was a remarkable speaker and in 1859, he toured in Illinois and Wisconsin with Fredrick Douglass. In 1860, he went on an extended tour in New England, and a Boston reporter noted at an abolitionist rally where he spoke just before Wendell Phillips that Douglas was "a good looking young man of color" and he "made a slashing speech of considerable ability." Frequently his name appears in newspaper accounts of meetings in the Black community in Chicago. With John Jones, Lewis Isbell, and William Johnson, he represented Cook County at the 1856 state Convention of Colored Citizens in Alton, Illinois, and chaired the committee to write a Declaration of Sentiments and Plan of Action for the convention.[46]

For the most part, the leaders of the community were born free, though Barney Ford and Lewis Isbell had been enslaved. A unique situation existed for Rev. Byrd Parker who was born enslaved, meaning that in his life, he was both a freedom seeker and a free person of color. Born in North Carolina in

1815, he first entered the historical record living enslaved in St. Louis in 1842, and he was evidently active in church work, as he was listed in records as Rev. Parker. In 1842 he married an enslaved woman named Caroline. He served as pastor at the St. Paul AME Church in St. Louis from 1845 to 1847 and 1851 to 1852. This is one of the churches that grew out of the religious work of Priscilla Baltimore, also called "Mother Baltimore." During his service, a substantial church building was erected. He left for Chicago in 1852 and became involved with Quinn Chapel, in part through occasional preaching and fundraising in Illinois and Wisconsin for the congregation's new building. At some point he purchased his freedom.[47]

A spirited preacher, Parker became widely known throughout the region and in Wisconsin. One newspaper reported on his sermonizing as that of a "Freedom Shrieker." He played a visible role in leadership in the Black community of Chicago and at a meeting of "colored citizens," he was "unanimously and enthusiastically" selected to represent the "Religious interests of Chicago" at the Colored National Convention in Rochester in July of 1853. He also was a participant at the first Convention of Colored Citizens in Illinois in October of that year. At the end of 1853, he helped organize a mass meeting of Black citizens gathered to express support for the work of Frederick Douglass.[48]

However, Parker's unique situation arose from a very public accusation of bigamy. As noted, in 1842, he married Caroline in St. Louis, and she was manumitted in that same year, evidently after the marriage. In 1851, a young woman named Jane Johnson, who was also from North Carolina, came to teach school in St. Louis and for a while lived with Byrd and Caroline Parker. She was twenty-one. Both Byrd and Jane moved to Chicago and eventually were married. When Byrd left St. Louis he sought a divorce from Caroline, but the Missouri courts refused to recognize the legality of a marriage of enslaved persons. So, Byrd and Jane likely concluded that the first marriage had no legal standing. However, in January of 1854, Caroline came to Chicago and publicly accused Byrd. He was arrested for bigamy.[49]

The leadership of the Black community issued a public letter of support for Byrd in the *Chicago Tribune*, Caroline left Chicago, and the case was dismissed. The letter was signed by William Johnson, H. O. Wagoner, Henry Bradford, James Bonner, Lewis Isbell, John Jones, and several others. They noted in the letter that Parker also had the support of Bishop Paul Quinn and other leaders of the African Methodist Episcopal Church.[50]

This situation is compelling in regard to the oppression that kept enslaved people out of the legal system, both in terms of registering something as basic as a marriage and then having no recourse to change or challenge what may or may not be the case. Probably because of this very public confrontation involving a minister and community leader and similar dilemmas, the legal standing of marriage emerged on church agendas. In 1858, the Wood River Baptist Association dealt with the following question: "If a slave man is married to a slave woman, and should they be separated by their master, or by making their escape into a free state, and marry another, is he or she guilty of bigamy?" In response to this concern, the Association concluded the following: "Resolved, that we believe the marriage of slaves to be morally binding, yet we do not believe it to be legal. We would, however, caution the churches to look well into the matter before they act."[51]

In concert with the activist work of key male leaders of the Black community were the actions by a group of women at Quinn Chapel to provide food, clothing, and shelter for arriving fugitives. They were referred to in the records of the church as the "Big Four." It is probable that Emma Atkinson and Joanna Hall, both active in the life of that congregation, were part of this activity. It is possible that the other two may have been Mary Jones and a woman known only as "Aunt Charlotte."[52]

Little is known of the full identity of Aunt Charlotte, but a young white girl growing up in Chicago later wrote of an unexpected encounter with her. Caroline Kirkland was the daughter of the editor of the *Chicago Democrat*, and years later, recalled meeting a woman who bought herself, her husband, and her son out of slavery before coming to Chicago. As a child of five or six, Caroline went with her nurse to see a woman in a particular neighborhood. She noticed that Charlotte's house was darkened and upon entering, saw sixteen bodies asleep on the floor. She wrote: "They were fugitive slaves, caked with mud, scratched and torn with briers, and showing through their rags marks of the most brutal ill-treatment." Charlotte told them that it would be necessary to wake them up in the middle of the night to enable to continue their journey. Although a young child, Kirkland had never forgotten the sight of these "sojourners in the dark."[53]

As a constant and growing stream of freedom seekers came to and through Chicago in the 1840s and 1850s, Black and white involvement was at times interconnected. Dr. Charles Dyer regularly collaborated with leaders in the Black community, starting in the 1840s. Years later, a Chicago abolitionist recalled: "He was often seen in close and earnest converse with the colored barbers of the town." Zebina Eastman remembered that for years it was well-known by Lewis Isbell, William Johnson, and other leaders in the Black community that collaboration with the white boat captains, Augustus Walker and Chesley Blake, was a good option, and "that both of their steamers were safe places on which to stow fugitives."[54]

The White Activists in Chicago

White activists, however, continued to assist freedom seekers through their own networks. By 1845, Aaron Gibbs, a native of Litchfield, Connecticut, settled in as the first full-time dentist in Chicago. He carried strong antislavery opinions and soon connected with Dr. Dyer to become directly involved. Over the years he was a public advocate for the Underground Railroad in Chicago and known as a source of financial support for the work.[55]

In 1845, Dr. Dyer was in the same suite of offices as Calvin DeWolf. James H. Collins's office was across the hall. In 1846, Harvey Hurd was a young attorney starting out by studying in the offices of DeWolf (see Figure 3.11). He came from Connecticut with his brother Edward Hurd, who had a tailoring business. Harvey wrote out of his personal experience, "Dr. Dyer was at that time recognized as the leading spirit among the anti-slavery people of this part of the state, and our office might reasonably have been designated as 'The Chicago depot of the underground railroad.'" Harvey and Edward knew well and worked with Allan Pinkerton on assisting travelers and over the years met with John Brown. Harvey was remembered for many years at the reunion of old-timers in Chicago because of a unique connection with John Brown. He was close to the size and build of Brown and when Brown arrived in Chicago with the twelve freedom seekers from western Missouri, it appears that Mary Jones and Allan Pinkerton sent him off to get a new suit for Brown. He may have obtained this from his brother who was a tailor. Chicagoans speculated that this was the suit John Brown wore at his hanging.[56]

Harvey recalled another occasion, in 1846, when white activists outside the city brought several runaway slaves to their offices in the center of Chicago. They had recently left the South and reached the networks of the Underground Railroad in northeastern Illinois. At the time, Hurd had his sleeping room in the back of the offices. The escapees were given new clothes and taken to another location. However, shortly after this, the US marshal arrived

Fig. 3.11 Harvey Hurd. Blanchard,
Discovery and Conquests of the Northwest.

convinced that slaves were present; and Hurd let him to see that they were gone. The marshal believed that they would try to escape on a lake steamer leaving that morning for Canada. Hearing about all the three fugitives, a large crowd gathered on the docks to witness the possible escape. This may well have been at the lumber yards and docks of Sylvester Lind. With the crowd and the marshal's men present, Hurd witnessed a successful sleight of hand where the three were intermingled with Black workers loading wood for the steamer and after carrying wood aboard, they were "safely stowed away."[57]

Some white abolitionists, although not directly involved with freedom seekers, were very helpful to the workers on the Underground Railroad. Edwin Larned grew up in Rhode Island, graduated from Brown University and took up a teaching position near St. Louis in 1840. He settled in Chicago in 1847 to join a law firm and, two years later, he married Frances Greene, the daughter of a Rhode Island senator for whom he had worked. Years later, after her death, he married Calista Blanchard. From the beginning of his career, he was a strong antislavery advocate and became well-known in Chicago for his oratorical skills. His first great public speech was in opposition to Stephen Douglas in mass meetings following the passage of the Fugitive Slave Act in 1850. He worked with George Manierre in the defense of freedom seeker Moses Johnson. In 1860, he worked with Isaac Arnold in the defense of Joseph Stout, one of those indicted in the great Ottawa Rescue Case involving the freedom seeker, Jim Gray. In April of 1861, Lincoln appointed Larned the United States attorney for northern Illinois and one of his first official acts was to dismiss all the changes pending against Chicago activists who had been brought to court for assisting freedom seekers. In all of this, although close friends with those directly engaged with assisting travelers, Edwin Larned's involvement was primarily in the court room.[58]

Some white men, such as Sylvester Lind, used their positions of power to aid freedom seekers. A lumber baron, he organized his company, Lind and Dunlap, in 1849 and had forests and mills in upper Wisconsin and Michigan. With these, he had a lumberyard and docks on the Chicago River. Working with activists in Chicago and across the region, he arranged to have freedom seekers placed on his ships and carried north to the mills, where other ships completed the passage to Detroit and Canada. A very successful businessman, Lind's initial contributions started Lind University, which became Lake Forest College.[59]

Interviewed in 1890 about the Underground Railroad, Lind discussed his close work with James H. Collins, Philo Carpenter, and Dr. Charles Dyer. He recounted one incident in which Carpenter stopped by his home late at night. Carpenter knew that Lind had a lake steamer leaving for Canada the next day, and he told him, "Mr. Lind, I've got four gentlemen locked up in my barn and I want you to help me get them to Canada." Lind agreed to make arrangements and, traveling to the boat with Carpenter, he found that only the cook was on board. The cook, a "good anti-slavery man," immediately

Fig. 3.12 Allan Pinkerton. Blanchard,
Discovery and Conquests of the Northwest.

agreed to hide the travelers, provide them with food, and see them safely to
Canada.[60]

Others in the rapidly growing white community in Chicago saw the need
for both abolition and assistance for travelers. Among these were the family
of Allan Pinkerton who moved to Chicago in 1847 (see Figure 3.12). The family had assisted freedom seekers from their home in Dundee and Allan, along
with continuing work with white activists, developed regular contact with
leaders in Chicago's Black community. The Pinkertons were among a number of immigrants from Scotland that settled across the Chicago region in the
1840s and 1850s. Additional activists emerged among German immigrants,

especially from Chicago's small Jewish community, almost all of whom came from Germany. As was the situation with Dutch immigrants directly south of Chicago, these recent immigrants were resettling in large part because of religious and political controversies and discrimination in Europe. These experiences may have provided some level of empathy for the plight of freedom seekers traveling through and some need to react to the reality of slavery in their newly adopted country. A strong voice in this direction was that of German immigrant George Schneider. Following warfare in the German states in the late 1840s, Schneider immigrated, settling first in St. Louis. In 1851, he came to Chicago to be editor of the *Staats-Zeitung*, a German language newspaper established several years earlier. The increasing national controversies over slavery led Schneider to publicly advocate for abolition, and with the influence of the newspaper, the German population in the upper Midwest became strongly antislavery and supported abolitionist policies. The *Staats-Zeitung* was second only to the *Western Citizen* in its positions on abolition. In a later memoir, Schneider wrote about the Underground Railroad and, although not providing details about specific freedom seekers, admitted to his deep involvement with the networks of support in Chicago.[61]

Abraham Kohn, one of the first German Jews to settle in Chicago, was well-known as an abolitionist, served as one of three Jewish delegates at the 1860 Republican National Convention, and was elected city clerk of Chicago in 1860. Kohn, along with Michael and Henry Greenebaum, Leopold Meyer, and Bernhard Felsenthal may all have reached beyond their public abolitionist sentiments to collaborate in assisting freedom seekers. Meyer reported on one specific incident in 1853 when Henry Greenebaum led a group of Chicago citizens to liberate a freedom seeker who had been arrested at the intersection of Van Buren and Sherman, at the south end of the station for the Chicago and Rock Island Railroad. It's likely that they interfered with an effort to take this prisoner back into slavery in Missouri. These activists also assisted in calling a mass meeting for all German residents of Chicago to join in the abolitionist movement.[62]

As new immigrant groups were settling in northeastern Illinois in the late 1840s, with some supporting the work of abolition and the Underground Railroad, established Black and white activists were engaged with political and organizing concerns in addition to providing assistance to travelers. In the Black community, support was coalescing for new congregations, one Baptist and one in the African Methodist Episcopal tradition. Community meetings were regularly held, in relation to national and state conventions and to support the efforts led by John Jones to overturn the "Black Laws" of Illinois.

White activists provided leadership in the Northwestern Liberty Convention in 1846. Meeting in Chicago, it opened with words from Dr. Dyer and the active participation of L. C. Paine Freer, Zebina Eastman, and James McClellan. From outside Chicago other speakers included Owen Lovejoy from Princeton, Samuel Cushing from Crete, Ichabod Codding from Lockport, and the Black Canadian-based journalist, Henry Bibb.[63]

These white activists supported the growth of the political movements that were increasingly proabolition and sought to influence the work of the state's constitutional convention in 1847. A state convention for the Liberty Party met in Hennepin in 1848, in part to select delegates to the national convention to be held in Buffalo. At the state convention, nine delegates were selected to represent Illinois. Of these, six were directly engaged in assisting freedom seekers: Charles Dyer, James Collins, and James McClellan of Cook County; Owen Lovejoy of Bureau; Moses Pettingill of Peoria; and John Cross of Lee County. Also in that year, the Chicago abolitionists led the state's Liberty Party; they nominated Dr. Dyer to run for governor and Philo Carpenter for mayor. However, these candidacies were swept into movements leading to the formation of the Free Soil Party and neither ended up in elective office.[64]

A Visible Underground Railroad

By 1845–46, both the networks and the language of the Underground Railroad were in place, particularly among white abolitionists in Chicago and the region. In September 1846, the *Western Citizen* wrote, "The Northwest branch of the great subterranean thoroughfare has been doing brisk business the present season and we understand that the stock is several per cent above par. A dividend will probably be declared soon." Newspapers and journals based in Chicago included reports about arriving fugitives, the activities of slave catchers, and various forms of announcements, occasionally on assisting freedom seekers. Because of the press activity, an increasing number of Chicagoans were aware of the Underground Railroad and likely knew some of the participants. With the growth of the Black community, after 1845, such reports and events regularly mention participation by both white and Black activists.[65]

Many of the freedom seekers coming through Chicago fled from enslavement in Missouri. Missourians understood that Chicago was often simply a stop on the way to Canada. Early on, in 1842, the St. Louis *Organ* newspaper noted that "The depredations of abolitionists upon our citizens are becoming more frequent and daring daily. Accounts from all parts of the State convince us that a regular system has been adopted by the abolitionists in Canada." By 1845, the business of transporting freedom seekers on boats on Lake Michigan going to Detroit was well-known.[66]

The different views of slavery in Chicago and St. Louis were clear and often bitterly expressed. One resident of St. Louis, possibly a kidnapping spy, was in Chicago and wrote to the St. Louis *Reveille* newspaper in 1845, pointing at the underhanded work of Capt. Walker, the most visible of the lake captains. To begin, he identified Dyer, Carpenter, Collins, Freer, and DeWolf as ring leaders of the Underground Railroad. He gave account of Dyer collaborating with Capt. Walker to smuggle four travelers on the *Great Western*. "Dr. Dyer stated, as the *Great Western* left the wharf, that he had placed the slave he had rescued on board, with two others, and as he was going on board, a fourth came and he put him on board, and the Western had sailed away with them. Whereupon the abolitionists gave three cheers for Dr. Dyer, the *Great Western*, and Capt. Walker. And then they departed to conduct fresh schemes to rob their fellow-citizens of their property."[67]

Opinions in St. Louis condemned Chicago as the center of "slave corruption." At one point, the *St. Louis Republican* headlined "Look to your Slaves," arguing that there were "scoundrel agents" in their own city seeking to lure slaves away. The paper mentioned several cases and gave as an example the experience of James Bissell. This slave owner lost four slaves and after sending agents after them, found that they had made it to Chicago. He then received a letter from Chicago, signed by "Anti-Slavery," which he shared with the St. Louis paper:

James Bissell, Esq. : —Dear Sir—

I have the satisfaction to inform you, that John and Lucy arrived safely here, via the underground railroad, and have left for Canada by steam. They love liberty and are among friends. I communicate this information

that you may be relieved of further expense in their behalf. Is it not your
duty to dissolve your connection with Slavery?

Truly yours, &c., "ANTI-SLAVERY"[68]

One of the most famous fugitive slave notices, prominent in the exhibits of
the Library of Congress, notes "$200 Reward. Five Negro Slaves." This notice
from St. Louis reinforced the assumptions about Chicago. After full descriptions of the "Negro man, his wife, and three children," it announces: "It is
supposed that they are making their way to Chicago, and that a white man ac-
companies them, that they will travel chiefly at night, and most probably in a
covered wagon." The fugitives were identified as Washington and Mary Reed
and their children: Fielding (12 years old), Matilda (6), and Malcolm (4).[69]

In 1851 the editor of the *Belleville Advocate*, in a town a few miles east of St.
Louis in Illinois, reflected the opinion held in many places in Missouri: "We
of the South do not regard Chicago as belonging to Illinois. It is as perfect a
sink hole of abolitionism as Boston or Cincinnati."[70]

A favorite foil for the abolitionists and especially for the white activists
was Judge Lewis C. Kercheval, serving in the Chicago courts. A Kentuckian
by birth, he was proud of his heritage and a proponent of the rights of slave
catchers, especially those from his home state. He was also well-known for
his hatred of people of color, and he was an alcoholic. One reporter wrote,
"When sufficiently sober to have a recollection he gloried in the memory of
a time in the dim past when his grandfather has owned a mulatto girl.... In
honor of his native state and his grandfather, he felt bound to indulge the pre-
sumption that every runaway negro belonged to some Kentuckian."[71]

In 1845, a freedom seeker from Missouri, a young man named Jim, was
captured and brought before Judge Kercheval by the notorious constable
Henry Rhines and Jim's supposed master from Missouri. However, "a number of prominent Abolitionists" heard of the case and immediately descended
on the court. Dr. Dyer arrived with more than twenty Black and white residents to sit in the court and the streets outside were packed. James Collins
stepped forward to defend Jim and engaged in an eloquent, extended opening statement. He demanded that the court must have legal proof that slavery was official in Missouri and after a good bit of back and forth, the judge
sent for a copy from somewhere of the Statutes of Missouri. The hallway and
courtroom were filled with protestors and Rhines, heavily armed, was overwhelmed by the crowd. It was all a setup. Daniel Davidson, a colleague of

Collins entered the room, Jim was advised to leave, and in the chaos, which ensued, Rhines was "run over" and Jim escaped, heading for Canada. One reporter wrote, "The crowd was jubilant, Rhines utterly disconsolate and demoralized, and Kercheval chagrined and indignant."[72]

The crowd marched to the law offices of Collins and celebrated. In response to what he saw as an unruly mob, the mayor called for a meeting of all the "law-and-order" members of the community. Appropriate resolutions were prepared to condemn the abolitionists and activists, however, no doubt led by Collins, Dyer, and others, the meeting was turned around and clearly supported Chicago as an "asylum from oppression" for those seeking their freedom. Some felt this was the moment in 1845 when Chicago's abolitionist and proactive reputation was publicly confirmed.[73]

Later in that same year, two young men were arrested as fugitives and Collins and his good friend George Manierre were asked to defend them before Judge Kercheval. Among the activists watching the trial was Allan Pinkerton. At the end of the second day of deliberations, Pinkerton announced his need for a good drink. And, of course, that he did not want to drink alone. He invited Kercheval, knowing that the two fugitives would be safely locked up in a kind of cell at the back of the judge's offices. It so happened that the offices which served as the court room were on a second floor just above a saloon. So, they adjourned to the lower floor, and "a second drink seemed as necessary as the first, and a third more refreshing than either." Pinkerton's generous hosting suggests he knew his judge well. Meanwhile, an old friend organized a rescue. Upon returning upstairs, Kercheval found his prisoners gone; Collins, Pinkerton, and others all pled total ignorance as to how this could have happened. And two more people took off for Canada.[74]

The visibility of the Underground Railroad grew in the late 1840s, when an increasing number of reports on freedom seekers coming to and through Chicago appeared in newspapers. The accounts often mentioned collaborations of white and Black persons in confrontations and rescues. Some of these reports were short and factual. Others were more heated, as in the report of an incident in 1846 when four freedom seekers were seized on the street in the middle of the day. A crowd of Black and white people, almost a mob, watched events as legal proceedings to return the four Missouri travelers started. As the proceedings got confused, a crowd of Black men appeared "with clubs and other weapons," the four were taken outside, and then "a strong guard of determined Blacks formed around each and escorted them to a place of safety." This created such a disturbance in Chicago that the mayor called for a public meeting to discuss how to prevent such disruptions. His meeting was itself disrupted by a crew of abolitionists who took over and turned the conversation toward discussing the means for assisting fugitives who might come to Chicago.[75]

In 1846 one of the most celebrated stories in Chicago's Underground Railroad traditions occurred. An escapee from Kentucky who was living with and working for Dr. Dyer was seized by his former master and held tied up in a room in the Mansion House hotel. Dr. Dyer found out where he was and, bursting into the room, immediately cut the ropes of the captive. The young man sprang to the window and disappeared. The enslavers followed Dr. Dyer out of the hotel and attacked him with a large bowie knife. Dyer was carrying only a cane but was able to use it to good account and with one blow knocked down his attacker. The cane was shattered. Shortly afterward, citizens of Chicago presented him with "a splendid gold-headed cane, with appropriate inscriptions commemorating the occasion." The cane itself was a gift for Dyer from a Virginia slaveholder visiting Chicago, who offered the cane with the admonition that slave owners ought to stay in the South and deserved to be cracked over the head if they were fool enough to come to Chicago. The gold head for the cane cost ninety dollars, with almost all of that coming from the Black community. It was a substantial tribute to Dr. Dyer from his "colored brethren," whom he sometimes referred to as his "fellow complexioners."[76]

Following the uproar created by this event, a public meeting was held with close to three hundred men and women in attendance. James Collins wrote to a friend of the success of the meeting and the passage of resolutions condemning slavery and slave hunting. Collins felt it was a strong indication that the tide of opinion was turning in favor of the abolitionists. He also noted that in the past two weeks another thirteen travelers were on their way to freedom and that was "a fair prospect of plenty of business for our 'Underground Railway.'"[77]

In the spring of 1848, slave hunters from Missouri kidnapped Abram Ross in Chicago. Ross had escaped from his enslavement, settled in Chicago, and worked as a delivery man for Philo Carpenter. Late one night in early June, two men barged into the home of Nelson White, an elderly Black man living on State Street. They came in "with pistols and a bowie knife," and demanded to know the whereabouts of Ross. The frightened man indicated that Ross was upstairs. The slave catchers rushed to the room and immediately grabbed a couple in bed. They stripped off their clothes and tried to drag them out of bed, only to find they had the wrong people. Meanwhile, Ross was in bed in a nearby room, heard the commotion and tried to escape. After managing to get onto the roof of an adjoined shed, he was grabbed and gagged and taken off into the night. A number of Black and white residents were aroused and gave chase but were unable to catch the kidnappers. Paine Freer recalled years later that he and Dr. Dyer took off in a wagon in pursuit of the kidnappers hoping to rescue Ross. However, when they reached Ottawa, they found the party had already left on a boat down the Illinois River. Recalled Freer: "We gave up the chase, but at Peru the negro made his escape. He pretended that he was sorry he had run away and would be glad to go back to slavery. He was locked up in the boat and his supper was sent down to him. With the eating knife sent with his supper he took off the lock, opened the door and went ashore before the boat left the landing. He was back in Chicago almost as soon as we were."[78]

Later that year, a traveler apprehended in Chicago was brought before Judge Kercheval, under the original federal Fugitive Slave Act created in 1793. In his defense, several of Chicago's longtime white activists appeared, with James Collins serving as his defense attorney. A motion was made to disregard the original arrest. As new papers were being prepared, the handcuffed man was last seen alone with Dr. Dyer. Evidently, Dyer was able to remove the handcuffs and urged the man to jump out of a nearby window. Court officials reappeared and when they asked what had happened to the assumed prisoner, Dyer replied, "He has sunk into the bosom of the community."[79]

In 1849, Lucinda Seymour escaped from St. Louis with her husband. They had a frightening time crossing the Mississippi, and upon landing on the Illinois side, she found that they were about eight miles outside of Alton, Illinois. They borrowed a wagon and a sympathetic farmer's wife gave them some peaches and her son took them to the home of an older Black man in Alton. From there, they received assistance at various places leading eventually to Chicago where they found help getting to the lake steamer under the command of Capt. Blake. With Blake, they traveled to Detroit and then over the river into Windsor, Ontario. Lucinda is in the iconic photograph (see Figure 3.1 at the opening of this chapter) of the group of freedom seekers still living in Windsor, Ontario, in the 1890s.[80]

In May of 1850, two Kentuckians from Louisville known today only by their last names, Churchwell and Throckmorton, arrived and announced that they had "capital invested in Chicago, the former in a family named Allen, the latter in a boy named George, a waiter at the Richmond [hotel]." The slave hunters stayed at the Tremont Hotel and evidently, their purposes became well-known. Although they obtained an arrest warrant from the United States deputy marshal, they were unable to catch anyone. A newspaper announced that the boy, George, was "safe over the border. The Allen family are also safe, and the Louisvillians may go home."[81] Note that the news report intentionally misspells "Louisvilleans"!

Near the same time, Calvin DeWolf recalled an incident involving Dr. Dyer and another traveler from Missouri. At the time, the public hospital in Chicago, controlled by county commissioners, would not admit Black patients. However, it came to Dyer's attention that the man, now living in the city, was in desperate need of care and possible surgery. He contacted a commissioner named O'Bryan and affirmed that he was aware of a Henry O'Bryan in need of care. Since Dyer had raised the concern, the three commissioners signed off on admitting Henry O'Bryan. Unknowingly, they violated the rules established by the County . . . because of the use of an Irish name.[82]

Fugitive Slave Act of 1850

A watershed for the Black community and for the Black and white activists of the Underground Railroad was the passage, on September 18, 1850, of the federal Fugitive Slave Act., Often referred to and denounced in popular discourse as the "Fugitive Slave Law," this act was part of the Compromise of 1850, a bundle of laws that settled some territorial questions, admitted California as a free state, and significantly strengthened the existing federal laws concerning fugitive slaves. Before 1850, although there were federal statues addressing issues with "fugitives," responses were basically seen as state and local concerns and varied across the country. The Fugitive Slave Act effectively nationalized the directives and responses for capture and return.[83]

Citizens and law enforcement officers anywhere in the country were directed to assist, under threat of fine and imprisonment, individuals seeking to capture or recapture their "property," people quaintly referred to as persons "held to service or labor," who managed to escape from bondage. Failure to assist in the capture of a fugitive could lead to a fine of $1,000 or six months in jail, or both. Once captured, a judicial hearing was needed to confirm that the correct "property" had been recovered. Incredibly, an officer of a court finding that the held person was indeed a runaway would receive an administrative fee of ten dollars, and one finding that the held person was free resulted in receiving a fee of five dollars! The great impact of the law was a clear indication that it was in force throughout the country. Its passage terrorized Black people across the northern states, creating fear for settled families as well as for freedom seekers traveling toward Canada. Black and white activists understood that providing assistance was more dangerous than before. With the growth of the Underground Railroad, many places throughout the North had become fairly safe for settled refugees and for those going to Canada. The new law meant that all such places, including Chicago and northeastern Illinois, no longer were outside the reach of slave catchers and kidnappers.

A few days after the passage of the Fugitive Slave Act, over three hundred Black and white residents of Chicago met at Quinn Chapel to respond to the outrage. The meeting was in the hands of Black leadership and they created a Vigilance Committee with regular patrols to watch for and confront slave catchers. This had "seven divisions of six men each" to patrol parts of the city and to "keep an eye out for interlopers." The groups paralleled the seven districts of the recently expanded police department. The resolution coming out of the meeting declared, in part, that as "colored men," they would stand together to resist any move to condemn them to slavery. They declared that they were not advocates of violence, but they would defend fugitives and free people of color at whatever cost. "We who have tasted freedom are ready to exclaim with Patrick Henry, 'Give us liberty or give us death;' and 'Resistance to tyrants is obedience to God.' We will stand by our liberty at the expense of our lives, and will not consent to be taken into slavery nor permit our brethren to be taken."[84]

A few days later, another community gathering of Black residents resolved that they would not "fly to Canada," but that they would stay in Chicago and "defend themselves." For the emancipation activists in Chicago, not only did they need to continue their tenacious efforts on numerous fronts to advance their community, fight against the Black Codes, and assist freedom seekers, but they also needed to prepare for armed and violent responses to the forces arrayed against them.[85]

However, a good number of individuals and families, including some who were settled and owned property, departed for Canada. Quinn Chapel lost close to half of its membership in October and November of 1850, with the vast majority of those who left going to Canada. Reflecting the biracial collaboration developing in the city, Mary Jones recalled that Dr. Dyer, Zebina Eastman, John Jones, Paine Freer, Calvin DeWolf, Henry Bradford, Lewis Isbell, Henry O. Wagoner, and others worked together to assist residents and travelers to head for Canada. During this commotion, one of the Black barbers in Chicago, a man named Jackson, was terrified when his former master entered his shop for a shave. He was able to leave without being seen and managed to quickly leave the city.[86]

The Common Council of Chicago met October 21st, voting their objection to the Fugitive Slave Act and directed Chicago officials and law enforcement to not assist in following the law. They resolved in part that this law was "an attempt to impose infamous duties on conscientious citizens and compel them to do the devil's work under the guise of constitutional obligation."

Their quick response to the passage of the Fugitive Slave Act, reflective of intense abolitionist sentiments and activism, placed Chicago as the first northern city to challenge the new federal law.[87]

The Common Council called for a public meeting the next evening, expecting to receive affirmations of support from various parts of the city for their action. However, Stephen Douglas requested time to speak and after holding forth for three and a half hours, he turned the energies of the gathering into supporting the federal laws. Several days later, the Common Council reversed its actions to defy the Fugitive Slave Act. This reversal was then followed by a large assembly called for by the abolitionists and in response to the oratory of James Collins and Edwin Larned, and a series of resolutions were adopted to condemn the act. Finally, by early December, the Common Council again voted to assert that if residents of Chicago were assisting "fugitives from oppression," in so doing they were not committing treason against the government. In this series of meetings, there is no evidence that any Black leaders addressed the groups. So, however clear-eyed the Black community was, some white opinions in Chicago churned back and forth in response to the new law.[88]

Earlier in 1850, the white activists in Chicago had formed the Committee for the Relief of Fugitive Slaves in Canada. This group included James Collins, Paine Freer, Philo Carpenter, Sylvester Lind, George Manierre, James McClellan, Jr., and other white activists. As an additional tangible reaction to the Fugitive Slave Act, and a reflection of growing relationships, on November 11th, the white committee invited John Jones, William Johnson, and Lewis Isbell to join in their efforts.[89] The collections for refugees appeared to be not only for those in Canada, but also for those traveling to Canada, and this marks a formal collaboration of efforts by white and Black leaders in Chicago. Moreover, such gatherings also created the opportunities to compare notes and develop plans for aid to arriving freedom seekers.

Since the mass meeting of September 30th at Quinn Chapel, the Vigilance Committee was making its presence known, as reflected in the case of Mr. Hinch mentioned in Henry Stevenson's story of his journey up the I&M Canal. The *Chicago Democrat* also noted, perhaps in response to the same incident, that the Black population of Chicago was "up in arms" and slave catchers needed to be alert to the "threat of tar and feathers." Several weeks later, the *Western Citizen* reported on a group of Black Chicagoans who pursued a slave owner who captured a person he once had held in slavery. About five miles out of town, they rescued the captive and sent him on his way to Canada.[90]

Other communities in northeastern Illinois reacted vigorously to the passage of the Fugitive Slave Act. Following the passage of the act in September, abolitionists in Somonauk called for a mass meeting to consider responses. Close to three hundred people showed up and supported a strong resolution that declared the Fugitive Slave Act to be "a base violation of the Constitution," that supporters of the law are "traitors to Freedom," that the law is "at variance with the laws of God," and that they would "agitate! agitate!" until this law is repealed. It is intriguing to note that, although there was a widespread understanding that families in the community provided assistance to freedom seekers, this meeting and its resolutions did *not* advocate direct support for fugitive travelers.[91]

In July of 1851, Henry Bibb, editor of *Voice of the Fugitive*, based in Sandwich, Ontario, traveled to Chicago to attend the Christian Anti-Slavery Convention. He shared with his readers observations about the Black community. He preached at Quinn Chapel and seemed pleased that it was "a crowded house" that Sunday morning. He noted there were about two hundred Black persons in Chicago and no school for Black children since they were able to attend white schools, as seemed right and obvious. Bibb wrote, "There is no city in the western or middle states where there is less prejudice, or where people of color have better friends, than in Chicago."[92]

The Anti-Slavery Convention for which Bibb came to Chicago had been called for at a similar convention the previous year in Cincinnati. Now, this second gathering, in 1851, had around 250 participants from the northern states with more than half from Illinois. At the end of the convention, Henry Bibb was asked to speak, continuing the tradition of antislavery groups having a former fugitive slave on the program to give witness to the horrors of slavery. Unlike almost all the antislavery groups and meetings that had been held across northeastern Illinois, this Chicago meeting was not a white-only gathering.

The Illinois delegates included many of the activists. Owen Lovejoy and John Bryant attended with eight others from Princeton in Bureau County; Rev. John Cross was there; as were Ezra Goodhue and four others from Plainfield; L. S. Bartlett from Beebe's Grove, a neighbor of the Cushings; one of the Blodgett's sons and three more from Downers Grove; Rev. John Payne from the Ivanhoe church and seven others from Lake County including Amos Bennett; and Deacon Strong, William Paxton, and fourteen others from Aurora. The large Chicago delegation included Philo Carpenter, William Taylor, Zebina Eastman, and Sylvester Lind. Most significantly, they were joined by John Jones, Barney Ford, and six others from their Baptist congregation and Rev. George William Johnson from Quinn Chapel. This is another indication that Chicago leaders and their wives continued to reach across racial lines in their work for abolition and to assist those traveling through.[93]

Henry Wagoner was also in attendance at the Convention and immediately following it, sent a letter to *Frederick Douglass' Paper*. He wrote that Henry Bibb addressed the people "to a very good effect," but that it would be very helpful to the Black residents of Chicago if he, Douglass, also could come soon to lift the spirits of the people who are "all anxious to hear your enchanting powers."[94]

Another incident involving strong responses by Black and white residents in June of 1851 is reflected in an extended set of articles in Chicago papers and picked up in press around the country. The articles reported on a freedom seeker, Moses Johnson, who had been snatched off the street in "broad daylight." Slave catchers claimed he was William Johnson, an escaped slave from Lafayette County in Missouri. When brought to court, George Manierre and Edwin Larned were the lead attorneys for Johnson defending him based on the arresting description along with several legal technicalities. The warrant used by the slave catcher described a fugitive who was five feet eight inches and "copper colored," and Johnson was five feet five inches and "very Black." The trial lasted for three days, and the press reported that large numbers of white and Black residents gathered both outside and within the court room. Harvey Hurd was there, serving as a clerk for the court and he remembered Allan Pinkerton in the vicinity with around fifty armed men. The marshal had half a dozen deputies guarding Johnson and ready for trouble. The whole event was so intense that immediately following the successful defense of Johnson, the Black citizens of Chicago held a meeting to pass resolutions and present silver cups of appreciation for the passionate work of Manierre and Larned. The leaders involved in the response included Barney Ford, George Johnson, Alexander Smith, William Johnson, Henry Wagoner, and Rev. Abram Hall. In presenting the silver cups, the Black leadership wrote, "We also feel gratified, gentlemen, to think the law has been observed, and order maintained, while at the same time, the slaveholder has been defeated, and liberty has triumphed; and that the best feeling exists on the part of the citizens, all of which, we think, will tend to strengthen the cause of freedom in Chicago." Because of the strong press coverage, the incident with Moses Johnson was pointed to by proslavery interests across the Midwest as a "standing disgrace to Chicago," and it was heralded by abolitionist forces as a strike for justice and safety for those seeking their freedom through Chicago.[95]

A particular connection reflecting Black and white relationships involved Paine Freer and John Jones in September of 1852. Their friendship developed over the years since Jones arrived in Chicago. Freer, in his capacity as an attorney, represented Jones in arranging for a curious bill of sale for a freedom seeker named Albert Pettit, a relative of Jones. Albert was in Chicago, but his enslaver followed him to Chicago, captured him, and announced he was willing to sell him. The contract identified James Pettit of Summerville, Tennessee, as Albert's owner and described Jones's commitment to set him free. Many years later, Freer recalled Jones's work among white and Black abolitionists to raise the funds to buy Albert's freedom. So, the funds were raised, the contract signed, and Albert was free.[96]

Because of his connections among white and Black residents in the city, John Jones was able to run, along with other businesses, what he called his "General Intelligence Office." This served as a place for obtaining loans, managing house rentals, and arranging for the payment of taxes. It also functioned as an employment agency for "stewards, cooks, waiters, seamstresses, chambermaids, and girls to do general house work." In 1854 and well into 1855, Jones ran advertisements for employees. It is very likely that the office was a not-so-subtle cover for finding jobs for fugitives. When Jones was advertising for his employment and real estate office, he offered as a reference Paine Freer.[97]

Black Emancipation Activism

As seen in the previous examples, Chicago's Black residents reacted strongly to the passage of the Fugitive Slave Act, acted decisively in support of freedom seekers facing kidnapping and return, and collaborated with white residents on a variety of concerns. Intimately connected to these were ongoing efforts to oppose the Black Laws and to foster community empowerment. Reflecting this broad set of issues, in December of 1852, a mass meeting gathered under the leadership of Jones, Wagoner, Johnson, Byrd, Bonner, and Rev. Hall to petition for the fundamental rights of citizenship for Black residents. [98]

Leadership in the Black community, particularly through the work of John Jones, Henry Wagoner, and H. Ford Douglas, kept abreast of national concerns and issues for Black people. A practical reflection of this was the regular contact maintained with Frederick Douglass. Douglass, through his continuous traveling, speaking, and communicating through his newspapers, helped connect Black leadership across the country. Not only did he publish letters from Chicago leaders, but he also had Jones, Wagoner, Johnson, and Bonner as his agents for *Frederick Douglass' Paper* in 1853 and 1854.

In July of 1853, a national Colored Convention met in Rochester, New York. This was energized in part by the leadership of Frederick Douglass affirming constitutional rights: "we are ... American citizens asserting their rights on their own native soil." The participants in the Convention considered a wide range of issues faced by Black people in the United States. Chicago's Black community elected four activists to attend: John Jones, James Bonner, H. O. Wagoner, and Rev. Byrd Parker. These four were elected at meetings of the "colored citizens" of Chicago at Quinn Chapel in early June.[99]

The demands for action and change articulated at the national convention helped set the agenda for the first meeting of the Convention of the Colored Citizens of Illinois in October 1853. However, this meeting was also in response to actions of the state legislature earlier in the year. In February 1853, the legislature passed An Act to Prevent the Immigration of Free Negroes into This State. The bill was the formal response by the legislature to the directive from the 1848 state constitution and also, in part, a reaction to the perceived support given to the increasing number of freedom seekers entering the state. This built upon the existing draconian measures in the Black Codes in the state that were further complicated by the Fugitive Slave Act, all of which drew strong reactions not only from Black leadership but from the increasing white abolitionist sentiments across northern Illinois. [100]

Meeting in Chicago, the thirty-three delegates to the Convention of the Colored Citizens of Illinois included twenty from Chicago. John Jones was elected president, and other leaders in the proceedings were the activists Wagoner, Bonner, Barquet, Isbell, Parker, William Johnson, and Rev. Hall. Jones's brother-in-law, Alfred Richardson of Alton, addressed the convention, another example of the close connections among those engaged in so many aspects of emancipation activism. The Chicago meeting adopted a series of resolutions reaffirming the injustices of the Black Laws in Illinois and the recent anti-immigrant law and urging their constituencies toward self-sufficiency and land ownership. There were major denunciations of slavery and its attendant evils and a "soul-stirring" address by Frederick Douglass. The writers of the final resolutions adopted by the Convention used language from the Rochester and earlier national conventions in regard to issues of emigration and their sense of citizenship: "We will plant our trees in American soil, and repose in the shade thereof." Following the Convention, they issued a letter to the People of Illinois asking for the rights for citizenship, voting, a peaceful home, full access to education, and, simply, entry into the state. "We ask for no special privileges or peculiar favors—we ask only for even-handed justice." [101]

Following the 1853 Convention, Black leadership in Chicago weighed in on a national controversy about positions being advocated by Douglass. The *Chicago Tribune* published their resolution of support, in which they wrote, "We regard Frederick Douglass as an able champion and defender of the rights of the colored people of the United States, and that they, the colored people, will promote their true interest by giving to his efforts as an editor and lecturer their active sympathy and approval." Support for this was widespread and included that of the activists Jones, Wagoner, Bonner, William Johnson, and Rev. Byrd Parker. [102]

In November of 1853, John Jones wrote to Douglass's paper describing the organizing underway for Black involvement and political pressures across Illinois. In this letter, he identified leaders in several communities and in

Chicago pointed to the support and work of Bonner, Wagoner, William Johnson, Rev. Byrd Parker, Henry Bradford, and several others. He wrote of the people's enthusiasm for councils and conventions for Black people at the state and national level, and of their cry for "ACTION! ACTION!" He added: "The underground railroad is doing a fair business this season. We received eleven passengers last night, and two the night before, and we hear of others on the road. We will take care of them, and see that they are snugly shipped for Queen Victoria's land."[103]

In these several years following the passage of the Fugitive Slave Act, Black leadership in Chicago continued efforts to aid freedom seekers, organize for potential armed resistance to slave catchers, oppose the Black Codes, build churches and other community institutions, and encourage participation in state and national conventions. Another component in this emancipation activism came with the organizing of a lodge of the well-established Prince Hall Freemasonry movement. The Chicago chapter of the African American Freemasons was initiated in 1852 with ten charter members included Henry Bradford, Lewis Isbell, and John Jones, established as the North Star Lodge.[104] Through the 1850s, these community leaders were in regular touch with Black men in lodges in Missouri, Kentucky, Louisiana, and Indiana. In 1857, a front-page notice in the *Chicago Tribune* gave the names of these individuals.[105] A similar process had emerged in the Black population of St. Louis leading to the creation of the Union Association, a "secret" organization akin to the Masonic lodges, and there is evidence suggesting contact with the Illinois based lodges.[106] A Freemason lodge developed in Alton in 1856, and the third lodge in Illinois was chartered in Springfield in 1857. The lodges came into existence both to organize and uplift local Black communities, but also were very deliberate in their operations as secret societies and sources of opposition to slavery and support for travelers from the South. Bradford, Isbell and Jones, the three brothers-in-law, each served as "Worshipful Master" of the aptly named North Star Lodge in the 1850s.[107] A lodge meeting in 1858 was advertised with H. Ford Douglas as the guest speaker.[108]

Support from Congregations

During this time, churches continued to supply moral and practical support for Black and white activists. As already seen, both Quinn Chapel and Zoar Baptist Church were intimately involved with activism. As early as 1844, white Baptists had split over the issues of slavery and abolition. Well into the 1850s, although several churches provided significant support for freedom seekers, there was far from total agreement as to role for churches in this civil disobedience. The Presbyterians in the city experienced increasing controversies, culminating in late 1852, when some members of the First Presbyterian Church decided to stand firm in their support for abolition and for freedom seekers. This was in part a response to the ambivalence of the national-level Presbyterian Church and the desire for more direct church autonomy in such matters. In response, the Presbytery of Chicago removed a total of forty-eight people from their membership. This included Philo Carpenter, who had been a dedicated Presbyterian, and he then worked with others in the group to create the First Congregational Church. The first deacons of the new church were Elishe Clark and Philo Carpenter, and over time, the congregation was referred to in some circles as "Carpenter's N——r Chapel." As was the case in many communities across northeastern Illinois, the Congregational Church in Chicago was one of the key bases for the networks of the Underground Railroad.[109]

In April of 1853, the several Congregational churches in Chicago and northern Illinois formed a Chicago Association. Its initial Declaration of Principles included this key section: "We believe that slave-holding, or holding our fellow beings as property, is an immorality in practice, and the defense of it is heresy in doctrine."[110] The Association was composed of First and Plymouth churches in Chicago, along with churches in Fremont; in Carroll County near the Mississippi (formed in 1838); Lyonsville, now Indian Head Park in Cook County (1843); Millburn, in Lake County (1841); and Crete, in eastern Will County (initially organized in 1839). Although these six congregations had a collective membership of around two hundred, each would be significant as a place of support for abolition and for freedom seekers.[111]

In many areas, the activities of the Congregationalists in support of abolition were very public. With the creation of the Congregational Association came the monthly publication of the *Congregational Herald* which continued until 1861. Filled with news about life and concerns within the congregations, it also regularly included articles and news items about the two pressing public issues of the day: temperance and slavery.

In one of its first issues in 1853, the *Congregational Herald* included an article on the recently enacted state laws on Black settlement in Illinois and the demand for repeal by the new Chicago Association: "Resolved, That the late law passed by our Legislature, (called the "Black Law") prohibiting the immigration of free colored people to our State, is a most flagrant violation of every principle of justice, and at war with the spirit and precepts of Christianity, and repugnant to every dictate of humanity." Another issue included an announcement from a church group in Detroit on the settling of twenty-five fugitives in Canada who escaped from Kentucky with the note that "the Underground Railroad is in good order." The August 1853 issue carried a brief summary of a presentation by Frederick Douglass given during one of his frequent visits to Chicago, observing that it was "a truly eloquent and powerful speech."[112]

Coverage in Newspapers

Although publications like the *Congregational Herald* carried some reports and news related to antislavery concerns and the movement of travelers, the daily newspapers continued to be the main source of information for the supporters of abolition and freedom seekers. Throughout the 1850s, the *Chicago Tribune* provided regular updates in articles that reached from short, spare reports to richly detailed stories, and even included occasionally mocking, ironic, impassioned, or strangely elliptical reflections. One of these reflections is seen in an article that headed the news columns on a spring day in 1853. Under the heading, "A Dark Affair," the article started, "Catching a runaway slave was not reputed to be an easy thing in Chicago, several years ago; and from the result of an attempt made here during the past week, we suppose it has not improved."[113]

In this "dark affair," a freedom seeker from Missouri settled near Chicago and over seven years found a real measure of success living in Illinois. He held good farm with livestock and prosperity, elements looked upon with envy by his neighbors. His former owner arrived, and in cahoots with the envious neighbors, gave papers to the US marshal to have this man arrested. However, others got wind of the intent and "desiring to show their great regard for the constitution," showed up at the marshal's office at 11 o'clock at night and offered to help bring in the fugitive. One of the citizens carried an "ugly looking shooting iron," and another prominently carried a "gold cane, which he had received as a reward for certain services rendered in a similar case." The latter was a not-so-subtle reference to Dr. Dyer. There were "sundry whisperings and winks that could not be mistaken." The marshal was "overcome by such a manifestation of patriotism," and the slave owner was overcome by such a deep sense of modesty suggesting he could not really be the owner of the man, that the whole matter of capture and arrest was dropped. The supposed owner took the Rock Island line back to Missouri and the *Chicago Tribune* noted that upon his arrival there, he would no doubt have things to say about Chicago.[114]

In November 1853, the *Chicago Tribune* noted a strong reaction to the loss of slaves in two Missouri counties. In Howard County, in central Missouri, a mass meeting gathered in response to "numerous and repeated acts of disobedience and outrage" by slaves in the county. White leaders felt that the presence of free people of color and slaves able to hire out their time created significant dissatisfaction within the enslaved population, some of whom were running away. Therefore, the white leaders created a six-person committee to inform free Black residents to leave the county and lax owners to gather up their slaves who were out for hire. All this was to happen within two weeks. Meanwhile, in Marion County, near Hannibal and the Mississippi River, a group of twelve slaves escaped leading to a county-wide meeting and the formation of the "Marion Association" to hunt down slaves and pursue all legal means against the runaway slave "and his ally, the abolitionist."

The *Chicago Tribune* responded to these reports carried by the *St. Louis Republican* by declaring that, in fact, the Marion County fugitives came through Chicago and were now safely in Canada. The paper pointed out that quite regularly, Missouri slaves passed through Chicago and the process would continue "so long as slaves prefer freedom to bondage" and were willing to take the necessary risks. The paper noted that holding public meetings and establishing new patrols would not solve the problems of Missouri, because "the more a free spirit is fettered, the more will it seek to throw off its fetters." The article concluded recognizing that Chicago people were in fact providing aid to fugitives. It is not just the abolitionists, for there were in Chicago proslavery people who sought to enforce the Fugitive Slave Act, but when confronted by runaways seeking food and clothing on their way to freedom, they still had "the hearts of men" and were willing to help.[115]

Newspapers across the country carried details on the passage of the Kansas-Nebraska Act at the end of May 1854. This act created the territories of Kansas and Nebraska, but in so doing, mandated "popular sovereignty" to decide whether these would become slave or free states. It not only effectively repealed the Missouri Compromise but led to the struggles of "bleeding

Kansas," heightening all aspects of the controversies around slavery and adding to the pressures for freedom seekers to flee and activists to help. In June of that year, the *Chicago Tribune* noted in response to this added pressure that the Underground Railroad in the city had rapidly increased its business and to help secure its work, "the officers and passengers on the road [were] furnished with 'irons' to be used against all who may have the audacity to interfere with trains or passengers."[116]

An intriguing example of the occasionally extensive coverage by the press and of the Missouri and Chicago connection involved a freedom seeker named Turner (first name unknown) in the summer of 1854. In the previous winter, while living in Missouri, he approached George Taylor, captain of the Mississippi River steamer, the *Belfast*. He convinced Taylor to buy him and then allow him the flexible time to pay for himself by hiring out his own time. Taylor agreed and later said that he really did not think of Turner as his slave, but rather as one "to whom he had lent money to buy himself."[117]

Turner went on his way, periodically sending money to Capt. Taylor. He arrived in Chicago but was slow in sending payments to Taylor. Feeling he would lose his investment, Taylor obtained papers from the governor of Missouri to have Turner arrested and returned to slavery. Three professional slave catchers from St. Louis took the papers and headed north.

Meanwhile, Turner had been in Chicago for four or five months, working with horses and freight wagons. The reasonable course of action for the slave catchers was to come to Chicago, give the papers to the US marshal and identify Turner. If the marshal did not do this or if some local citizens rescued him, then the federal government "would have been bound to indemnify his owners for his loss, in accordance with the provisions of the Fugitive Slave Law."

However, rather than visiting the marshal, they saw Turner on Wells Street near Jackson and sought to grab him. After gaining a firm grip, they hauled Turner down the street, when he suddenly tried to break free and almost got over a fence. He lost his coat, but one of the attackers dropped a gun, which Turner managed to pick up, but never used. He almost broke free again, shaking off two of them. However, one stuck him with the end of a revolver, bloodying his arm. Finally, Turner was able to run. After a half of a block, two of the catchers were surrounded by a crowd suggesting that they should back off. The third man went running after Turner, fired a shot at him, and waved papers and shouted that he owned the man. After taking the shot, he was seized by police and immediately taken to the jail. The other two were arrested in a saloon. All three were charged with assault with a deadly weapon and attempted kidnapping. On the way to the jail, they were followed by a large and agitated crowd, anxious to make sure they did not escape.[118]

Turner managed to get to a house on Jackson, near Wells, and went inside. A few minutes later he was seen on an upstairs porch. He had the fresh wound on his arm, spoke pleasantly, and affirmed that he did not know his pursuers and, in fact, did not want to know them. That evening he headed for Canada and the *Chicago Tribune* noted that he "consequently is now in a much more pleasant position than his attempted captors."[119]

The *Chicago Tribune* covered the trial of the slave catchers in detail, commenting very pointedly about the defendants: "The slave catchers are men of very unfavorable appearance. Their countenances almost warrant the belief in the minds of almost all who have seen them that they are specially designed for slave catching.... Their faces lack the expression of intelligence and mental acquirements, but contain all that is animal and ferocious. They are of the real Legree stamp."[120]

However, before the trial could be completed, through the collusions of the district attorney, the sheriff, and others, the three were removed from jail, taken to Springfield, and put before a sympathetic judge who found that they had been unjustly accused and jailed. They slipped back to St. Louis as free men. All this activity was followed by the press in St. Louis and one paper declared that outside of Chicago, "any court or commissioner in all of Christendom" would have ruled on behalf of the slave hunters. The paper went on to say that the citizens of Chicago were so thoroughly supporting abolition, that Black activists operated with the "entire possession of the sympathies of the people."[121]

In autumn 1854, a group of fifteen freedom seekers successfully escaped from Missouri with the help of a free man of color who lived in Alton on the Mississippi and arranged for small boats to carry them across the river. Once in Illinois, they traveled by night in "a closely covered wagon" until they arrived north of Peoria and then were able to move safely during the day. The group included three young families with children and several single men, all of whom had been able to earn some money while enslaved and then used the funds to pay for their travels. Their guide declared that he did this work full time and made the journey many times, always taking "his 'train' safely through to Chicago, from which they could safely pass on to Canada."[122]

The group of fifteen arrived safely in Chicago, followed closely by slave catchers "in hot haste for their human prey." On the way, the slave catchers acquired the necessary papers from the governor of Illinois to call out the military. It was a "deliberate and deep down plan to humble Chicago" and to remind them to be subject to the power of the slave owners. As the *Free West* dryly reported, the slave catchers evidently felt the right "to steal those babies and the men and women for service in Missouri, and the girls for prostitution."[123]

With their paperwork from the governor, the slave catchers arranged for a detachment of the National Guard to march through the center of Chicago. It was intended as a kind of declaration that the national laws about fugitive slaves would be enforced. In response, Chicago citizens, Black and white, filled the streets, seeking to see what caused all this "fuss, feathers, and bearskins." From a distance, the *New York Daily Times* reported the events under the headline: "Slave Excitement – Military Called Out." [124]

All the while, the fugitives, the fifteen, were not found and were not seized. *The Daily Times* concluded: "no negroes can be arrested, much less carried away from Chicago," and "at the close of the day the militia retired—the people retired also—and no arrests were made, and no blood was spilled. The fugitives remained in town a day or two, and then were shipped off in a body to Canada on the cars of the Michigan Central Railroad." [125]

Thus ended this great effort to whip Chicago into shape on the business of dealing harshly with runaways. However, after all the potentials for confrontation and slave catching, The excitement just faded away.

Newspaper coverage was extensive on occasion, as with the reports from the *Chicago Tribune* and the *New York Daily Times*. Fairly often, there were simple announcements, like this one from the *Tribune*, also from 1854:

For Freedom
  Twenty fugitives from Slavery left this city on Wednesday evening, by the Underground Railroad, for Canada and Freedom. The stock of that corporation is rapidly rising in this market.[126]

By this time in 1854, slave owners in Missouri were painfully aware of the growing sophistication of the networks of support that had emerged across the river in Illinois. In August of that year, the *St. Louis Republican* noted that "negro stealing, once fraught with much risk, was now comparatively easy. Branches of the subterranean line lead from St. Louis to Chicago." The process of "negro stealing" was described, or perhaps imagined, in an article on the "Underground Railroad," stating that it was alive and doing well in St. Louis, with groups of Black residents in the city who were in correspondence with abolitionists. The white abolitionists were providing funds and advice and the Black residents were "constantly running off slaves," and it was clear that Chicago was the spot for the "centralization of negro-stealing." As further proof, the article summarized a letter purportedly written by a recently escaped woman in Chicago and sent to an enslaved woman in St. Louis. In this letter, she proudly shared her escape, identified other enslaved persons who should leave, and announced her plans to walk on Chicago's lakefront with some white ladies. In St. Louis, a rival newspaper argued that this was an exaggeration of reality, but the *St. Louis Republican* stoutly defended its case against Chicago. They were convinced that Chicago was to blame for the formation of associations of Black activists who were collaborating with white leaders to make the Underground Railroad successful.[127]

Across Northeastern Illinois

From 1845 through 1854, activists around the rest of northeastern Illinois continued their work, closely engaged with Black and white leadership in Chicago. South of the city, networks were well established with coordinated support, a small Black community grew in Joliet, and Dutch families settled in the Calumet area.[128] To the west, new sources of support developed in DeKalb, Kane, and DuPage Counties. To the north of the city, new residents encountered freedom seekers in Lake and McHenry Counties, with the growth of a Black community in Waukegan.

Southwest of Chicago, activists in the small settlements in LaSalle County were connected to those in Ottawa, on the Illinois River. Ottawa was eventually the key commercial point on the I&M Canal for the county and an active center for the work of the Underground Railroad. The ongoing networks in LaSalle County were strengthened by the organizing and leadership of William Brown Fyfe and his wife, Mary, and the arrival in 1851 of the family of John and Martha Hossack.

William Brown Fyfe, a resident of Ottawa, was over many years involved with freedom seekers and well connected with activists in La Salle and Livingston Counties. Fyfe developed a map of the routes from La Salle County to Chicago, Detroit, and Canada and gave copies to freedom seekers. He

created a map of routes followed by freedom seekers in the two counties leading into Ottawa reproduced in Siebert's book, *From Slavery to Freedom*. His
extensive written materials are one of the great sources for details and understanding of the work of the Underground Railroad in northeastern Illinois
including a series of articles for the *Pontiac Sentinel* in Livingston County
written in 1889. Also, he is one of the few activists who specifically mentions
the strong support of his wife, Mary. He indicated they were in this work together and she was "a true friend of the poor slave." At the time of his death,
Fyfe was honored not only for his writing about the "anti-slavery days," but
also for the personal involvement of his family in assisting freedom seekers.[129]

   John and Martha Hossack came to Illinois in 1838 attracted by the possibilities for work on the I&M Canal. Living near the canal in Cook County,
and then in Gooding's Grove (near Lockport), John managed construction
contracts on the Canal. By 1849 he was engaged with lumber business on the
canal, and in 1851, with grain shipments on the canal. In 1854, John and Martha built a lovely residence on a bluff overlooking the Illinois River in Ottawa
(see Figure 3.13). Through these years, the family was actively involved with
aiding freedom seekers, often at their own home. In addition, John traveled
regularly on the canal and had several encounters with freedom seekers on
the canal. Even some of their eight children became involved. They were active members of the Baptist church in Ottawa and the congregation became
openly antislavery by the late 1850s.[130]

   One account of the Hossack's involvement was written by their son Henry,
in 1917. They provided transport from Ottawa northeast to Harding or to
Newark on the way to Chicago. He recalled that "Father had a closed carriage and I or one on my brothers drove the slave, secure from observation in
the back seat, and we traveled at night." In addition, in a letter to his friend,
William Fyfe, John Hossack wrote directly about several instances of support
for freedom seekers. Fyfe framed these and other stories in the context of
Hossack's strong commitment to the work of the Underground Railroad.[131]

   The established activists in LaSalle County found new collaborators in
small towns just south in Livingston County and on the roads to Chicago
in Kendall County. Moses Rumery settled in Livingston County in 1854,
coming from Maine, and soon was recognized as a radical abolitionist, with
at least one documented encounter with freedom seekers. Two years later,
he was serving on the State Executive Committee with Henry Wagoner, the

Fig. 3.13 John and Martha Hossack House, built 1854, current view. Author's photo.

Black abolitionist from Chicago, and others for the planning of a State Radical Abolition Convention.[132]

In Peru, to the west of Ottawa, in the spring of 1854, two free men, traveling with papers on a river steamer from St. Louis, were kidnapped and charged with being horse thieves. Local residents immediately intervened to rescue the men. They continued on their way to Chicago and although another attempt was made to seize them in Ottawa, the local authorities had been alerted and provided protection.[133]

Heading toward Chicago from LaSalle County, accounts note that from 1850 to 1854, freedom seekers found help from Dr. Townsend Seeley, who was living near the road from Ottawa to Yorkville. This is the same Dr. Seeley who, in 1844, "purchased" the only slave ever sold in Kendall County and set him on his way to Canada. His son, Edmund Seeley remembered, "The first person that was brought to our house was a woman of very fine appearance, with hair as straight as an Indian, although she was very black. She had been raised in one of the first families of St. Louis, but she was afraid she would be sold south, and thought she would take her chances of getting to Canada. She was very much a lady in every respect."[134]

In the early 1850s, the Seeley family was host to Fredrick Michel who escaped from St. Louis with his wife and several friends. He was a mason with skills that enabled his master to send him out to labor for fees. Edmund Seeley remembered that he fashioned a weapon for defense out of the end piece of a farm scythe, made a sheath for it and looked "quite formidable" with the weapon at his side. Fredrick could write and carved his name into a board in the Seeley's barn, which was there to be seen for many years. After several months, Fredrick and his family continued their journey toward freedom in Canada.[135]

Near the Seeley's was the home of Deacon Isaac Whitney and his wife, Susan. They came from Massachusetts in 1834, and he served as a leader in the networks of the Underground Railroad in the region southwest of Chicago. Their son Lucius remembered an incident at their farm in 1845. A friend of the family living on the Fox River in LaSalle County came to their house late one night with six travelers. They were warmly received and stayed in the house during the day to avoid being noticed. Lucius was charged with keeping watch to make sure that no neighbors happened to come by. Unfortunately, while eating dinner, the neighbor whom his family was most concerned about, a settler from Kentucky, stopped by to manage some business affairs. The freedom seekers were quickly hustled into the loft of their cabin and told to be "perfectly quiet." The neighbor came in, took care of his business with Lucius's father and then went on his way. After he left and with great relief, Lucius recalled that as darkness came his father hitched up the horses to his wagon and took their visitors on to other friends on the road going to Plainfield.[136]

Lucius Whitney recalled several other specific instances involving travelers, also during the late 1840s, some of whom he ended up directly guiding on to safe locations on the way to Chicago. One incident involved providing some provisions for a large group of fifteen to twenty freedom seekers. At another time, they were visited by three men traveling on their own, heading to Canada. A year later, they were very surprised to be visited again by one of the three who indicated he had made it to Canada and found that it really was the place of freedom he had hoped for, and so he returned to the South to rescue his family.[137]

Also near the Seeleys and Whitneys were the families of Thomas Wright and George Barnard. In 1851 or 1852, they hosted three Black women: Kate, about twenty-eight; Julia, about forty; and Massey, fifty-eight. Massey carried a picture of her daughter living in Chicago and the three were intent on reaching the city as soon as possible. Although it was a cold winter day, Wright arranged for the women to leave for Deacon Goodhue's in Plainfield. They loaded in his new sled with buffalo robes and hot bricks for their feet and off they went. After an encounter with a proslavery family, they reached Goodhue's home in Plainfield and later went on to Chicago and Canada.[138]

Movement through Kendall County was not always successful. On at least one occasion, a traveler ended up in the custody of the sheriff. In January and February 1845, Sheriff Cornell placed advertisements in a local paper announcing he was holding James Alexander Campbell, a Black person "supposed to be a runaway slave." Campbell could be turned over to someone with documentation or would be otherwise disposed of. He may have been from Kentucky, but his origins and his fate are unknown.[139]

By 1850, there were a scattering of Black families and individuals in Will County. It is probable that they responded to the needs of freedom seeking travelers coming through the county, but currently, there is no direct evidence of contact with these Black families. Although few in number, the African Americans in Joliet and across Will County were organized well enough that in 1853, they sent two delegates to the First Convention of the Colored Citizens of Illinois: August Hill of Joliet and William Liverse of Lockport.[140]

Into the 1850s, although freedom seekers traveled through and near Joliet, some on the I&M Canal, there is little direct evidence of involvement by white residents of Joliet. Some local traditions hold that support included the use of the American House hotel that stood at Bluff and Jefferson. Two of the key white figures in Joliet were Dr. R. E. W. Adams, who settled in Joliet in 1836, and George Woodruff, author of the *History of Will County, Illinois*, one of Joliet's best-known citizens and a strong abolitionist. Adams was one of only six delegates from northern Illinois at the organizing meeting of the Illinois Anti-Slavery Society in Alton in 1837. Both Channahon and Lockport continued to see freedom seekers traveling through on the I&M Canal (see Figure 3.14). Through the 1850s, freedom seekers traveled east across Will County following the Sauk Trail.[141]

Directly south of Chicago is the area known as the Calumet region. Both in Illinois and Indiana, the region includes the watersheds of Lake Calumet and the Little Calumet River. The area was crossed by the old Detroit-Chicago Road, initially opened by the federal government in the 1820s. For persons leaving Chicago overland to move toward the east, the crossing of the

Fig. 3.14 I&M Canal Headquarters, built 1836–37, current view. Author's photo.

Little Calumet River over the Dolton ferry or bridge was essential. The ferry and bridge were located where the current Indiana Avenue bridge crosses the Little Calumet River and the Calumet-Saganashkee (Cal-Sag) Channel. In the 1840s, Chicago was a small city that occupied essentially the area of today's Loop, or downtown area. Ironically, freedom seekers leaving Chicago had to go south for fifteen miles to cross the river and then head east under the southern edge of Lake Michigan and northeast toward Detroit. About four miles south of Chicago, the Gardner family opened a tavern on the Vincennes Trace, also known as Hubbard's Trail, in the present-day neighborhood of Washington Heights. Purchased by the Wilcox family in 1844, family records indicate the tavern and barns were an occasional stopover for freedom seekers. Immediately north of the Wilcox property were six parcels owned by Dr. Charles Dyer at the point where the Vincennes Trace merged with the Detroit-Chicago Road. Because of this, it is very likely that Dyer had contact with the Wilcox family, the Doltons, and other families settling near the Detroit-Chicago Road at the Little Calumet River, and, later, with Dutch settlers. Such connections through business and land-related concerns were useful in providing aid for freedom seekers traveling south out of Chicago. [142]

At the Little Calumet River, freedom seekers traveling from Chicago initially used a ferry and bridge and likely had contact with white families who settled there in the mid-1830s, including George and Olive Dolton. Within a few years, there were several waves of settlement in the area by Dutch immigrants. By 1850, some in the small Dutch community in Roseland and along the Chicago Road were passionate about aiding freedom seekers. Key among them were Cornelius and Maartje Kuyper, and their friend, Jan Ton (see Figure 3.15). Ton immigrated with the Kuypers in 1848. In their group of travelers was Aagje

Fig. 3.15 Farm of Jan and Aagje Ton, on the Little Calumet River,
ca. 1900. Author's photo. collection.

Vander Syde, whom Jan married in 1853. Also in 1853, the Tons acquired land
from George Dolton on the banks of the Little Calumet, several blocks east of
the bridge. This was at the extreme southern edge of present-day Chicago.[143]

Both Kuyper and Ton spoke English, and this, no doubt, was important
both in working with other local folks like the Doltons and in communicating with freedom seekers. Cornelius Kuyper prided himself on being a wel-
coming figure for slave catchers coming through the region. On more than
one occasion he would open his home to them and make a considerable show
of being helpful, while, at the same time, housing sought-after fugitives in his
own home or barn. Years later, his granddaughters delighted in retelling his
stories of hunting runaway slaves while he in fact had them hidden. Kuyper
would then carry the fugitives in his wagon on to the Ton farm on the Little
Calumet River. Going to the east, on occasion, Jan Ton waited until nightfall
to take fugitives by wagon to the next stop. Sometimes this was "Homan's
Bridge" in nearby Hammond, Indiana, or they would travel further on to
Green's Tavern in Tremont.[144]

DeKalb, Kane, DuPage, and western Cook Counties form the western
part of northeastern Illinois, with all west of Chicago. Starting in the late
1830s, settlers formed abolitionist groups and support networks that developed across county lines and into Chicago.

DeKalb County

In DeKalb County after 1845, abolitionist sentiments strengthen across the county, and by the late 1840s, after Cook County, DeKalb had the largest number of subscribers to the *Western Citizen*. Although abolitionist sentiments were strong across the county, there were relatively few encounters with freedom seekers. In the village of Sycamore, in the northern part of the county, the family of Deacon West, and others connected with the Congregational Church, assisted freedom seekers.[145]

In the early 1850s, a group of seven travelers, two parents with their five children arrived at the West home. The Wests made beds on the floor for all and gave them dinner. The next day, they recruited the help of a neighbor who shared their sympathies and with two wagons, they carried the seven to St. Charles; from there, they traveled on to Chicago. About a year later, the West family received a letter from one of the daughters of the family indicating they were doing well in Canada, she had learned to read and write, and they could not thank the West family enough for "helping them on their way to freedom."[146]

Dr. Horatio and Eliza Page were close friends of the Wests. He was the first physician practicing in DeKalb County. They arrived in 1838, and they were charter members of the Congregational Church in Sycamore and strong abolitionists. They appear in the 1850 Census with a seventeen-year-old Black man in their household named John Shepherd. He was born in Massachusetts, as were the Pages, and was the one Black resident in the county. Shepherd may have been a settled refugee from the south and it is very likely that the Pages were directly involved with assisting travelers.[147]

In the early 1850s, a Universalist Church was established in Sycamore. Paralleling the Congregational Church, it carried a strong abolitionist orientation among its members. Among these was the extended family of Rudolphus and Mary Burr. They were solid antislavery advocates and subscribers to the *Western Citizen*. Burr family traditions hold that they assisted freedom seekers by hiding them in a "small stone-lined room" under the back porch. This was most likely a storage cellar of some sort and not built particularly as a hiding place. A great-grandson received the name Howard Freeman Kelsey. Freeman was not a family name, but the family feels it may have been used to honor the family's involvement with the Underground Railroad.[148]

Somonauk, near the southern edge of DeKalb County, grew on one of the main roads reaching from Chicago into the northwestern corner of Illinois and the booming lead mining region around Galena. George and Ann Beveridge settled in Somonauk in 1842 and were instrumental in establishing the Somonauk United Presbyterian Church. Organized in 1846, the congregation was composed of friends and the Beveridge's extended family, most of Scottish and Scotch Irish heritage. George and Ann were strong abolitionists and actively engaged, along with their three sons, in responding to the needs of occasional visitors over the years. In 1849, the Beveridge's welcomed Rev. Renselear French as the new pastor for the Presbyterian Church. French arrived with his wife and several children, including a young son, Albert, and stayed with the Beveridges for an extended period. Years later, Albert wrote about his father's and their congregation's strong positions against slavery. In this recollection, he noted their home was a "station" and wrote of an incident in which one of the church deacons carried three runaways "under a load of green cut corn" in his wagon. Another time, around 1853, he vividly recalled an instance of being in church with seven or eight "negroes" sitting in front of the pulpit. His father, the pastor Rev. French, saw strangers enter the back of the church and immediately invited the congregation to stand for prayer. As the full church stood up, the strangers demanded of a deacon in the back if there were any fugitive slaves in the church. They were invited to look, saw the full church and left. Albert wrote: "I remember the ashy frightened look on the faces of those negroes, and their humble manner." Years later, at a celebration of the history of the Church in Somonauk held in 1925, Dr. Oscar Schmidt, president of the Chicago Historical Society, offered this romanticized image of the work of the activists: "To ask for a map of the routes of the 'railroad' is to ask for a map of the routes by which the wily fox evades the hounds."[149]

Henry Boies, a contemporary of the Beveridge's and author of a history of the county, wrote about one encounter in 1852 when the family was visited by a "gentlemanly stranger" who kept inquiring about what they might know about aiding runaway slaves. Finally, the stranger directly pressed Ann Beveridge as to whether or not she ever provided shelter. One story says she answered curtly saying: "Yes and in spite of your oppressive laws, I will do it again whenever I have an opportunity." Unbeknownst to her, the stranger was a doctor from Quincy making connections among families providing aid across northern Illinois.[150]

To the northwest of Sycamore is Mayfield Township, home to the Townsend, Nickerson, and Nichols families. All were deeply involved with travelers and part of a congregation of the Wesleyan Methodists. This was an antislavery church and members were vigorous in assisting fugitives. Later in his life, William Nickerson reflected on this period and how he "assisted in forming the 'underground railway." He recalled an occasion when his neighbor, Ira Nichols, carried a freedom seeker, a young man about twenty-five years old, under a load of sacks of grain, from his farm in Mayfield to a market in St. Charles. Nichols drove through Sycamore and on the street was the owner of the young man standing with a deputy United States marshal and offering a $500 reward for the runaway.[151]

William and Agnes Deyoe settled to the west of Mayfield, in South Grove Township, having moved from New York State as firm abolitionists. In the early 1850s, they were assisting freedom seekers. One time, when two travelers arrived at their door, William felt it might be unwise to deal with them directly and asked a worker on the farm to take the men by wagon to the farm of a relative in Mayfield. He said to his worker: "Look neither to the right nor to the left. Do not look behind you or you will become a pillar of salt but drive directly to Joshua Townsend's house and back up to his cellar door." The freedom seekers were delivered successfully.[152]

In the summer of 1854, South Grove was a way station for a three-generation family of travelers. In an article in the *Sycamore True Republican* in 1884, the story was recounted by a resident of Ogle County who had accompanied Solomon Shaver, a well-known Underground Railroad activist in Ogle County, as he led this family across northern Illinois.[153]

In June 1854, a man with his wife and two children and his wife's parents arrived in Illinois near Rock Island. The man escaped from Missouri several years earlier, settled in Canada, and returned to "risk liberty and perhaps life in securing his wife and children from bondage. It was liberty or death with him." He found his family and spent several days planning their escape. They managed to escape late one night and found themselves being pursued by slave catchers with dogs. They eluded the dogs by walking in a stream while looking for a wagon waiting for them. The hunters saw the wagon before they did and the driver immediately took off, leading the slave catchers to eventually catch an empty wagon. This deception enabled the group to escape and reach the Mississippi. After crossing the Mississippi River, they continued east along the Rock River and connected with Solomon Shaver, living in Ogle County west of DeKalb County. Known to all as "Uncle Sol," he intended to move north from the Rock River heading for Bryon, where there were others willing to help. However, the trip became longer than anticipated. Uncle Sol set out with a four-horse team and wagon and his passengers, heading for a small town known today as Polo, Illinois. There he stopped to pick up a friend, and in the town, he purchased a large cloth he planned to use as a flag on a pole attached to the wagon. He planned to head north, but there were rumors that up in Mt. Morris, threats were in the air that anyone assisting fugitives would be arrested. Well, he was determined to see his passengers to safety and would do so "with his flag flying."[154] They managed to get through Mt. Morris unmolested and arrived in Byron, on the Rock River, on the Fourth of July. They found the antislavery folk having a giant picnic and those folks asked if Uncle Sol could take the passengers on further. All agreed and the group continued east into DeKalb County and ended up at the Wesleyan Church in South Grove Township. Here, they found "true anti-slavery men," and the next morning the extended family headed east through Kane and DuPage Counties to reach abolitionists in Chicago.[155]

Kane County

As was the case in other parts of northeastern Illinois, most of the activist families who settled in Kane County in the late 1830s and 1840s were still there in the 1850s. Families in Elgin continued to be of help to freedom seekers and the Congregational Church remained one of the centers for abolitionist activities. In St. Charles, community leaders continued to be involved with the Kane County Anti-Slavery Society, and from time to time, there were freedom seekers traveling through. In one documented instance, as noted earlier in the chapter, the family of Deacon West in Sycamore brought to St. Charles a group of seven travelers.

In response to some internal church politics, in 1846, the lay leadership of the Congregational Church in Elgin supported new resolutions reflecting the congregation's commitment to denouncing slavery. In the same year, one morning, a large wooden coffin appeared on the steps of the church with a note attached for the pastor: "You will need this if you don't stop talking against slavery." The church rallied around its pastor who told his son to put the coffin on the woodpile, saying, "This will make good kindling."[156]

Aurora saw the greatest activity west of Chicago, both in relation to free-dom seekers and issues of abolition. By 1850, there were two known Black residents in Kane County, living in Aurora. They were Phoebe and her son, Gill, who arrived in the late 1840s, with Phoebe as the "servant" of a family from South Carolina. Rev. D. R. Miller was pastor of the Congregational Church from 1849 into 1852 and called the church the "union depot" for the Underground Railroad. He carried two strong memories of events around 1850.[157]

Rev. Miller recalled that on one occasion, a woman came to the parsonage confessing that she and her husband sought to escape to Canada and were being closely pursued by their master and overseer. They had been lost in the woods and then separated from each other. She had had nothing to eat and was now desperate, both for food and to find her husband. Rev. Miller took her in and arranged for a member of the congregation to take her to Downers Grove, most likely to the home of the Blodgetts. Miller noted that the woman had a very light complexion, "as white as most women." Later that same evening, a man appeared at his door, who also appeared to Miller to be white. However, after some time he determined that this person was the woman's husband, and in the early morning hours, he escorted him to the house in Downers Grove.[158]

Near the same time as this encounter, Rev. Miller recalled being alerted by friends in Ottawa that fugitives were headed toward Aurora, and soon he was visited by a woman and two men. Slave catchers arrived looking for them and sought to hire men in Aurora and Naperville to assist in the hunting. No one was sure what to do with the hidden visitors, so Rev. Miller finally realized he would have to act. A neighbor had a six-passenger carriage, which he borrowed. He had his wife and the "colored woman" dress alike and sit together, with the men hidden under blankets in the back of the carriage. They rode on to Naperville where they were stopped by two men, one holding the horses and the other approached the carriage. His wife moved her veil and he saw that she was white and assumed the other woman was also. The two men let them pass.[159]

Reaching the streets of Chicago, the woman traveler was stunned to see her master on the sidewalk. The two men also recognized him and moved to prepare their guns for defense. Miller noted, "They were armed to the teeth, saying they would never go back alive." He drove on to the home of Philo and Ann Carpenter and learned from Ann that her husband was in the downtown. Ann Carpenter told Miller, "I do not know what we shall do, there is great excitement in the city. The slaveholders are here and our house and Dr. Dyer's are watched day and night." The three were hidden at the Carpenters home and Miller found Philo Carpenter, who was also very concerned with the high level of activity by slave hunters. Miller then went to see the Black barber Lewis Isbell and another Black businessman and asked them to gather a group of men to help. Forty Black men armed themselves and went together to the Carpenters' home to provide safe passage for the freedom seekers. They brought a covered wagon which was used for transport and the three were taken to a lumber yard and warehouse on the Chicago River. This was most likely the property of Sylvester Lind, whose vessels regularly sailed up Lake Michigan. After being safely deposited there, the next day, they were on a ship toward freedom.[160]

Both before and after the ministry of Rev. Miller, the Congregational Church was the center of activity in Aurora, the "union depot," as he called it. It was in this church that abolitionist leaders gathered in 1854 and held one of the first political meetings that referred to itself as a gathering of the "Republican Party." Many of the great antislavery speakers came to speak at the church, including John Cross, Ichabod Codding, Salmon P. Chase, John Hale, and others.[161]

Also, in 1854, the church was the site for a scheduled debate between Senator Stephen Douglas and the great abolitionist orator Frederick Douglass. Notices went out announcing that they would be speaking. However, both men arrived in Aurora very sick. Stephen Douglas needed two men to help him off the train, and Frederick Douglass was so sick that local doctors told him not to speak at all. A huge crowd gathered in the church, and the afternoon was filled with confrontations and attempts at speaking by supporters of both Douglas and Douglass. Finally, Frederick Douglass managed to speak for a short while. A church member wrote that in those thirty minutes there was eloquence "which those who heard can never forget."[162]

DuPage County

The well-established networks in DuPage County continued to receive and assist freedom seekers traveling through, particularly through the activists in Naperville, Downers Grove, and Lombard. In 1853, a major development in the County reflected the controversies that were underway across the county. Across Illinois, individuals and families from New England and New York with abolitionist commitments were moving away from the Presbyterians and toward Congregational churches. Parallel to this shift, within the Methodist churches, starting in the 1820s, a substantial group of clergy and lay members left to form the antislavery Wesleyan Methodist Church. In 1852 and 1853, leaders of this new denomination met to establish the publicly abolitionist "Illinois Institute." They purchased property in the County adjacent to the village of Wheaton and over time this became Wheaton College. Clearly reinforcing their intentions, Rev. John Cross, pastor of the Wesleyan Methodist congregation in Wheaton, became the first president of the institute. This, of course, was the same John Cross who played such a major role in fostering networks of support across much of the Midwest.[163]

Because of the networks Cross helped establish, his own notoriety through the various antislavery societies, and his connections among a variety of congregations, it is highly likely that in the early years of the institute, freedom seekers received temporary shelter. Courses began in the fall of 1853 for this "anti-slavery progressive school in a beautiful rolling rich prairie country."[164] Following Cross, the next president was Lucius Columbus Matlack, another ardent abolitionist. In late 1857, Johnathan Blanchard became president, coming from Galesburg, Illinois, and earlier from Cincinnati, Ohio. In Galesburg, he had been president of Knox College and in both places he and his wife, Mary, had been actively involved with networks of the Underground Railroad. Blanchard Hall is the original main building for the college and named to honor this president (see Figure 3.16).

Ezra Cook, a student during these early years and one of many Wheaton College students who went off to serve in the Civil War, recalled that attitudes within the town and the college were very supportive of any assistance provided to fugitives. Attitudes were so strongly abolitionist that it was not necessary to hide the temporary presence of freedom seekers at the college. Cook noted, "With hundreds of others, I have seen and talked with such fugitives in the college chapel."[165]

Throughout the 1850s, in DuPage County, there continued to be what the newspapers called "anti-slavery meetings." These meetings kept widely felt abolitionist commitments in the public eye and served as convenient ways for those involved with assisting freedom seekers to stay in touch. Chicago-based Black activists like John Jones and H. Ford Douglas were regular speakers at such events.[166]

Fig. 3.16 Blanchard Hall, the original main building at Wheaton College. Courtesy of Buswell Library Archives and Special Collections, Wheaton College, IL.

Boone, McHenry, and Lake Counties

During the 1840s, there was relatively little movement by freedom seekers through the northern counties. In Boone County, there is no standing tradition and no available documentary evidence on the movement of freedom seekers. Belvidere was on one of the principal roads from Galena to Chicago. It is probable that some travelers came through Boone County and Belvidere, but there are no specific references.[167]

Among the first non-Native settlers in McHenry County was the family of Samuel and Laura Terwilliger. Coming in 1836 from New York State with one son, they had three children born in Illinois by 1841. Later in life, Samuel was identified as a Republican. A few miles to the northwest were John and Mary James, who came from New Hampshire in 1846. They helped start the Greenwood Baptist Church in 1847 and built Windhill Farm in what is now Woodstock. Strong local traditions hold these two locations and several more in the county as places of assistance. The current documentary evidence in support of these claims is slight.[168]

However, among the travelers through McHenry County were Caroline Quarlls and Joshua Glover. As mentioned in a previous chapter, Caroline reached Milwaukee, and then traveled south around Chicago. This brought her through McHenry County on her way to Elgin. Joshua Glover was a freedom seeker who escaped to Racine, Wisconsin, and after living there for two years, was captured, beaten, and jailed as a runaway. Abolitionists came to his defense, which lead to a series of nationally noted court cases. When Joshua first traveled to Racine, he came up through Illinois, along the Fox River and through McHenry County. Both Caroline and Joshua avoided travel through Chicago given the dangers of slave catchers.[169]

East of McHenry, in Lake County, was the family of Amos Bennett, who arrived in 1834. He was involved in the colored conventions in Illinois and likely was involved with freedom seekers. Although a very strong abolitionist movement developed in the County, there are only a few recorded instances of engagement with freedom seekers outside of Waukegan. Lake County is the only county in northeastern Illinois that has no "conductors" listed by Siebert.[170]

One probable stop was the roadhouse-tavern known as the Mother Rudd House. Milwaukee Avenue starts in Chicago and angles northwest and north toward its namesake in Wisconsin. Much of it follows the Des Plaines River. At a place where it crossed the Des Plaines, the road intersected with a road from McHenry County going east into Waukegan. At this site, a roadhouse-tavern was established in 1844 as a stopping point about halfway between Chicago and Milwaukee. Eventually owned by Eratus and Wealthy Rudd, it was called the Mother Rudd House. Local traditions maintain that freedom seekers were accommodated in the roadhouse and related buildings.[171]

The Ivanhoe Congregational Church in present-day Mundelein and the Millburn Congregational Church were organized by Rev. Flavel Bascom, one of the early advocates for abolition in Chicago. In the mid-1840s, the pastor at the Ivanhoe church was Rev. Joseph H. Payne, also a strong voice for abolition. In August 1845, the Ivanhoe congregation adopted several resolutions responding to growing public sentiments for abolition. They affirmed a view of slavery "as a most daring sin against God," to never allow "slave-holding ministers to preach in our pulpits," and to never invite "slave-holding members in spirit or practice to Christian fellowship in the church." The congregation went on to note with "great grief and abhorrence" that millions are held in bondage by "men professing Godliness."[172]

In the northern part of the county, the Millburn church called William Bradford Dodge as their minister in 1844. The son of a distinguished Puritan family, Dodge came from Salem, Massachusetts, where, in the 1830s, he was principal of a predominantly Black school and president of the Anti-Slavery Society of Salem and Vicinity. Because of family connections and an invitation to lecture for antislavery groups in the West, Dodge and his wife Sarah Dole Dodge moved to Millburn and joined the small church. Soon after they arrived, the congregation invited him to become minister. He served for eighteen years as pastor of the Millburn church.

Although the congregation already held antislavery views, their commitments were reinforced by Rev. Dodge. As with the Ivanhoe church, in 1845, this congregation passed a resolution condemning slavery. In the spring of 1845, Dodge, with other Lake County ministers and laymen, called for a county convention for prayer and consultation on moving forward to "suppress slavery, intemperance and Sabbath desecration." Joining in this call were Joseph Payne of the Ivanhoe church and more than twenty other leaders. At their convention in Libertyville in the summer of 1845, Ichabod Codding, the great antislavery orator, spoke. Along with Codding were a choir from Chicago singing antislavery songs and an appearance by Sojourner Truth. In 1846, they organized a Lake County Anti-Slavery society and Dodge was elected president.[173]

At the Millburn congregation, the family of William and Margaret Bonner helped transport travelers into Wisconsin. Church members provided horses and wagons for transport "from Millburn to Somers [a township just north in Wisconsin]. On the morning after such trips, Bonner's son John and his nephew James Bonner had the responsibility to clean up and curry the horses lest neighbors become suspicious from the muddy animals."[174]

By the mid-1840s, a unique community grew at Lake Zurich. Initiated by Seth Paine, a man of "much ability and marked eccentricities," this community emerged as an American example of the work of Charles Fourier, a French Utopian Socialist. Fourier advocated the importance of cooperation, communal living, and women's rights. Paine's effort for a utopian community included building the House for Humanity, a residence for homeless people. An abolitionist organizing meeting in March of 1846 led to the Lake County Liberty Association and Seth Paine served as its first president (with Henry Blodgett as secretary). Paine was a fierce advocate and traveled with Owen Lovejoy and Ichabod Codding, going to such places as abolitionist gatherings sponsored by Allan Pinkerton in Kane County. Local tradition holds that Paine and his friends in Lake Zurich welcomed occasional freedom seekers, having them stay at the House for Humanity. Although there is no direct evidence, this hospitality seems probable.[175]

Local history in Lake County includes the story of Kuhn's Rock. Next to an old road, this twenty-ton granite rock carries a legacy as an Underground Railroad signpost. Nearby was the cabin of the Kuhn's family; local tradition holds that fugitives were directed to the rock and thus to their cabin. Located in the path of Interstate 94, the rock was moved. However compelling its original appearance was, there is only local tradition in support of the claim.[176]

Waukegan is on a main coach road from Chicago to Milwaukee. By 1845, thrice weekly stagecoach service ran between the two cities, traveling along Green Bay Road. Waukegan residents participated in antislavery conventions in the 1840s and in the formation of the Liberty Party in Lake County. Thus, it is not surprising that stories emerged about the movement of freedom seekers and the provision of support for them in Waukegan. Local traditions point to the involvement of James Cory, owner-publisher of the *Waukegan Gazette*, a paper known for its support for abolition, and that of Henry W. Blodgett, who grew up in Downers Grove, the son of Israel and Avis Blodgett. Blodgett came to Waukegan in 1845, and "was constantly in the front line of anti-slavery agitation." His life is well documented and probably because of his public life and elective offices, he most likely kept some distance from illegal activities. There is no direct evidence of Cory or Blodgett's work with freedom seekers.[177]

However, two white families in Waukegan were involved. Charles and Sarah Lindsay emigrated from Ireland, arriving in Waukegan in 1848 with four children and several other relatives. Charles was a merchant in town and although his name does not appear among the active abolitionists, friends remembered that "more than once in ante-bellum days he aided the fugitive slave in making his escape to Canada." By 1850, Philip and Sarah Blanchard settled on the western edge of Waukegan after traveling from New York. They were relatively close to the family of Amos Bennett, the first Black settler in Lake County. They came with eight children, including a daughter named Sarah, born in 1837 in Albany. Sarah remembered fugitives hidden in the basement and taking food downstairs to them. In addition, she recalled they had a separate "root house" used to store vegetables and from time to time, escaping slaves were hidden there.[178]

Almost unrecognized is that by 1850, there were a small number of Black families and individuals, twenty-eight in total, living in Waukegan. The 1850

Census lists most of these as northern born or born in Illinois. However, several are noted with their births in Tennessee, Virginia, and the Carolinas.[179] These residents of Waukegan were familiar with Black families in Chicago. In 1856, Mary Ann Shadd, editor of the *Provincial Freeman* published in Sandwich, Ontario, while traveling with Frederick Douglass, met with friends in Chicago and later visited "the good Mrs. Medlin and family" in Waukegan. Confronted with serious encounters with slavecatchers, Black activists in Chicago may have brought fugitives north to Waukegan to board lake steamers. By 1860, this Black community diminished to thirteen, probably in response to the long-term impact of the Fugitive Slave Act.[180]

Two additional stories of freedom seekers are based north of Chicago. In 1848, Frederick Douglass's newspaper, *The North Star*, carried an account of a strange court case in Woodstock, in the center of McHenry County. Two freedom seekers from Missouri were kidnapped in Wisconsin by two slave catchers. Traveling south, the catchers and their captives were brought before a magistrate in Woodstock who determined that he had no jurisdiction since the so-called slaves were illegally brought into Illinois and thus, they were discharged as free men. However, at the insistence of the slave catchers, the two "men of color" were rearrested on the charge of horse-stealing. The claim was that they took the horses when they left Missouri. The story in the *North Star* focuses on "the Negroes vs. the horses." In hilarious and perhaps factual detail, the legal arguments unfolded positing both the horses *and* the fugitives as property and raising the question as to which property stole which. Did the fugitives steal the horses as property or did the horses carry off, stealing the fugitives as property in the process? The fugitives were released from their captivity, and the slave catchers were arrested for kidnapping, having to pay a major fine to free themselves. They promptly left town, the fugitives headed for Canada, and the correspondent for the *North Star* wrote, "The horses, I understand are to be tried tomorrow for stealing the Negroes."[181]

Also in the region north of Chicago unfolded the unusual journey of Malinda Fountain. In 1851 she was enslaved as a "chamber maid and body servant" for a family from Memphis traveling by steamboat on the Mississippi. When it arrived at Galena, at the far northwest corner of Illinois, Malinda decided it was time for this family to "nurse their own children, black their own boots and comb their own hair, or pay for having it done." So, she escaped off the boat dressed in her master's suit while the family slept. She immediately found support in Galena and was hidden for some time as "the whole country around was soon filled with advertisements, offering a reward for her apprehension." Traveling across northern Illinois from Galena, she came through McHenry and Lake Counties or just to the south through Elgin. She went directly from the region on to Canada. When her story was published, she was clear in sending a message back to her furious owner that he need not look for her; that she was happy "in the enjoyment of *British liberty*"; and that if she ever choses "to return to *American slavery*, she will let him know."[182]

Vigilance in Chicago and across the Region

Across northeastern Illinois and in Chicago, growing support for abolition, the substantial networks of assistance, and the strength of Black leadership served to undercut the Fugitive Slave Act. There was an increasing sense of Chicago and the wider region as a place of sanctuary. However, the need for ongoing vigilance was clear. Again and again, Chicago newspapers carried warnings about the work of slave catchers in the region. Typical was the warning from one paper in response to the arrival of travelers from Mississippi: "We caution all interested to be on their guard, and ready for an emergency."[183]

Although support for the movement of freedom seekers was a relatively open process, the call for caution and discretion was always warranted. Slave catchers were about, but they, too, needed to be on their guard. Black and white leaders in the city had substantial experience with the courts and with their own capacity to generate physical protection for travelers and physical threats for slave hunters. As noted in several of the stories in this chapter, freedom seekers were often armed and ready to defend themselves physically with force and to use their arms against slave hunters. The use of arms and the threat of violence is covered in a number of news accounts and personal reminiscences. Violence was a clearly accepted alternative if needed to defend journeys to freedom.[184]

In June of 1854, the *Chicago Tribune* commented on the success of the Underground Railroad. As a corporation, it could easily be compared with the fast growing "upper ground" railroads, although there was no real interest in stocks or dividends. This railroad had a crew of "trusted conductors," and well-situated stations.[185] However, the paper also noted that on this particular railroad, passengers were well-supplied "with 'irons' to be used against all who might have the audacity to interfere."[186]

Reinforcing the sense of success for the networks operating in Chicago and the region was an event that occurred several months later. A young woman, carrying her small child, escaped from Monroe County in northeastern Missouri with her husband, who lived in bondage in a nearby county. The two parents crossed the Mississippi arriving in Rock Island where they found help to get on a train to Chicago. To get to the river, they had taken two of their master's best horses and he came hotly after them. He tracked them to Rock Island, but once he arrived and discovered they had left for Chicago, he gave up, knowing how difficult it would be to retrieve them.[187]

However, the antislavery and antikidnapping atmosphere in Chicago and across northeastern Illinois was not always a guarantee of safety. Slave catchers prowled the streets and main roads, and constant care was needed. A young girl living in the city in 1854 vividly remembered a terrifying day when a refugee family was almost destroyed. She lived near State Street and recalled an incidence with a free man of color who purchased his wife's freedom. They had twin girls, but slave catchers somehow discovered that they were born "less than eight months after their mother's freedom." They found her master who used this technicality of the timing of their conception to immediately claim the children as his property. The slave catchers, returning to Chicago, found the family and grabbed the children. The mother heard them screaming and raced out of her home and held on to the back of the wagon bearing her children. A crowd soon gathered, and the slave catchers were forced to obtain a warrant. By this time, the children were rescued, placed in a small boat, and rowed out into the lake. The catchers searched a lake steamer leaving that night, but they did not know that later it stopped in the lake to pick up the children who were taken on to safety in Canada.[188]

Leaders and Travelers

By the mid-1850s, Chicago reached fifty thousand residents with a Black community of more than five hundred. The booming city was a place of choice for Black settlement and a strong community emerged, particularly around the two vital Black congregations, Quinn Chapel of the African Methodist Episcopal tradition and Zoar Baptist Church. With a remarkable group of Black leaders and collaboration among Black and white activists living in the city and across the region, there were well-established networks of support for those who decided to settle and for those who pushed on to Canada.

The movement of freedom seekers to and through Chicago was strongly supported and, to the frustration of slave owners, efforts to capture or recapture former slaves were often thwarted. The passage of the Fugitive Slave Act in late 1850 exacerbated the legal ramifications around escapes and attempts at recapture. Both slave catching activities and networks of support were more deliberate, the threats of force were more obvious, and the work of Black and white activists was more collaborative. Black leadership in Chicago was not only effective in their support of freedom seekers and in initiatives to strengthen their community, but they were also a rising voice in national concerns through meetings and antislavery newspapers.

CHAPTER FOUR

Open Secrets and Railroads, 1855–1861

James and Narcissa Daniels

O F ALL THE GROUPS of freedom seekers passing through Chicago, perhaps the most famous is the group that travelled under the direction of the radical abolitionist John Brown. Through the 1850s, the cross-country movements of Brown intersected with activists in Chicago. In the traditional story, in March 1859, Brown arrived in Chicago on his celebrated journey of liberation for eleven slaves from western Missouri. In Chicago, he had the help of Allan Pinkerton, who later became the famous detective, in getting the fugitives on to Canada and safety.

This story is found in Chicago and Illinois histories framed as a key event orchestrated by John Brown. In Northern newspapers, the focus was on Brown, and the "slaves" were often minor characters in the story of his triumph of distance and daring. At least one Southern paper went further, suggesting the slaves were essentially conned into leaving by agents of the Underground Railroad. However, several of the key elements are incorrect in almost all the traditional accounts.[1]

In the fall of 1858, Jim and Narcissa Daniels, living enslaved on a farm in western Missouri, were worried about their immediate future following the recent death of the man who owned them. His children were determining what do to with his estate, including the disposition of the enslaved people. It was possible that they, along with their two children and their baby on the way, would be sold to a slave-owning planter living in Texas. The farm where Jim and Narcissa lived was near the border with Kansas, and because of this proximity, they hoped to find assistance from antislavery activists, so they could escape (see Map 4.1). Jim Daniels made brooms as a trade on the side and, having permission to do some local traveling and selling as a broom salesman, he crossed the border into Kansas. There, he contacted George Gill, whom he heard was in the abolitionist camp, hoping to receive help to save his family. Gill was a friend of John Brown. Brown was looking for an opportunity to liberate a group of enslaved people and reacted quickly to the one presented by Jim and Narcissa.[2]

On December 20th, Brown and a contingent of twenty men rode into Vernon County, on the western edge of Missouri. Breaking into two groups, they found eleven people ready to go with them. The enslaved persons included Jim, Narcissa, and their children; a widow with three children; Sam Harper and his young brother; and Jane Cruise, a woman separated from her husband. Jim and Narcissa knew the others, whom they most likely recruited.[3]

The freedom seekers traveled with John Brown and his escorts, stopping at the homes of activists in Kansas, Nebraska, and Iowa. Moving through Des Moines, Grinnell, Iowa City, and other towns, the band was warmly received in several places. However secure the band of freedom seekers moving with Brown may have felt, there was almost always a posse on their trail. After traveling across most of the state of Iowa, they boarded a freight car on a Rock Island train headed for Chicago. Before leaving Iowa, the eleven had become twelve, with Jim and Narcissa having a baby along the way, aptly named John Brown Daniels.[4]

In March 1859, three months after their liberation from Missouri, the group reached Chicago. The freedom seekers stayed with the family of Henry and Susan Wagoner while Brown and the other escorts stayed with John and Mary Jones. Brown was well acquainted with the Wagoners and Joneses. There was concern about the dangers for Henry Wagoner if he were too publicly associated with the assistance of freedom seekers. Therefore, they called on Wagoner's friend Allan Pinkerton to assist with moving the escapees. Pinkerton came to the Jones home and brought his son, William, who recalled years later also going to Wagoner's mill and seeing the crew of white "western men" in rough clothes along with the fugitives. Pinkerton raised several hundred dollars to pay for a train ride to Detroit for the freedom seekers, John Brown, and a few of his men. They crossed safely into Canada on March 12, 1859, after a total journey of close to one thousand miles over eighty-two days (see Map 4.1). Along the way, in Springdale, Iowa, Sam Harper and Jane Cruise were married, with a local Quaker justice of the peace performing the ceremony. Years later, the Harpers were photographed in what became one of the iconic images of Black settlement in Canada (see Figure 4.1).[5]

Map 4.1 Jim and Narcissa Daniels, with their children and a few friends, escaped their enslavement with the help of John Brown, the radical abolitionist. They traveled from western Missouri across Iowa and Illinois, staying with John and Mary Jones in Chicago before continuing on to freedom in Canada.

Action and Refuge in Chicago and the Region

In the handful of years before the outbreak of war in 1861, the networks of the Underground Railroad were fully matured and functioning well across northeastern Illinois. Through their church connections, antislavery societies, and years of experience, the people in the networks, both Black and white,

Fig 4.1 Samuel and Jane Harper, in the 1890s in Windsor, Ontario.
They traveled with the Daniels in the famous journey from western
Missouri in 1858–59. Schomburg Center for Research in Black
Culture, New York Public Library Digital Collections.

provided effective and relatively safe assistance for freedom seekers. Across the northern part of the state, well settled by families from New England, New York, and other northern states, the activities of the Underground Railroad were open secrets. One Chicago paper observed that in addition to those traveling through, other freedom seekers decided to stay in Chicago "believing they will be as safe as they would be in her Majesty's the Queen's Dominions."[6]

Small Black communities and individuals living throughout Illinois were in regular contact with Black activists in Chicago, particularly through the African Methodist Episcopal and Baptist churches. Some freedom seekers continued to travel basically independently of these networks before reaching Chicago. Refugees were living openly in Chicago and activists who assisted freedom seekers traveling through the region were discrete but not fearful. Periodically, slave catchers were very visible in the streets and on the wharves of Chicago, but they were easily avoided. In addition, the threat of violence so often felt by freedom seekers was, in a real sense, reversed in Chicago, with the threats often directed against slave catchers by armed residents. Incidences involving confrontations with slave catchers often included physical threats, as noted in the previous chapter, particularly after passage of the Fugitive Slave Act.

A memorable example of the hostility toward slave catchers involved an incident with Lewis Isbell and two freedom seekers from Missouri. One morning, on a wintry day early in 1855, the US marshal came into Isbell's barbershop in the Sherman House hotel to tell him about two fugitives seen in Chicago and he needed Isbell's help. Joseph Bagsby and James Calvert, from Missouri, were the supposed owners of the two and came to Chicago searching for them. They declared to the marshal that they had seen the two and asked him to arrest them.[7]

Isbell took immediate action, recruited a dozen strong Black volunteers, picked up the two freedom seekers and took them all to a deserted cabin on the edge of Chicago. When the marshal returned to Isbell's shop in the afternoon to go searching, they went to the place of the original sighting and, of course, the two were gone. That evening, Isbell went to see Bagsby and Calvert and asked how much they would pay for help in capturing their two slaves. They were willing to pay him $250 for the two. Isbell recalled telling them to keep their money, and to be ready in an hour to go with him to the place where they were hiding.

Isbell then returned to the cabin alone and instructed the men to come out of the cabin when they saw Isbell arrive with the owners in his sleigh. He directed them to "give them a good trouncing. Don't kill them, but shake them up."[8]

Upon returning to the hotel to get the two Missourians, Isbell insisted that they go without guns and even searched the two men to be sure them were unarmed. As they got into the sleigh a third man rushed up and Isbell immediately said they would not go if this third man was part of their group. Bagsby pushed off the third man and unbeknownst to Isbell was given a revolver. When they arrived at the cabin, they stopped at some distance and as they crossed the snow-covered ground, the fourteen men rushed out of the cabin and attacked Bagsy and Calvert. As the incident began, Bagsby pulled out the revolver and shot four times at Isbell, missing with every shot. After being severely beaten and with little urging, Bagsy and Calvert decided to return to Missouri without their intended captives, having "expended two months' time and two to three hundred dollars."[9]

Additional incidents from 1855 reinforce that Chicago was close to being a "safe haven" for freedom seekers. It is likely that everyone knew someone who knew someone who helped freedom seekers. In August of that year, in recounting the unsuccessful efforts by a Kentucky slave owner in Chicago, the *Chicago Tribune* trumpeted: "Valiant Kentuckian! Didst thou not know that the soil of Chicago was free ground, and that the air from our prairie was so pure that he who once has breathed it never again becomes a slave?" The slaveowner was trying to regain possession of his property, with the help of a Kentucky lawyer who had recently established himself in Chicago. The paper also noted that members of Chicago's Black community might appear helpful to visiting slave catchers, but the main intent was to impress on them the possibilities of vengeance and injury if they sought to capture their property. In a similar situation, the *Chicago Daily Democrat*, not a friend to the abolitionist movement, reported on a fugitive "sought in Chicago" in 1855. There was a frustrating search, warnings to the hunters, assistance for the fugitives, and then they simply disappeared into freedom.[10]

The small Black community was well organized, not only when force was needed, but also to attend to a variety of needs within the community and in support of freedom seekers. Along with the churches, the North Star Lodge, collaborations with white abolitionists, and a few other social groups, in the Spring of 1855, Black leadership formed the Anti-Slavery Society of Chicago "comprised principally of colored citizens." However, there is little evidence that this group actually got underway alongside everything else going on in the Black community.[11]

In these years before the Civil War, the contrasts were increasingly stark. Relative safety in Chicago and northeastern Illinois was more apparent and the constraints of slave-owning and slave-hunting in Missouri and other states were more obvious. Throughout the late 1850s and into the early 1860s, the newspapers of Missouri continued almost daily publication of fugitive slave notices, right next to the notices for the sale of livestock. See for example, a page from an issue in October 1860 of the *Daily Missouri Republican*, with a $400 reward notice for "a Negro man named Gus"; an ad for B. M. Lynch, a seller of "all descriptions of negroes suitable for the Southern markets"; a sales ad for a "likely negro boy," and "a negro girl, 16 years old, a very good servant in every respect"; and an announcement seeking the return of a small flock of sheep who strayed.[12]

Northeastern Illinois was overwhelmingly white, but there were small numbers of Black families and individuals living across the region in the late 1850s. Along with the growing Black community in Chicago, there were established Black families in Waukegan, to the north of Chicago, and in Joliet, to the southwest. In addition, a small number of Black families and farm workers lived in and near Ottawa in LaSalle County, and another handful were spread across the region. Other than the work of Black activists in Chicago, the connections and relations of these other settled families and individuals with the movement of freedom seekers is largely unknown.

In the spring of 1856, Mary Ann Shadd, the editor of the *Provincial Freeman*, published weekly in Sandwich, Ontario, visited with friends in Chicago. She was the first Black woman newspaper editor in North America and was impressed with what she saw during her visit. In mid-May, back in Canada, she wrote, "Underground railroad operations in Chicago, are no longer in the hands of the great merchants of that city, if they ever were, but when fugitives arrive, a society of colored men meet, put their hands in their pockets and provide for the passage of their brethren to Canada."[13]

Shadd met with leaders in the Black community, and they clearly communicated with her their willingness to provide direct support. These Black leaders were well-connected with the white activists led by Dr. Dyer who continued to provide aid, often in collaborative efforts.

Within the Black community in Chicago, the members of Quinn Chapel continued as a focal point for assistance. In late 1856, building from an existing small Baptist congregation, key activists joined together to create an enlarged congregation, established in December as Zoar Baptist Church. William Johnson was elected clerk and one of three trustees, along with Henry Wagoner and Henry Bradford. John Jones was elected treasurer with F. Bowen, J. Johnson, and J. H. Marshall serving as the first deacons.[14]

Also in November 1856, a second "State Convention of Colored Citizens" gathered in Alton for further response to the Black Laws of Illinois. The meeting was called for in September by a group of Chicagoans including Johnson, Bradford, Barquet, and Isbell. As the first convention in Chicago in 1853 was attended by mostly Chicagoans, for this gathering, most were residents of Madison County and Alton, including C. C. Richardson. Representing Cook County were John Jones, William Johnson, H. Ford Douglas, and Lewis Isbell. Jones and Isbell were related to the Richardsons and at the convention, Jones spoke warmly of his connections with Alton. Although the gathering focused on the ongoing impact of the Black Laws and on forming a statewide repeal association, the occasion provided opportunities to discuss current concerns for assisting freedom seekers. This gathering again reflects the multiple concerns of these emancipation activists who were working together on a wide range of issues for Black residents and travelers.[15]

Not only did freedom seekers continue to receive assistance from residents in Black communities across the state, but also from others while en route to Illinois. Particularly up and down the Mississippi River and in the many towns along its reach, the racial mix was rich. White settlers, including many foreign born, free people of color, Native Americans, and persons enslaved were engaged in work related to the great river and its commerce. In this diverse context are the stories of Barney Ford and John Stella Martin, both held in bondage but acting independently, working on riverboats. Communications among people of color, both enslaved and free, enabled reports of options for freedom to percolate into enslaved communities. A woman corresponding with the *New Orleans Picayune* complained that "free negroes employed on our finest steamers are nearly all trained and paid to use their influence" to entice "our servants to abscond." She claimed they would identify at Cairo enslaved persons most likely to seek escape and pressure them to leave as the steamers traveled up the Mississippi. She had herself lost a slave to a free man now living in Chicago, and she complained that he made good money convincing enslaved persons to abscond and has a house where "he receives his colored friends."[16]

Although Chicago had become increasingly proabolition and open for freedom seekers, these sentiments were not shared by all residents of the city. In 1856, William G. Stewart, proprietor of a hotel at Clark and Jackson, married a woman from Kentucky. This woman owned an enslaved woman named Mrs. Sylvia Young who escaped and successfully resettled in Stratford, Ontario. They shared some correspondence, so Mrs. Stewart knew where Mrs. Young was living. The newly married Stewarts hatched a plan to try to draw Mrs. Young back into their control. Mrs. Stewart wrote a letter which oh so sweetly urged Mrs. Young to return for the sake of the children who loved her, and she would receive her freedom in two years. Meanwhile, Mr. Stewart wrote to the constable in Stratford to enlist him in a plan to deliver Mrs. Young to Ohio, where she could be captured. The good constable could make $200 for his cooperation. However, the constable delivered Stewart's letter to the local magistrate and the whole affair became public. So, amid the spirit of abolition in Chicago, the Stewarts were denied the hoped-for return of their slave.[17]

As was the case since the beginnings in Chicago, one strong alternative was passage on lake boats to Detroit. This continued along with the increasing use of the railroads. John Weiblen, a justice of the peace in Pennsylvania through most of his later career, as a young man worked on lake steamers out of Chicago in 1855 and 1856. As part of his work, he managed conditions for any fugitive slaves that ended up on his boat, which usually stopped at Collingwood, a port on the Canadian side of Lake Huron. He vividly recalled one incident involving a gentleman from Georgia traveling with his wife, two children, and an enslaved woman servant. All appeared to be going well with the family and the dutiful servant until the boat docked at Collingwood. As they came off the boat, the gentleman and his wife led, with the servant and the two children following. "As soon as the slave girl reached the dock she stepped back from the two children and declared to her master saying 'Massa, I am free.'" He tried to get her to return to the boat to fetch something from their state room, but the young woman refused and again announced that she was free. They offered many promises, but it was to no avail, she was now free and that was that.[18]

The perception of Chicago as a substantial center for the Underground Railroad not only grew across the Midwest, but also reached into the western territories. This role for Chicago was certainly assumed by George Clarke, a militant proslavery advocate in Kansas Territory who offered in 1856 a fifty-dollar reward for the return of "my negro woman, Judy." In his published notice, he wrote that she might still be in Kansas, but more likely "she already secured a passage on the under-ground railway to Chicago." That view of Chicago's role was seen in a variety of ways. From Tennessee, the *Nashville Democrat* was clear that "fugitives from service" were all heading for "that hot bed of treasonable *Abolitionism and corruption*, Chicago."[19]

Over the years, Dr. Dyer enjoyed the distinction of being referred to as "president" of the Underground Railroad in Illinois. However, he did not have exclusive claims to the title. Peter Stewart, a stalwart supporter of freedom seekers in Will County since the late 1830s, found himself in 1857 riding on a train from Washington, DC, to Baltimore in the same car with President James Buchanan. Stewart was sitting near the president and a woman in the car asked if he would change seats with her, so she could sit near the president.

> Mr. Stewart, with the bluff and hearty manner for which he was noted, says: "Madam, I am the President."
>
> "Indeed!" says the lady, "Of what are you president?"
>
> "Of the underground railroad, Madam," he replied, as, with great politeness and good humor, he complied with her request. [20]

Freedom Seekers Living in Chicago

As Chicago continued its explosive growth, due now largely to the impact of the railroads, many of its newest white residents were firmly abolitionist in their interests and politics. Among these was Ernst Schmidt, a noted German American medical doctor and socialist. Born in 1830 in Bavaria, he emigrated to the United States in 1849, part of the flood of Germans escaping the political upheavals of 1848–49. After time in New York, he settled in Chicago in 1857, developing a large medical practice, especially with the poor. He was active in abolitionist circles, working with Black and white leadership. It is likely that he was directly involved with freedom seekers. He knew John Brown, worked actively for Lincoln's election, and cofounded Chicago's first Jewish hospital.[21]

In 1857, the openness in the region was reinforced in the national consciousness due to a confrontation involving the radical congressman Owen Lovejoy. Lovejoy, who was present at his brother Elijah's death in Alton,

Illinois, in 1837, was a powerful voice for abolition in the state and the country and was active in the networks of the Underground Railroad. Over the years, he worked closely with many of the key white and Black activists in Chicago. A longtime resident of Princeton, in Bureau County, he served in Congress from March 1857 until his death in 1864 and was a close friend and loyal advocate for Abraham Lincoln. Lovejoy was one of the outstanding orators among the abolitionists. His sentiments sparked some controversy and led to a confrontation on the floor on Congress and a great speech.

This controversy stemmed from an encounter with a freedom seeker who is known to history as "Old Mose," who lived in Chicago but had been central to an encounter just west of LaSalle County. Earlier in 1857, this gray-haired freedom seeker reached the region as the property of his master, a Mr. Lombard from Mississippi, with some sort of promise that he would be given his freedom. However, Lombard was slow to take any steps in that direction, and Old Mose acted on his own behalf and headed for Chicago. He made an overnight stop at the home of Owen Lovejoy in Princeton. Soon after arriving in Chicago, he found employment in the lumber business with some success.[22]

Lombard believed Lovejoy had directly intervened and was responsible for Old Mose leaving his "employment." He published a nasty letter addressed publicly to Lovejoy, threatening to bring Lovejoy's involvement all out into the open on the floor of the House of Representatives. He handed his grievances over to O. R. Singleton, a congressman from Mississippi. Singleton, perhaps more scheming than hysterical, held back on attacking Lovejoy over his supposed seduction of Old Mose into freedom. Rather, he waited for a debate in the House about using federal funds to pay for the jail fees of locked up fugitive slaves, and then attacked Lovejoy. He accused Lovejoy of being a "Negro-stealer," having directly supported the freedom journey of Old Mose and thus removing him from being the property of Lombard.

In reaction to this attack, Lovejoy presented one of his greatest speeches in Congress; his words were picked up by abolitionists across the country. On the floor of Congress, he admitted having helped Old Mose and was proud of it. He described how an older man, whom he did not know, arrived at his door, he fed him and after a few hours put him on the train to Chicago. Since now he was accused on "negro stealing," he felt an obligation to respond to the charge.

If the object is to ascertain whether I assist fugitive slaves who come to my door . . . I march right to the confessional, and say, I do.

Is it desired to call attention to this fact? Proclaim it then upon the house tops. Write it on every leaf that trembles in the forest, make it blaze from the sun at high noon, and shine forth in the milder radiance of every star that bedecks the firmament of God. Let it echo through all the arches of the heavens and reverberate and below along all the deep gorges of hell, where slave catchers will be very likely to hear it. Owen Lovejoy lives in Princeton, Illinois, three-quarters of a mile east of the village, and he aids every fugitive that comes to his door and asks it. Thou invisible demon of Slavery, dost thou think to cross my humble threshold, and forbid me to give bread to the hungry and shelter to the homeless! I BID YOU DEFIANCE IN THE NAME OF MY GOD![23]

The same spirit of resistance came in a contemporary finding by the Illinois Supreme Court. In late 1857, a suit was filed against the Illinois Central Railroad for allowing the slave of a Missouri master to board a train in Cairo and travel to Chicago (where, of course, he promptly disappeared). This went to the state supreme court, which sided with the railroad and determined that since slavery was illegal in Illinois, there was no need to honor the wishes of the slave owner and the railroad had been in its rights to issue a ticket. The court referenced the 1850 Fugitive Slave Act, but ruled that since this was federal law, it did not apply to a case brought in Illinois courts. This court case became widely known across Illinois and in abolitionist circles as another Chicago example of nullification. It reflected the argument emerging across the northern states that states and local jurisdictions had the right to set aside, or "nullify," the federal law when they had fundamental disagreements with it.[24]

The impulses to act quickly to defend the rights of freedom seekers is well reflected in the encounter of Samuel Thompson and Samuel Gantz with the engaged citizens of Chicago. In August of 1857, Thompson was returning to his farm near Monmouth, Illinois, with Gantz, a sixteen-year-old. Years earlier, in Pennsylvania, Thompson met Gantz's mother, a free person of color, traveling on her own. He ended up adopting her young son and, after visiting Pennsylvania, was now returning with him to his Illinois farm. Seeing this young Black man with an older white, a crowd of Black Chicagoans gathered and immediately assumed that a child was being taken into slavery. Over the course of several days, with near riots and confrontations occurring, finally the courts, the sheriff, Calvin DeWolf, Allan Pinkerton, and Black leadership were all involved. After several attempts to convince everyone of the ordinariness of this situation through the court and the intervention of Pinkerton, young Samuel Gantz was able to convince a group of Black men that he in fact was free and wanted to go home with the man caring for him. The *Chicago Tribune* concluded its coverage of the whole encounter with the observation, "We cannot blame the colored men of this city for the jealousy with which they watch any thing that looks like an attempt to take one of their color back to slavery, that bitter, crushing, terrible slavery, which so many of them have suffered."[25]

From the late 1850s, some freedom seekers settling in Chicago for a significant period do not appear in the historical record. The Census and other records of 1860 are not particularly helpful since these individuals and families could have been in Chicago for years and then gone by census time, and, of course, some chose not to be interviewed or recorded, given their refugee status. An example of the elusiveness of records is the story of Warren Carter, known only from his official Civil War Pension file.

Carter had been enslaved in Kentucky and he reported that he had been the property of John C. Breckenridge of Lexington. It is possible that this was the John C. Breckinridge then serving as vice president under President James Buchanan. Carter chose to escape in 1857 and went to Chicago, arriving in October 1858. He indicated in his army pension request that he lived in Chicago for several years before moving to Wyanet, west of Princeton in Bureau County, Illinois, from where he enlisted. In Kentucky and in Bureau County, he was working on farms, but there is no indication of his work during his time in Chicago. There is simply no record yet uncovered to support his mention of having lived in the city.[26]

In 1858, an interesting measure of the strength of abolitionist sentiments is reflected in a situation with criminals mistaken for fugitives. In January, three young Black men were arrested in Chicago for robbery. However, they were logged into the jail as "fugitives, escaped from their masters." A jail employee, without checking on the facts of the arrest, raised the alarm that fugitive slaves were being held, and steps were taken to free the prisoners. Only later did the public learn that, in fact, thieves had been released.[27]

In September of that year, the *Chicago Tribune* announced on page one: "U.G.R.R. – The directors of this line of road who, from necessity and choice, keep dark about its affairs, from time to time demonstrate that the line is open." Under this opening was a brief description of a young couple—he was thirty, she was nineteen—traveling to Canada. The bounty was $700 and slave catchers were close at hand. Their place of lodging (it appears likely they were with John and Mary Jones) was being watched but they managed to safely leave Chicago, reach Detroit, and cross over to Windsor in Canada West.[28]

On February 21, 1859, a group of seventy freedom seekers arrived in Chicago, after traveling through Iowa from Missouri. Heading for Canada, they were heavily armed and made it clear to any who were interested that "They said that they had worked for white folks a great many years for nothing, and thought it was about time to be doing something for themselves."[29]

In November 1859, a small-town Missouri paper reported on the departure of eleven freedom seekers from La Grange, on the Mississippi River north of Quincy; they called it a "Negro Stampede." The freedom seekers stole a flat boat to cross the river, and the paper admitted that now locally they were experiencing what was so well noted by St. Louis newspapers. In their small community they now saw "the third or fourth successful stampede in the past three or four months. This fact leads us to the conclusion that there is a regular underground railroad established from this place to Chicago, Ills. and that the company have an agent or agents in this city."[30]

In that same direction, the *St. Louis News* pointed to agents of the Underground Railroad in Kansas, Iowa, Illinois, and Michigan colluding to recruit fugitives and carrying them to Canada. The latest "Negro exodus," in November 1859, included twenty-six persons and, at that rate, Missouri would soon lose all its "negroes." A week later, the *Chicago Tribune* reported on an Underground Railroad group arriving with thirty passengers, "five from the vicinity of Richmond, Virginia, twelve from Kentucky, and thirteen from Missouri. The thirteen from Missouri were sold to go down the river the very day they started. They are now all safe in Canada. A stalwart six-footer and a Sharp's rifle were the only guards."[31]

Along with the willingness of freedom seekers to defend themselves, the sentiment to use force was shared by Chicago residents. In early 1860, a young family escaping from Mississippi, a couple with a young child, were in hiding in Chicago until "the treachery of a negro" exposed them. Taken to court with the help of a federal marshal, they were ordered to be returned. The federal officials and slave catchers feared that abolitionists would try to rescue the family and so removed them in secret. Rapidly after the court judgment, a large contingent of residents formed to storm the jail to release the family. However, upon hearing of their departure, the group decided to hunt down the informer. According to the account from the *Chicago Inter Ocean*, "There must have been four hundred to five hundred people in this mob, white and black, women being as plentiful as men." They found the man, and in a vacant lot just off Harrison Street near the downtown, they upended a large cart, lashed a strong beam across the shafts of the cart and put a rope noose around the man's neck. At that moment a group of policemen appeared, managed to rescue him from a lynching and fought their way out of the crowd, carrying him to safety.[32]

Also early in 1860, Chicago's Black community's connections with national issues was reflected in a fundraising "festival" on behalf of the Black families most affected by participation in the Harpers Ferry raid led by John Brown. Several women, including Susan Wagoner and Sattira Douglas organized the festival. One of the speakers for the event was H. Ford Douglas whose oration "did ample justice to the heroes of that memorable event."[33]

During 1860, there were a fairly large number of newspaper reports on freedom seekers in Chicago. One from January noted, "Two colored men and three colored women from a plantation near Jackson, Mississippi, were passed through Chicago." Another in May announced, "A colored man, James Mann, raised a balance of $220 here to free his son then in slavery in Virginia. Previous to this he had paid $2,400 for himself, wife and two other children."[34]

In November, the *Chicago Tribune* ran a series of front-page articles on "The Eliza Grayson Case." Eliza and her sister Celia escaped from their owner, Stephen Nuckolls, in Nebraska City, Nebraska, near the Missouri border, in November of 1858. Nuckolls, with friends and slave catchers, pursued them across Iowa, creating an uproar all along the way. Confrontations led to court cases in several communities throughout 1859. Eliza and Celia traveled across northern Illinois and made an impression on some who assisted them in Kane County.[35]

In late 1860, Nuckolls learned that Eliza had settled in Chicago, and he came after her. He found her and even though he had the help of local authorities, he simply did not understand the situation in Chicago. One of those he hired was a local scoundrel named Jake Newsome. With Jake's help, Eliza was arrested, but as she was transferred to another jail, an aggressive group of Black Chicagoans descended, grabbed Eliza, and she was on her way to safety in Canada.

Not only were all the details laid out in the press, but *Chicago Tribune* reporters wrote two stunningly satirical, cynical articles about the whole affair. After her escape, the first headlined: "THE UNION AGAIN THREATENED. The Colored Person Loose." They ridiculed Nuckolls' efforts to reclaim his property. She was locked up, escaped, and became "one very lively bit of darkness going east by the U.G.R.R."[36]

Responding in kind of the *Tribune* articles, the *Nebraska City News*, of Nebraska City, Nebraska, declared: "Eliza is in the papers—two weeks ago she was in a free-love and freedom-loving brothel in the very Black Republican city of Chicago." However, she left there and made it to Canada, no doubt "to finish her existence in a house of ill-fame." The paper expressed amazement that somehow the crazy abolitionists felt this route was better than to stay put as a slave in a "home of luxury and plenty."[37]

Soon after the front-page excitement with Eliza, another compelling freedom seeker story emerged in early 1861 connected with the family of a well-known Congregational preacher and his wife, Dr. Joseph and Emily Roy. In the spirit of the antislavery declaration of the Chicago Association of Congregational Churches, Plymouth Congregational Church formed in 1853 and by 1855, called to the pulpit the energetic twenty-eight-year-old preacher, Joseph Edwin Roy. Rev. Dr. Roy not only was strongly abolitionist but threw himself into the life of the growing city and led the congregation for five years. He knew deeply the commitments of his congregation and "It did not hurt us to be called the 'n—' church and the pastor the 'n—' preacher." Freedom seekers in Chicago often found support and protection from the Roys.[38]

In 1860, he left the church to serve as a Midwest leader for the American Missionary Association. In that capacity, on one occasion in early 1861, he and his wife were staying at the Orient Hotel in the middle of Chicago. Working in the hotel was a free man of color who had purchased his freedom, and then helped his wife to escape from slavery. His wife was also employed at the hotel. Slave hunters learned that she was in Chicago and appealed to a US marshal to find and arrest her.

The marshal came to the Orient Hotel with a bloodhound used for tracking. The hotel's proprietor, although a Democrat and not an abolitionist, could not manage the idea of seeing the woman returned to slavery and so immediately sent word for her to go the Roys' room in the hotel. Emily Roy hid the woman in a small closet and placed a large dresser in front of the door, with a writing desk close by. After being detained by the hotel owner, the marshal and bloodhound searched the building and came to the Roys' room. Sitting at the desk, Emily Roy welcomed the marshal in. Although the bloodhound was attracted to the dresser, the marshal did not ask to move it and after a short while left. The woman remained hidden for two days until well after the marshal and dog left town. Contemporary records suggest this was the last time a bloodhound was used to track freedom seekers in Chicago.[39]

Also, in early 1861, Dr. Roy remembered a dramatic encounter involving Dr. Charles Dyer, perhaps embellishing the details. He recalled Dr. Dyer being so desperate to get a young man safely on a train to Detroit that he dressed him in women's clothes, veil and all. With the disguise in place, they traveled Dr. Dyer's buggy through the city in the middle of the day to reach the first rail station beyond the city. This was about seven miles from Chicago, and they reached the train in time to "put him on board for the land of freedom."[40]

Amid all these activities, a reporter for the *New York Daily Herald* summarized the work of the Underground Railroad in Chicago. He saw it as a very well-organized group of activists led by two men, one white and one Black, both "men of means." He probably meant Dr. Dyer and John Jones. He continued his description, saying that they have the active support of about two hundred white men and around one hundred Black, all divided into groups of ten. Communications were very effective and whenever word was given on the arrival of travelers, an organized contingent of men met that train and responded to whatever situation arose. He called it a "formidable abolitionist organization." Formidable as the Underground Railroad may have been, the regimented structure was unlikely. The collaboration was an open secret, an association across racial lines that could and did, in fact, respond to a great variety of needs. However, it may best be seen as far more fluid, as all the evidence suggests that responses were of a great variety. As freedom seekers arrived, some were alone and anonymous, others well-organized. Some came with advance notice and contracts while others sought flexible and creative assistance. With all of this, it was clear that Chicago was both a destination and a way station for folks on their way to freedom. [41]

Northeastern Illinois

From 1855 forward, white activists across northeastern Illinois continued assisting travelers and often directed them to Black and white leaders in Chicago. Most of these activists settled in the 1830s, stayed where they settled, and did the work of the Underground Railroad for years. As was the situation in Chicago, the movement of freedom seekers across the region was generally discrete but in the open, in the daylight, and often the result of their own independent actions. This diversity of movement is reflected in the stories of Andrew Jackson and Mary Wagden.

Andrew Jackson was enslaved in Mississippi, the name-sake son of a wealthy planter. When about twenty-eight years old, he escaped and made his way to Illinois, where he spent the winter of 1858 living with the family of Lorenz and Mary Ott in Deerfield, in Lake County north of Chicago.[42]

He traveled from Marshall County, Mississippi, on the border with Tennessee, where the plantation owner, Andrew Jackson, lived with sixty slaves. Of these slaves, thirty-five were female, most of child-bearing age and eight of the sixty were listed in the federal Census of 1860 as "M," mulatto. There were several of the right age to be his mother, and he decided to take his father's name. During his time in Deerfield, he shared with his hosts that he came from Mississippi, he was the son of his owner, and while working on the plantation, he often saw his white sisters. [43]

Most likely, Jackson traveled overland to the Tennessee River and followed it north to the Ohio River. Crossing the Ohio, he traveled overland to the Chicago region. Traveling on his own, probably going around the city of Chicago, he reached the home of Lyman and Clarissa Wilmot in Lake County. They came from New York with strong abolitionist commitments and settled near Deerfield with a large family. Jackson arrived in winter and because of the difficulty of further travel at the time, he had to stay locally. The Wilmots could not host him; not only did they have seven children, but already had several boarders, including the local school teacher. To manage through the winter, they brought him to the home of Lorenz and Mary Ott. At the Ott home, Jackson helped with home chores through the winter which enabled the Ott children to go to school. Years later, Samuel Ott, a teenager at the time, remembered this winter with Andrew Jackson and the stories he told about his life in slavery and his escape. [44]

Jackson shared with his hosts that as the master's son he had some flexibility and access to information and thus developed a strong desire to be free. He told them that soon after he ran off, his master came after him with slave catchers and bloodhounds, most likely while he was still in Mississippi. They caught him, tied him with a rope and made him walk alongside the horses. Over time he loosened his ropes and when his master was asleep, he slipped away into the woods. He lived, almost starving, in the woods nearby for many days and on several occasions heard his master and others in the woods searching for him. He stole corn from the fields and remembered a time that he took fresh loaves of bread from a house.

After an extended period near the plantation, he finally took off and headed north, eventually reaching the farmlands north of Chicago in Lake County. Jackson stayed through the winter and was a good worker, not only with the household chores, but also with managing the horses. During this period, the family taught him to read and write. He had carpentry skills and he "made a nice gate of stout wood" for the fencing in the front yard. He said the gate would last until all "the slaves were free," and that Mr. Ott should destroy the gate when that day of freedom came. When spring came, Lorenz Ott provided Jackson with a new suit of clothes and money to pay for passage on a steamer to Canada. Lyman Wilmot traveled with Jackson to Chicago. Upon reaching Canada, Jackson wrote back to tell the Otts that he had arrived safely.[45]

William and Roxana Nickerson, longtime residents of Mayfield Township in DeKalb County, vividly remembered a very cold winter night in 1860, when they received as visitors a woman with a young child. Brought to his door by a stranger who then abruptly left, the woman said to William, "I am told that you are a friend to the colored people." Thus, they met Mary Wadgen. The Nickersons came from Connecticut and along with farming, William served as the first minister of the antislavery Mayfield Wesleyan Methodist Church. He helped form the Republican Party in the county during the 1850s and in later years served as Supervisor of the township. Mary Wadgen had a complex history of movement across the United States. Born enslaved in Virginia in 1842, her father may have been her master or another white man living on or near his farm. She was sold out of Virginia and ended up in Wilkerson County, Mississippi, as the property of a white woman named Mary Watkins. At some point, she decided to go for her freedom; perhaps she herself had been raped and was pregnant. She reached Iowa and there in 1858 gave birth to her daughter. In 1860, traveling east from Iowa, she reached DeKalb County and the home of the Nickersons.[46]

Consulting with others in their church, they realized it was too wintry for Mary and her daughter to continue traveling. Then they discovered she had papers testifying to the fact that she was a skilled cook and realized that they might find a position for her, even if it was temporary. Nickerson recalled many years later, "We went to Sycamore and found a home for her in Dr. Page's cellar kitchen. She remained there for four months and then we sent her on her way to Canada."[47]

Dr. Horatio and Eliza Page settled in Genoa in 1838 and he was the first physician practicing in DeKalb County. They moved close to Sycamore, were charter members of the Congregational Church there, and, over time, became among the wealthiest families in the county. The Census of 1860 notes that living with the Pages was Mary A. Wadgen, twenty-eight, born in Virginia, with a daughter named Mary, aged two, born in Iowa. They are listed, mother and daughter, as mulatto. Mary and her daughter are two of the seven Black residents noted in DeKalb County in 1860.[48]

In the years immediately before the Civil War, LaSalle County was the scene for two powerful stories reflecting the issues and experiences shaped by the conditions of American slavery and the burdens of the federal laws. In October 1859, public conversation in Ottawa and across the county, as was true across the country, focused on the stunning news of John Brown's raid at Harpers Ferry. Brown and his men moved into Harpers Ferry in the early morning of October 17th, and confrontation led to blood and chaos. However, in that same week, the conversations in Ottawa were overwhelmed by details of two local situations, one concerning a local man named Berkley and the other arising from the arrest and escape of a fugitive named Jim Gray.

Berkley, a free man of color, worked on the farm of William and Mary Dickerman outside Ottawa starting in 1848. He was in their employ for years, and they were comfortable with his decision earlier in 1859 to go off to search for gold at Pike's Peak with a friend named Aaron Daniels. While they traveled through Missouri, Daniels suggested that Berkley pretend to be his slave so they would not be hassled along the way. Unfortunately, in St. Joseph, Berkley was discovered and arrested as a free man without papers. He was badly beaten, and Daniels lost his nerve and left his friend. [49]

Berkley obtained the assistance of a lawyer who communicated with residents of Ottawa, who sent assurances that he was in fact a free man and had been living as such in Ottawa. This, however, was of no help and Berkley was sold to pay for jail fees. He was bought for $1045 by a Missouri farmer who soon felt that he was a flight risk and took him to the St. Louis slave market. There he was sold to a slave trader planning to send him down river toward New Orleans to be sold again. Near Memphis, he managed to escape from the boat. Traveling north with another fugitive, "on their way through Tennessee and Kentucky they lived on potatoes, corn, &c., which they found in the fields." They crossed into Illinois, reached an area south of Decatur, and after being discovered, managed to escape a group of slave hunters. They traveled by foot all the way back to Ottawa. In the same week as Brown's raid on Harpers Ferry, two slave catchers arrived in Ottawa from New Orleans. They claimed to be from St. Louis looking for an Irishman wanted for murder. However, their real intentions were discovered, and Berkley was protected by friends.[50]

Residents in Ottawa and the surrounding area held several meetings to raise funds to enable Berkley to travel to Canada and safety. The final meeting of support was on October 17th, the same day as the raid on Harpers Ferry and just a few days before Jim Gray was brought to Ottawa. At that gathering, one resolution reflected the moral outrage that kidnappers would try "to abduct from our midst an intelligent and worthy young man not charged nor suspected on any crimes or offense, for the purpose of inflicting upon him the untold horrors of chattel slavery." These community leaders in Ottawa were determined to protect Berkley and publicly declared that they supported his decision to go to Canada, which he indeed chose to do.[51]

In this same month, a few weeks earlier, the notorious "Jonesboro Gang" in southern Illinois removed from an Illinois Central train a freedom seeker whose kidnapping became the occasion for a nationally followed court case in Chicago. The gang of a dozen or more fellows was headquartered in Jonesboro in Union County under the leadership of the former postmaster, John B. Jones. His second in command was J. W. Curtly. The gang started years earlier, when, with accomplices, Jones began kidnapping people of color on the trains. By 1859, the gang was well in place under Jones and Curtly. The *Jonesboro Gazette* reported their efforts, including the capture of a Black man riding on the Illinois Central, who had with him a "trunk of good clothes and $56." It turned out he was an enslaved person traveling on business of behalf of his master and he was released.[52]

Immediately following this and other kidnappings, on October 5th, 1859, the Jonesboro Gang ran into Jim Gray. He had been living enslaved on a farm near New Madrid, in the southern corner of Missouri, on the Mississippi River. Along with two friends, he decided to escape. Leaving on September 4th, they traveled about forty miles north, making their way across the Mississippi near Cairo. At some point, they boarded an Illinois Central train. In Perry County, more than eighty miles north of Cairo, they were attacked, and Gray was captured.

Departing the train, the kidnappers took Gray to the sheriff in Perry County while they searched for his owner. However, this sheriff refused to cooperate, and the kidnappers had to return south to their own stomping grounds and place him in the jail in Jonesboro, Union County. B. G. Root, a resident of Tamaroa, in Perry County, witnessed the initial kidnapping and took the Illinois Central directly north to see Judge John D. Caton, chief justice of the Illinois Supreme Court, residing in Ottawa. Root described the situation to the judge, and Caton issued a writ of habeas corpus, demanding to know the reason for the capture and holding of Jim Gray.

When confronted with the writ, the sheriff in Union County was furious because he saw no reason for upstate, "Abolitionist judges" to interfere in local matters. No doubt urged on by Jones and his accomplices, he wanted to simply ignore the writ, but a local judge urged compliance. In the meantime, Gray's owner, Richard Phillips, living in Cape Girardeau, Missouri, arrived in Jonesboro and joined the intensity. Rather than defy the judge, the locals decided to head north to Ottawa. The group included Jim Gray, the sheriff, Phillips, and nine men serving as bodyguards. The contingent stopped first in Springfield and appeared before US Commissioner Stephen A. Corneau who issued a writ for the arrest of Jim Gray under the Fugitive Slave Act. This, of course, now gave a legal "cover" for the kidnapping on the train. At the same time, Corneau sought to appoint Isaac Albright (one of the kidnappers!) as a deputy US marshal, but that did not happen.

Leaving Springfield, the group boarded the Illinois Central train north to LaSalle. There, they changed trains for the short ride east to Ottawa. They had to go on foot through the streets of LaSalle from the Illinois Central station to that of the Rock Island line. "The appearance there of the phenomenon of a negro tied with a cable, and driven by half a dozen men, with murderous weapons in their hands, inflamed the populace, and more especially the Irish laborers on the Canal basin, in the highest degree. The latter were with difficulty restrained from mobbing the white men and setting the negro free on the spot."[53]

They continued to Ottawa to appear before a judge and discovered a very large crowd gathered at the court house to view the proceedings. The court was packed. Judge Caton immediately ruled that the original arrest, that is, when Jim Gray had been kidnapped and turned over to the sheriff, was illegal. However, he then ruled that under the writ issued in Springfield, there was reason to hold Jim and ordered the marshal to do so. The marshal prepared to take Jim back to the jail; however, in that moment, people in the packed court room began to cry out and push and pull, and one man was calling to Jim Gray, "seizing him by the arm and jerking him in the direction of the door. There was a rush and a hubbub about one minute in length, and Jim was gone. The crowd around the door was very great, and before the Marshal and his posse could gain the street, by the ordinary means of egress, there was no Jim in the city limits".[54]

Evidently, some thought had gone into the "rescue" and longtime activists were there to help out. William Hickok, from Troy Grove and deeply involved in assisting freedom seekers, was one of those present who helped Jim Gray escape. One news account held that Gray accidentally "fell through a trap door upon the line of the Underground Railroad." Actually, he was carried by buggy east out of Ottawa, then south across the Illinois River to the home of William Strawn, a committed abolitionist in La Salle County. A day or two later, two young men living in Seneca, on the Illinois River near Strawn, connected with Gray and traveled with him through "miles of swamp and forest" to the home of a Quaker abolitionist and then north to "other agents of the Underground Railway."[55]

In 1915, the *Journal of the Illinois State Historical Society* published an article on the rescue of Jim Gray and the life of John Hossack. This publication includes a retelling of the rescue effort. However, in contrast to the newspaper accounts of the day, the retelling reflects the post–Civil War romanticization of the role of the "Abolitionist" and the caricature nature often used in depicting the freedom seekers. In this version, it is Hossack himself who calls out to Jim Gray:

"If you want your liberty, come." Dr. Stout separated the negro from the Marshal, and Hossack threw himself in the way of the officer. A lane, lined by Abolitionists, made a path for the negro, which closed behind him, but his way was blocked at the door; Dr. Hopkins, an athlete, who had been standing outside, caught the negro by the shoulders and lifted him free of the crowd: Someone cried "the carriage" and, not seeing the gate, the negro leaped the fence at a bound, and plunged head first in and through the carriage, both extremities sticking out.... the wild black team sped away leaving only a cloud of dust, and a bewildered, baffled, angry crowd surging about the scene of the well-executed escape.[56]

A few weeks later, in mid-November of 1859, the *Ottawa Free Trader*, the widely read local paper, lumped three recent events together—John Brown's raid at Harpers Ferry, the support for Berkley, and the rescue of Jim Gray—convinced that the rule of law was collapsing in the country, chaos caused by the abolitionists. The paper noted that the New York *Courier & Enquirer*, in responding to this time of chaos, advocated that all those who agreed either directly or indirectly with John Brown and wanted to help fugitive slaves ought to be hanged. The *Free Trader* added, "This rule would hang a score or two of our Ottawa abolitionists."[57]

This then is the apparent end of the story of Jim Gray. Going forward, the public focus was entirely on those who helped him to escape. The key participants were arrested, and this became a nationally watched event known as the "Ottawa Rescue Case." Jim Gray became a mere reference point as "Jim," or as "the N——r Jim." He became the briefly mentioned occasion for telling the great story of the Ottawa Rescue, the work of courageous abolitionists.

From the dramatic rescue event in the courthouse on October 20, 1859, initially seven residents of Ottawa were arrested. However, the trial soon focused on the specific involvement of three persons in the rescue. The principals were identified as John Hossack, the prominent businessman, born in Scotland, and widely respected throughout the region; Dr. Joseph Stout, physician from New Jersey and the Cincinnati Medical School; and his brother, James Stout, a lawyer in Ottawa. All three were well-known and respected. When arrested and taken to the train for trial in Chicago, several hundred came to the station in Ottawa, speeches were given, and the crowd sent them off with three cheers.

The three arrived in Chicago, were placed under custody in the so-called Debtor's Quarters in the courthouse, and, within days, were visited by hundreds of Chicago residents. Their trials went into February and March of 1860, with the final determinations made in October 1860. Among the lead attorneys were Isaac Arnold and Edwin Larned. James Stout was acquitted. Along with court fees, Hossack and Dr. Joseph Stout each were fined $100 and sentenced to ten days in jail. Both during the trials and during the subsequent few days in jail, the prisoners, especially Hossack, were praised throughout Chicago. Mayor "Long John" Wentworth saw to it that accommodations and meals were well taken care of. During the afternoons of his confinement, Hossack was "paroled" from jail by Mayor Wentworth and driven around the city with the mayor in his carriage.[58]

Just prior to being sentenced, John Hossack delivered a speech that was soon in print and distributed across the country by the advocates of abolition. This received wide coverage in the North in the months before the outbreak of the Civil War. Hossack warmly admitted being an abolitionist, roundly attacked slavery and the Fugitive Slave Act, and concluded by saying,

> The jury have found me guilty; yes, guilty of carrying out the still greater principles of the Declaration of Independence; yes, guilty of carrying out the still greater principles of the Son of God. Great God! Can these things be? Can it be possible? What country is this? Can it be that I live in a land boasting of freedom, of morality, of Christianity?... I am guilty of no crime. I therefore ask for no mercy; I ask for justice. Mercy is what I ask of my God. Justice in the courts of my adopted country is all I ask. It is the inhuman and infamous law that is wrong, not me.[59]

At the end of 1859, the *Chicago Tribune* continued to follow the activities of the Jonesboro Gang that had kidnapped Jim Gray in October. The paper warned the public of the dangers of the "snares and traps laid for fugitives in Jonesboro (Union County) and other towns in Egypt." About the Jonesboro Gang and others, the paper said,

> Their business is to waylay the trains passing North, and seize all colored persons found on them. The County Judge and Sheriff of Union appear to be in partnership with these lawless wretches. The mode of procedure is to capture a negro, if one is found on a train, throw him into jail, and keep him there for a few days or weeks, waiting for a claimant to offer a reward for his capture. If a reward is offered, the negro is at once handcuffed and hustled out of the State; the blood-money is divided among the kidnappers, who proceed to set their traps for another victim. But if no claimant appears, the negro, instead of being liberated, is taken out of prison and

started down the Mississippi in charge of a portion of the kidnappers and sold to the first buyer.

The reports included an occasion when the Jonesboro Gang took a porter off a sleeping car and intended to sell him. Fortunately, a conductor was quickly informed and managed, revolver in hand, to rescue the porter.[60]

In January 1860, Chicagoans continued to read the news on the activities of John B. Jones and his gang. One report involved a freedom seeker kidnapped and held in the gang leader's house for several days before being taken south for sale. Another was that of a freedom seeker kidnapped and brutalized, then sold to Jones for him to then resell in the South. Then, on January 31st, the *Chicago Tribune* published a letter from John B. Jones, strongly objecting to all of which he was accused. He maintained he was "Negro stealing" in lawful ways and in fact it was the abolitionists, in the case of Jim Gray, who stole a Negro out of due process and thus "trampled the law and constitution of our State." Not only, in his judgment, did they "steal" Jim Gray from him, but they also deprived a citizen from another state of reacquiring his rightful property. It seemed clear to Jones that it was well within the law to arrest freedom seekers and "put them in safe keeping until their owners can get them."[61]

In a remarkable turn of events, under the heading "Whisky and Kidnapping," the *Chicago Tribune* reported on the strange deaths of both Jones and Curtly, the heads of the Jonesboro Gang. Reprinting a story datelined from Anna, Union County, on February 3, 1860, the paper reported that Curtly was a full partner with Jones in the terrible events involving Jim Gray and other kidnappings. The latest news was that Curtly recently took eight days to die "from the effects of exposure and bad whisky." Just before his death Curtly confessed that he was a murderer, had another wife with two children, and was guilty of many other crimes. All this so terrified Jones that "he fell on the floor fearfully convulsed, and never was sensible after, but lingered a week and on the very same day and hour one week later, died the most horrible of all deaths, lying on the floor. . . . He died as only those do who die of that fearful disease, the delirium tremens." The article concluded by noting that their deaths appeared to have ended kidnapping in the region. Others possibly attracted to kidnapping work witnessed this "closing scene of their lives, and the denunciation, 'as ye sow so shall ye reap,'" which was deeply imprinted on them all.[62]

Four months later, in June 1860, the *Chicago Tribune* reported on a kidnapping of a free man named James Waggoner born in Ohio. Two Virginia slave catchers operating in Ohio took him into Kentucky and sold him. In reporting the story, the *Chicago Tribune* saw this connection: "The beauties of kidnapping are not a monopoly of Illinois. The delirium tremens having carried off the two ringleaders in Union County, in this State, their immortal parts seem to have been transmigrated to the earthly tabernacles of a pair of incredible scoundrels in Ohio."[63]

Railroads and Kidnappings

Whatever brought them into Illinois, freedom seekers settling in and near Chicago or passing through benefited from the arrival of the railroads. Long after activists adopted the language of the railroads, the rail lines themselves reached from the east into Chicago and exploded across Illinois in the middle of the 1850s. Rapidly, they were put to good use for movement into, through, and beyond northeastern Illinois (see Map 4.2).

The earliest of the rail lines from the east connected Detroit with Chicago. This was enormously important for the movement of freedom seekers to the edge of Canada. The Michigan Central Railroad reached from Detroit to Lake Michigan in 1849 and to Michigan City, Indiana, in 1850, with boat connections to Chicago. The full line came to Chicago in 1852. The Michigan Southern Railroad also extended into Chicago in 1852. There were likely earlier uses of these rail lines by freedom seekers, but one of the first reported was a note in the *Free West* in late 1854 of a group of fifteen travelers from Missouri leaving Chicago on the Michigan Central. Charles Goodrich Hammond was the general superintendent for the Michigan Central and, several years later, personally responded to the plea of Allan Pinkerton to provide passage for the group of freedom seekers who came to Chicago with John Brown in March of 1859. Hammond provided a boxcar supplied with food and water for the trip to Detroit. Staff of the Michigan Central, perhaps at Hammond's direction, maintained a concealed room in the railroad's depot in Michigan City, Indiana. This was used for the protection of freedom seekers traveling on the Michigan Central and on the New Albany and Salem Railroad, which shared the depot. At least one of the regular trains out of Chicago had an especially prepared baggage car with a private room in it to accommodate freedom seekers.[64]

Within the state, the completion of the Illinois Central was a stunning opportunity. The trek from Cairo and the southern reaches of Illinois up to the Chicago region was always daunting, taking weeks, even months. With the coming of the rail line, the trip was overnight! The line from Chicago to Cairo was completed in 1855, connecting with steamboat service all the way south to New Orleans.

The Rock Island line, more formally the Chicago and Rock Island Railroad, reached from Chicago to Joliet in 1852, then west to Rock Island on the Mississippi in 1854. The river was bridged in 1856, with rail service west across Iowa. What became the Chicago, Burlington and Quincy Railroad was completed from Chicago to Quincy on the Mississippi in 1856. A line from Chicago to the Mississippi opposite Burlington, Iowa, was finished a year earlier. The Chicago and Alton line, under various names, reached from Alton and St. Louis to Joliet by 1855, with an extension into Chicago in 1856.

The expanding rail network provided for freedom seekers and for slave catchers the possibilities for far more rapid movement into the Chicago region and from Chicago to Detroit and Canada. The seriousness of this problem was seen by the mid-1850s with a failed attempt by the Illinois legislature to allow only free Black persons with papers to ride the trains (see Map 4.2).[65]

At the far southern end of the state, the *Cairo Times*, enthusiastic about the newly completed Illinois Central, saw that this was clearly not an emotion shared by slave-owners in Kentucky, Tennessee, and Missouri. They immediately understood how the new rail lines became rapid avenues for escape. In response the editors of the *Cairo Times* declared, "The impression has gone abroad that there is to be an underground railroad from this place to Chicago, and that Negroes will be induced to run away from Missouri and Kentucky. We assure our friends abroad that such fears are entirely without foundation." Directing its words to readers in Missouri and Kentucky, the *Cairo Times* declared that although they were part of a free state, "there are no abolitionists here . . . the climate doesn't agree with them."[66]

On the Illinois Central

In September 1855, the *Daily St. Louis Intelligencer* reported that a slave owner in Mississippi County in Missouri pursued his slave all the way to Chicago after the slave had successfully purchased a ticket from an Illinois Central agent. In Chicago, the "abolitionists had placed the negro beyond the reach of the

Map 4.2 Beginning in 1852 and continuing into 1861, some freedom seekers traveled to Detroit from Chicago on the Michigan Central Railroad (MCRR) and the Michigan Southern Railroad (MSRR). Starting in the mid-1850s, some came to Chicago on the Chicago & Alton Railroad (CARR); the Chicago, Burlington & Quincy Railroad (CBQRR); the Chicago & Rock Island Railroad (CRIRR); and the Illinois Central Railroad (ICRR).

owner." The paper went on to note that employees of the Illinois Central included "regular agents" of the Underground Railroad.[67]

In 1857 a young man named George Burroughs arrived in Cairo. A native of Canada, he was actively involved with refugee settlement, including work with "True Band" societies. As a young teenager, he worked with his father and others to form a True Band near Hamilton, Ontario. These True Bands were formed by African Canadians and recently settled refugees to counter what they saw as the ineffectiveness and counterproductive work of some white and Black activists who circulated in the northern states and Canada raising funds to assist Black refugees. True Bands sought to build an alternative to the "begging" they saw done supposedly on behalf of refugees, so they could provide direct assistance to those in transit and newly arrived in Canada and foster economic self-sufficiency.[68]

From such work as an African Canadian, Burroughs chose, or was encouraged, to go to Chicago in 1857 to become directly involved. He met a Canadian friend in Chicago, who suggested that they contact people of the Underground Railroad. It is quite possible they worked directly with Henry and Susan Wagoner and John and Mary Jones. From Chicago, the friend went to work with the Rock Island Railroad and Burroughs, as a seventeen-year-old, was employed by the Illinois Central. He became a car porter on the trains between Chicago and Cairo.[69]

On one occasion in Cairo, Burroughs tried to convince a slave to "flee for his freedom," assuring him of help. However, the young man refused to go with Burroughs because he knew Chicago and Canada were at war. His master read the newspapers from Chicago and read to him about the war, telling him that everyone in Chicago was getting killed. Burroughs tried to explain that his master was lying and that "Chicago was in the state of Illinois and Canada was a British dominion." However, his urging was of no avail. Another time, while in Cairo, he went onboard a New Orleans-based steamboat heading up the Ohio River. Burroughs met a man on his way to Louisville with his master and urged him to consider going for freedom. The man was willing but could not bear the idea of deserting a sister still in New Orleans. For almost forty years, he remembered that man and even his name, Charlie Gardner.[70]

Writing many years later of his work on the railroad, he noted a time he felt too many people were aware of his work and he was afraid to stop over at his usual hotel in Cairo. One night he walked near the depot when he saw what he thought was an animal in the grass. He recalled,

> It was when I got close up to it in the dark it spoke and then I knew it was a woman she asked me if I was a colored man. I told her I was she said you wont betray me she said I saw you standing by the freight house and thought you were a white man and when you started down the path I thought you had seen me I told her to follow me and be quick I took her to the porters room. There was a box for carrying extra bedding between 4 feet high I told her to get in the box and covered her up with quilts.[71]

Burroughs managed to get the box on board the train and as he did so, one of the conductors suggested he go and get some supper. He said he wasn't hungry, and also, he wanted to keep an eye on the sleeping car. The conductor was pleased to hear that since there were often runaways around and asked Burroughs if he had seen any. The porter replied directly that he had not. The next morning after arriving in Chicago, he found the opportunity to open the box and encouraged his "passenger" to get out. He was surprised to discover that she was a young girl about eight years old of "light complexion and very pretty." He gave her a comb and brush and some water to clean up a bit but realized that she was dressed so badly that it might be difficult to get her out of the depot. There were two police officers standing outside and he knew he needed to get past them. He coached the young girl to be very brave and quiet and out they went. One of the officers stopped them, but Burroughs told him quickly that she was his cousin and he had just brought her back from the country where "some poor white trash" had cheated her out of her wages. He seemed to have held them off for a bit, but as they walked into the city, the two officers followed. They finally slipped into an alley and Burroughs was able to get her to safety.[72]

James Wilson, a fervent white activist in Illinois in mid-century, as an eighty-year old resident of Centralia wrote to Siebert in 1895 summarizing the importance of this railroad-created community. The town was aptly named, as the central point for the Illinois Central as it ran north from Cairo and marked the split of the line that continued due north and the line that veered to the northeast to Chicago. Wilson indicated that that they worked hard to creatively use the Illinois Central. They identified a conductor who was sympathetic, willing to regularly hide travelers in freight cars with enough food to make the journey to Chicago. In addition, they knew conductors who would not challenge Black riders as to whether they were free persons. Because of this, they could occasionally place travelers into passenger cars.[73]

Another resident living northeast of Centralia provided details reinforcing the line's importance. After moving there in 1857, his father aided a "good many fugitive slaves," with almost all coming from Missouri. They regularly put freedom seekers on the trains to Chicago and "that was getting' em through fast, when they got 'em on the R.R."[74]

The Illinois Central was key in a complicated journey for a young woman and her two children fleeing bondage in south central Tennessee. In the Spring of 1859, she convinced her master, Garret L. Voorhies, Esq. of Maury, Tennessee, to allow her to travel some miles north to Franklin with her children to visit her mother. She was an attractive light-skinned person who could easily pass as white. Taking advantage of that, she purchased tickets in Franklin without question for the Tennessee and Alabama Railroad into Nashville. At some point she collected some funds, possibly with the help of her mother, to finance her journey. In Nashville, she easily obtained tickets on a river boat traveling to Cairo, Illinois. Once there, she purchased tickets on the Illinois Central to Chicago and with some assistance continued to Canada. Evidently to the great annoyance of a southern newspaper, while in Chicago, that place of refuge for "the deluded victims of Republican philanthropy," she wrote back to Voorhies, declaring her freedom. In response, Voorhies sued the Tennessee and Alabama Railroad since, of course, they were responsible for allowing her journey to freedom. He valued this mother and her children at $3000 and wanted his money.[75]

Also, in 1859, Jourden Banks ran away from a plantation in Alabama. He traveled north into Kentucky and crossed the Ohio River into Illinois. Moving secretly with a friend, they looked for the Illinois Central Railroad and followed the tracks north, walking all the way. After months of traveling, stopping to work, and being put in jail for a second time, Banks escaped and again following the tracks, ended up in the small town of Peotone in Will County. There, he spent time working on the farm of the Dean family. After several months, Banks went to Chicago, took a train to New York City, and then an ocean steamer to Liverpool in Great Britain. In 1861, abolitionists in England published his story as *A Narrative of the Life of J. H. Banks, an Escaped Slave, from the Cotton State, Alabama, in America.*[76]

John Stella Martin was enslaved in Georgia and later Alabama, but eventually convinced his owner to place him working on steamboats on the Mississippi River. While serving on board he ran across a fellow with free papers and "temporarily" borrowed the papers. He kept them just long enough to assist the fellow to obtain new papers in New Orleans and then had the original set for his own use. Posing as a free person, he worked for a steamboat captain whose boat ended up at Cairo, blocked by an icy river at the end of 1855. Convincing the captain that he had business in Chicago, he received a few days off. He arranged for his trunk to be taken to the Illinois Central station in Cairo and left the boat. He wrote years later that when arriving at the ticket office, "The ticket agent told me in a most insulting manner that he did not sell tickets to coloured people unless they got someone to vouch for their freedom."[77]

Martin reminded the agent that Illinois was a free state and that he had a right to a ticket unless someone proved that he was a slave, but this did not change his mind. He then suggested that the agent go and seek out the captain to confirm his claim to be a free person. However, the agent said his job was to sell tickets and not to look around for verifications. Martin left, reflected on what to do and decided to return to the station. As it happened, in the ticket office he found a gambling man from California who had been on his riverboat. Several days before, on the boat Martin advised the man to avoid a certain card shark. Now the Californian suggested he might be able to help Martin. So, he purchased his own ticket to Chicago and one for Martin. Remembered Martin: "In an hour more we were on our way to Chicago, where, without further accident, we arrived the next morning by eight o'clock, on the 6th day of January, 1856. I thus became a FREE MAN."[78]

On the Rock Island Line and Others

Although the greatest number of freedom seekers traveled north on the Illinois Central, there were incidents on other lines running to Chicago. Decades later, Emma Chapin, a longtime resident of Geneseo, on the Chicago and Rock Island Railroad line, recalled the involvement of her mother and father, along with others in town, in a variety of incidences. The last one she remembered was in 1855. The freedom seeker "was smuggled on the train when it stopped at the water tank, a little way below the station." The Rock Island bridged the Mississippi in 1856, and, as noted, was the line used in early 1859 by John Brown and the company of twelve freedom seekers from western Missouri.[79]

In the summer of 1860, a family enslaved on a farm in northern Missouri also escaped on the Rock Island line. The mother, father, and four children used the networks of the Underground Railroad in Iowa to slip across the state line and travel east to Davenport where they boarded the Rock Island and arrived safely in Chicago. Two years later, the father returned to Missouri and with the help of Union army officers was able to rescue a fifth child and return with her to their new home in Canada.[80]

In late June 1855, a freedom seeker known to history only as "Dick," arrived in Chicago, having traveled on the Chicago, Burlington and Quincy from the Mississippi River. He hurriedly left Burlington, Iowa, after his release from arrest as an alleged fugitive slave escaping from Missouri. In what came to be the only incident in Iowa of a person being held under the provisions of the 1850 Fugitive Slave Act, his situation gained dramatic attention. The governor of Iowa, leading abolitionists, along with slave catchers and lawyers were all caught up in the case. However, in a dramatic courtroom encounter, it became a case of mistaken identity. He was not the person being sought by owners in Clark County, Missouri. Thus, he was immediately released to the joy of a huge crowd and escorted to a ferry to cross over to Illinois and begin the rail trip to Chicago. One commentator noted that on this rail line, freedom seekers could be secreted on freight cars in Quincy and travel to Chicago going "right through without much local help along the route."[81]

The Chicago, Burlington and Quincy Railroad ran through Princeton, a widely recognized center for activism. Here, the work was headed by Owen Lovejoy, who was a minister, the brother of the martyr Elijah Lovejoy, a member of Congress, and a resolute abolitionist. One summer night, Rev. Lovejoy brought a young family with two children and two other young men to the Chicago, Burlington and Quincy stations northeast of the village. He added that "It was known that the conductor on the CB & Q RR that passed through Mendota about midnight was friendly to this competing line."[82]

A collaborator with Owen Lovejoy was John Howard Bryant, one of the most popular poets of the nineteenth century and a longtime resident of Princeton. He referred to his own home as one of the "signless stations on the weird and mystic route to freedom," and in one poem wrote, "Here hath the fleeing bondman found / A shield from hell's pursuing hound." One biography of Bryant notes that there were occasions when he had "as many as 15 slaves in his house at once," and collaborated with officials of the Chicago, Burlington and Quincy Railroad. In Chicago, this rail line had powerful connections with the Underground Railroad. Dr. Charles Dyer was well acquainted with its leadership and its chief engineer, Colonel Berrien, was also a strong abolitionist.[83]

By 1855, the Chicago and Alton line reached Joliet, with trains coming north from East St. Louis and Alton. From 1857 through 1861, the line operated under the name of the St. Louis, Alton and Chicago Railroad. Although it had a direct route and activists helped travelers in Alton, few stories have survived about movement on this railroad. One story is remembered of two freedom seekers traveling north, who for some reason left the train in Lexington, south of Pontiac. They were directed to the families of abolitionists who sheltered them for several days before sending them on toward Chicago. George Woodruff, the Will County historian, includes a highly romanticized story of an incident in Joliet with a young woman freedom seeker on the Chicago and Alton line, complete with danger and success.[84]

In May 1855, a young man named Edwin living near the Mississippi in Missouri seized his freedom and made his way to Alton. There he obtained a ticket on the Chicago and Alton line. His owner, Daniel Overall, figured that he might try to use the train and immediately upon Edwin's escape, Overall took the train into Illinois, stopping at Virden. For several days, he checked each train as it came through, and on a night train, he found Edwin asleep in a passenger car. He asserted his possession of Edwin, forced him to return to Missouri and immediately sold him.[85]

Kidnappings

Across the South and on journeys into the North, the movement of freedom seekers was always accompanied by the potential for capture and return. From the beginning, there were forms of "slave catchers," including men from the South hired to go after runaways, residents in northern areas interested in rewards offered, and officers of the law willing to use and misuse various fugitive slave laws. Starting in the 1820s and 1830s, the newspapers of southern Illinois regularly carried fugitive slave notices. These were posted by owners seeking their runaways and by county sheriffs and others who had happened upon runaways, arrested them, and were holding them for reacquisition by their owners. By the mid-1830s, newspapers in Chicago began carrying such advertisements.

As Chicago's reputation as an abolitionist hotbed and refuge for freedom seekers grew, the ads in Chicago newspapers stopped, although, as explored earlier in this book, fugitive slave notices in Missouri and other places occasionally mentioned Chicago as a destination. In the 1840s and particularly after the Fugitive Slave Act of 1850, increasing numbers of professional slave catchers came to the city. The press often referred to them as "man-hunters" and "Negro-stealers." In African American, African Canadian, and proabolition newspapers, their activities were most often referred to as kidnappings. This was also the language used among abolitionists and Underground Railroad activists. However, in the 1840s and through the early 1850s, in many American newspapers, the notion of slave catching was seen in terms of the return of property; human cargo to be sure, but property nonetheless. At the time the issue was perceived as theft, not kidnapping. In newspapers both

South and North, the language referred to fugitives and their escape or return. It was not until the late 1850s that Northern papers more often used "kidnapping," perhaps signifying a greater understanding that this form of theft involved human beings.

Since its inception, the *Chicago Tribune* reported incidences involving the capture of freedom seekers in Chicago and other places around the country. Most of the language used was of slave catchers and fugitives. However, from 1858 through the onset of the Civil War, reports in the *Chicago Tribune* were almost always under headlines about *kidnappings* or used that word in the article. This suggests an evolution in thinking and an assertion that freedom seekers, by getting North and to places like Chicago, were in their rightful conditions and environments as men and women and were being forcefully taken from where they belong. Not simply seen as captured or recaptured property, they were now clearly presented in Illinois as human beings being kidnapped.[86]

In reports about Illinois and Chicago, attention focused particularly on the work of kidnappers based in St. Louis and in southern Illinois, especially in Perry and Union Counties on the Illinois Central line. The kidnapping of Jim Gray was the most famous example of this focused attention.

In late 1859, the *Chicago Tribune* offered an editorial on a kidnapping case in McDonough County in western Illinois. In response, a letter to the editor, signed by "A Democrat," presented a succinct example of the opposing viewpoint. This writer held that it was inappropriate to refer to the confinement of a runaway slave as "illegal" and those responsible as "kidnappers." It was clear that confinement was a matter of "safe keeping" of property while the owner is located and to do otherwise not only was in opposition to the Constitution, but also an "act of bad faith toward the slave-holding states." A few days later, the *Chicago Tribune* countered with a detailed review of the current legal situation in Illinois regarding the status of fugitive slaves, affirming that any person in Illinois is a free person, the arrest of fugitives is "in violation of the law," and the use of Illinois jails to hold fugitive slaves is "illegal and unwarranted." This interpretation of the law was counter, of course, to the prevailing national "law-of-the-land" and in opposition to federal judicial opinions.[87]

Even though a strong abolitionist atmosphere held across northeastern Illinois and the networks of support for freedom seekers were broadly known, kidnappings were very visible in 1859 and 1860. From time to time, the Chicago newspapers contained notices like this one, which appeared on the front page of the *Chicago Tribune*:

Look out for This Man – a man about six feet high, thin face, light complexioned, slightly pock-marked, hailing from St. Louis has haunted this city for some days on the disreputable errand of hunting runaway n——. Would not object to kidnap a likely boy or two, probably.[88]

Chicago papers carried detailed stories of kidnappings, often to a dramatic effect. In August of 1860, the *Chicago Tribune* told the convoluted story of a freedom seeker from St. Louis who escaped to Chicago with his two children only to be drugged and almost kidnapped. Later that year, it carried the story of Thomas Leary, a Chicagoan of Irish descent kidnapped and arrested in southern Illinois because he looked like a Black person. Moreover, the reality and diversity of horrific kidnapping experiences is seen in the following stories of the Anderson brothers, the Armstrong brothers, and James Salter.[89]

In July of 1859, Dr. Frost, a resident in St. Louis, discovered that three of his slaves escaped and headed for Chicago. They were Washington and James Anderson, and their cousin, Henry Scott. The three traveled north through Illinois and sought assistance when they reached Livingston County. Quite early in the morning, abolitionists in Pontiac brought them to the home of Moses Rumery, a well-known activist on the road to Ottawa. They explained to Rumery that they were anxious to get to Canada as quickly as possible. Responding quickly, Rumery immediately took them to Ottawa where funds were raised to send them on to Chicago.[90]

Dr. Frost set up a reward of $2,500 for their return. Two former Chicago police officers, Charles Noyes and Charles W. Smith, learned of the reward and resolved to find the three if they were in Chicago. A young Black man named William Turner worked for Noyes. About three weeks after their escape, Turner, with the help of a boy sent from St. Louis who knew and could identify the fugitives, located the three. Noyes and Smith began an elaborate ruse to convince the three that good jobs were available and they were particularly well-suited for the work.[91]

In their scheme, Noyes and Smith outlined that Noyes was about to retire and wished to move from Chicago to a farm he owned in western Illinois. He wanted the three to come work for him and even took them to visit hardware stores to solicit their ideas on the best tools to buy for the farm. After this assumed shopping venture, Noyes and Turner took the three back to Noyes' lodging. Meanwhile Smith chartered a separate second-class car on the Illinois Central line to take the three back to St. Louis, and the three were bound and taken to the station.

At Odin, above Centralia on the Illinois Central line, they transferred to the Ohio and Mississippi Railroad with a direct line to St. Louis. The two ex-detectives took their hostages to Bloody Island, opposite St. Louis. A Black woman who knew them arrived in Chicago and reported that they were being held there and "cruelly whipped."

The three were delivered to Dr. Frost and for their shifty work, Noyes and Smith received a fee of $2,300 for their services and promptly returned to Chicago. There was a tremendous uproar in the city, especially within the African American community. Turner was put in jail for his own protection and held there as warrants were issued for the arrest of Turner, Smith, and Noyes. A court convened quickly, but Noyes had already skipped town with the $2,300. Allen Pinkerton and some of his associates joined the hunt to find Noyes. The courtroom was packed with Black and white residents and the situation was especially intense when Turner was brought in. Leading the anger expressed by the crowd was the brother of Henry Scott.

The night before, there was a large meeting at Quinn Chapel with about 150 people in attendance. Their anger was furthered by news that one of the brothers had died from the whipping on Bloody Island. Two nights later, a second large gathering was held at Zoar Baptist Church to consider the activities of Turner and discuss security needs in the community. That meeting accepted a resolution by Henry Wagoner that "a vigilance committee of fifteen should be appointed to investigate this matter." Noyes was never located, Smith was found guilty, and Turner was released with insufficient evidence and the suggestion he had been deceived by Noyes and Smith.[92]

On this same day, Dr. Frost wrote to the *Chicago Times* a lengthy letter explaining that there had been a great misunderstanding. In fact, he asserted, he had come to Chicago himself, after having sent detectives to look for "the boys." Then he himself interviewed them and they "were perfectly willing to come home with me, told me of all the hardships and troubles they had suffered, inquired after their friends and relatives at home, laughed and chatted merrily for half an hour, and then went fast asleep." There is no record that anyone in Chicago believed him.[93]

Tom and William Armstrong, ages sixteen and eighteen, were free persons of color living in Chicago. In March of 1860, they were hired by a Mr. Floy and a Mr. Charley Wyatt to go with them to southern Illinois to buy cattle and then assist in herding the cattle back to the Chicago region. They traveled south on the railroad and evidently passed over the Ohio River into Kentucky. The travelers stopped several times while the bosses inquired about the price and quality of cattle available, and they kept expressing dissatisfaction with the options they found. By the time they reached Jackson, Tennessee, Tom and William were seriously concerned and realized they were heading deeper and deeper into the South. They appealed to some residents of Jackson, indicating that they were free persons and supposedly assisting with cattle in southern Illinois. Those they had approached immediately realized what was happening and attempted to pay for the release of the young men.

Floy and Wyatt would have none of that and immediately headed for the woods and disappeared. This, of course, still left the two boys in a dangerous situation. However, a Tennessee attorney named Norwood stepped forwarded and offered the hospitality of his home. Within a few days, some white residents of Chicago were in Jackson, met with the boys and ascertained the truth of their dilemma. Some funds were collected to return them to Cairo and from there, the Illinois Central provided transport back to Chicago. The account of this in the *Chicago Tribune* concluded, "The noble conduct of the citizens of Jackson is worthy of all praise. Mr. Norwood especially deserves the grateful acknowledgement of every friend of humanity. He made no charge for boarding the boys several days. We trust the infamous scoundrels who attempted the outrage will yet be made to do the State good service behind the prison walls of Joliet."[94]

In July of 1860, three young men were kidnapped from the small town of Clifton, south of Kankakee, and taken to St. Louis. They were James Salter, and two friends, William and John, both free men. Kidnappers, in concert with four local men, tried to capture five Black men who worked on farms in the area. Two got away, but the others were captured and taken to the train stop, the confrontation arranged to occur just prior to the train's arrival. Local residents tried to intervene, but the conductor did nothing to stop the kidnappers and their captives from boarding. The group traveled by train to St. Louis, where they were thrown into a slave pen and brutally questioned. One man refused to respond at all, and the second continually insisted that he was a free man, unlawfully seized.[95]

The two, William and John, were tied up and whipped, with the intent of forcing the first to at least talk and both to confess to their status as runaways. They were also denied food to extract their confessions. "At last, both these men—one torn ruthlessly from his wife and children, and the other from a neighborhood in which his industry had made him respected, and each from a life of freedom and enjoyment—were sent South and sold."

The third man, James Salter, had in fact escaped from enslavement, and he ended up moving through a remarkable turn of events. He told his kidnappers that he had been the property of Aime Pernard, the owner of a farm seven miles outside St. Louis. They went to see his master, from whom he escaped five years earlier. Pernard sent James's mother to the slave pen to inquire about him and she reported back on his haggard and beaten condition. After negotiations, the master paid the standard $100 for a recaptured slave plus jail fees of $35. He and James returned to the farm and after two days of apparently remarkable conversation, Pernard decided to free James. He drew up free papers and went with James across the river into Illinois and bought him tickets to return by train to Clifton. At the heart of the conversation was Pernard's amazement at discovering that James wanted to be a free person and then agreeing that this was reasonable.

Several days after being abducted, James was home in Clifton. He came off the train waving his free papers in the air. A small crowd gathered to hear his remarkable saga of the slave pen, the return to the old farm, and the kindness of his former owner.

The *Chicago Tribune* editors used the occasion and notoriety of this story to attack the practices of the Illinois Central regarding kidnappings. Under a headline of "No More Kidnapping," they challenged the Illinois Central to discipline the actions of its employees. They asked, "Is it to be understood that, without the authority of court or the command of officer, the road becomes part of the kidnapping machinery which is kept in full play in southern Illinois?" In addition, in response to the initial kidnapping, in August 1860 the paper issued a powerful editorial, "The Last Great Outrage," on the evils of kidnapping and the demands for individual freedom and justice.[96]

In the Fall of 1860, these controversies about slavery and abolition were recast in a bitter political contest. In the November election, the northern states voted in support of Abraham Lincoln and the relatively new Republican Party. The southern vote split in support of Stephen Douglas and the Democratic Party and John C. Breckinridge and the Southern Democrats. It was further divided by votes for John Bell and the Constitutional Union Party which sought to take a neutral stance on slavery. In the political turmoil, the movement of freedom seekers to and through northeastern Illinois and the functioning of the networks of support continued. However, the compelling political furor tended to obscure any significant reporting about activities involving freedom seekers. That is, until the Great Chicago Exodus.

The Aftermath of the Great Chicago Exodus

As related in the opening of this book, just weeks after Abraham Lincoln's inaugural as President, an overzealous US marshal in Chicago was determined to capture and return refugees in Chicago who had escaped their enslavement in the South. In reaction to this, between seven hundred and one thousand freedom seekers left the city within a few days in early April 1861. The *Chicago Tribune* followed up its coverage of the Great Chicago Exodus by reporting in a small paragraph several days later: "About 300 fugitive slaves principally from Illinois have passed into Canada at this point since Saturday, and large numbers are reported on the way. Many are entirely destitute, and much suffering is anticipated, notwithstanding every effort for their relief."[97]

Douglass' Monthly summarized the whole process of the Great Chicago Exodus and included an observation from the *Chicago Democrat* about those persons who chose not to leave: "There are still many fugitives in the city, but they are generally those who are prepared to fight, but not to run. – They are willing to take the risk of staying here, but swear that they will never be taken back to bondage. If they are arrested they will die—but they will not surrender. These men live with their lives in their hands. – Their conduct may not be very prudent or advisable, but they claim the right to take care of themselves, and say they are quite able to do so."[98]

The *Detroit Tribune* commented on the great rush into Canada and noted that residents in Windsor, across the river, would be holding a public meeting in response. They hoped to discuss ways to support this large influx of newcomers from Chicago. The paper noted, "The houses and churches in Windsor have become filled to overflowing with the fugitives, as it is with utmost difficulty that sleeping rooms can be obtained for them." They sought to provide for those "who have fled from no crime, who have outraged no law of God, but whose only offense is the black skin that made them slaves."[99]

In striking contrast, a Missouri newspaper approvingly quoted the *Detroit Free Press* from that same day: "Several hundred darkies of all shades, ages, sexes and sizes passed through this city yesterday in route for the land of negro bliss and equality across the river. They came from Chicago, whence they were driven through fear of being run off south.... An excitement of a similar nature would be beneficial to this community."[100]

Paralleling this opinion, the antiabolition press of Chicago trumpeted that the city's reputation as a place of safety in the face of the Fugitive Slave Act had fallen apart, even if the abolitionists tried to continue their work. Some might see Chicago as the "real Canaan, where they might defy their masters and the Constitution." However, now with this great exodus, "The negroes, with their poverty-stricken wives and children, are thoroughly stampeded, and thrown, half starving, into a foreign country, while the Republican Marshal gets credit for executing the law, and the Republican press still keep up their level of philanthropy." Thus, the controversies and opinions on the movements of freedom seekers and the Underground Railroad continued to be complex and dramatic even as the whole country prepared for war.[101]

A week after the exodus, the *Chicago Tribune* uncovered a remarkable twist in the tragic story of the Harris family who had been whisked away and sent back into slavery by the actions of the new marshal Russell Jones. Evidently, a man passing himself off as a Missouri abolitionist had gained the confidence of a Mrs. Johnson, who was a resident of Chicago for many years. With his help, she arranged to have her daughter, along with daughter's husband and three children, secretly brought out of slavery. She paid $150 for his help, mortgaging her home to raise the funds.[102]

Mrs. Johnson's family was the Harris family. They were, in fact, assisted to escape from the farm outside St. Louis on which they labored. However, the supposed abolitionist who helped them was part of a kidnapping gang that included St. Louis policemen and retired police from Chicago. They made connections with the owners of the Harris family and arranged to acquire escape notices and then writs for their arrest. It appeared to be simply one more example of a regular kidnapping system in place between Chicago and St. Louis. This time, however, the whole country was on the brink of war, and the kidnapping of the Harris family precipitated the Great Chicago Exodus.

Amid all the details of the Great Chicago Exodus, the reports in the *Chicago Tribune* were filled with fury and irony. They wrote of this latest attempt to "save the Union" through sacrificing a family of five by returning them to "Chattelism." They noted that the Harris family had been fugitives for a month, and they made the grave "error" of stopping in Chicago to see

Mrs. Harris's mother, somehow naively assuming that as human beings they had some right to see her. And, of course, they saw that the rage expressed by "free people of color" in Chicago was totally out of line because, couldn't they see the plain "justice of the thing" in having a family ripped out of their home? As the country teetered on the edge of civil war, one *Chicago Tribune* reporter wrote that going to Canada was probably a good option for those "who cannot make up their minds to save the country by going back to their masters."[103]

The Ending of the Underground Railroad

Freedom seekers kept coming to Chicago in the early months of 1861, their numbers increasing due to the anticipated confrontations between North and South. The established mechanisms of support were there, in the work of white abolitionists led by the Dyers, Carpenters, and others and that of Black abolitionists led by the Joneses, Isbells, and others, all regularly in contact with one another. It was this regularity and connectedness that enabled the larger community to respond so quickly and effectively to the crises of April 1861.

The events in April saw the final intense assistance made possible through the networks of the Underground Railroad. As the whole country moved into a great Civil War, the strictures of the Fugitive Slave Act were now moot and simply ignored in northeastern Illinois. Black and white activists continued to welcome new refugees settling in Chicago and to assist those seeking to move to Canada. The days of discrete collaboration and illegal action were finally over, and the "Underground Railroad" business was finished.

It had been a remarkable journey. Thousands of freedom seekers moved to and through the region in the decades before the Civil War. Some arrived on independent journeys. Most made use of the networks established across Illinois by Black churches and related associations and by white networks often based in congregations and antislavery groups. Arriving in northeastern Illinois, freedom seekers found refuge with a strong collection of both Black and white activists, often working closely together. Most chose to continue traveling, looking to safety and freedom in Canada. Many left on ships or walked and rode overland around the bottom of Lake Michigan. In the last years, the expansion of the railroads created far more rapid means for reaching Chicago and beyond.

The range of stories throughout this book show the diversity of freedom seekers, traveling as individuals, in family groups, in both large and small parties committed to their common safety and success. It was an intensely practical, hopeful, and dangerous process. Travelers feared for their lives and for their loved ones, facing the terrors of possible capture and return to lives of enslavement. In response to their courage, young white and Black families and individuals settling in northeastern Illinois made their own judgments about opposing the laws of the land and decided to be of help. It was, all of it together, an unexpected movement of civil disobedience and an unrivaled affirmation of common humanity.

On Freedom Seekers

FRANK AND LUCY MCWORTER. New Philadelphia continued as a multiracial community for several decades and their family continued to live in the region. Frank died in 1854 and Lucy in 1871 and they are buried near the town site.[1] A section of Interstate 72 is recognized as the Frank McWorter Memorial Highway, and New Philadelphia was designated as a National Historic Landmark in 2009. This is now a site significant for historical and archaeological research.

Claiborn and Charity. We know nothing more of Claiborn and Charity, and yet their experiences were repeated hundreds of times in the stories of freedom seekers heading north and finding their way into Illinois, almost always seeking to reach the Chicago region. From the start of statehood in 1818 into the years of the Civil War, newspapers in Illinois contained notices from slave owners, like that which sought Claiborn and Charity, and parallel notices from county sheriffs announcing the runaways held in their jails.

John and Eliza Little. After moving around southern Ontario, with a brief stay in Buffalo, New York, the Littles finally settled in Queen's Bush. After twenty years, the close of their story connects with the fact that throughout his experiences, John Little proudly understood that he was "pure African," aware of the birth of his grandparents in Africa. He said, "There is no white blood in me; not one drop." In 1862, the Littles left Canada to take up a new life in Haiti, the one country in the Americas led by people of African descent.[2]

In 1856, the Littles were among over one hundred persons in southern Ontario, then called Canada West, interviewed by a Massachusetts abolitionist named Benjamin Drew. These interviews were first published in *The Refugee, or a North-Side View of Slavery* and used throughout New England abolitionist circles. More recently, this was republished as *The Narratives of Fugitive Slaves*. In addition, Canadian researchers have found evidence of the life and work of the Littles in Queen's Bush.[3]

John and Eliza spent months walking the length of Illinois. The title of this book honors that journey and the remarkable efforts of so many to embark on similar commitments to seize their own freedom. In addition, an observation made by John Little now serves as the opening for the Introduction to the Library of Congress digitalized collection: "Born in Slavery: Slave Narratives from the Federal Writers' Project, 1936 to 1938." John Little observed: "'Tisn't he who has stood and looked on, that can tell you what slavery is—'tis he who has endured."[4]

Caroline Quarlls. In 1846, three years after arriving south of Windsor in Sandwich, Ontario, Caroline married Allen Watkins. He was a freedom seeker who escaped from Kentucky after his first wife died. Caroline and Allen were instrumental in the development of the Sandwich Baptist Church congregation and in 1853, they helped build the still-standing historic structure. They built their own home a few doors from the church and had six children. Their descendants have played remarkable roles in the development of African Canadian and African American communities, especially in the Detroit-Windsor metropolitan region.

Barney and Julia Ford and Henry and Susan Wagoner. In 1860, the Fords moved to Denver and Barney Ford, after several financial setbacks, had a celebrated career in business and public life in Colorado. For a brief time, Henry Wagoner visited with the Fords and sent letters about Black people in the Pikes Peak Gold Region to *Douglass' Monthly*. After the outbreak of the Civil War, Wagoner was back in Chicago helping with recruitment for "colored soldiers."

Across the country, African American men active in the abolitionist movement and the Underground Railroad, like Henry Wagoner, engaged in the challenge of recruitment for the war effort, recognizing that this was a crucial step in the Black struggle for freedom. In this work, he joined with the efforts of Frederick Douglass, Martin Delaney, and John Mercer Langston, all of whom were more well-known both in that period and in our historical memory.

Later, Wagoner served in the Union army and at the end of the Civil War, he and his family permanently joined the Fords in Colorado. The two friends, and brothers-in-law, provided leadership for the rights of African Americans in the territory and then state of Colorado. Today, they are recognized as civil rights pioneers in Colorado history. The Fords' last home in Breckenridge is a museum and outside of the town is a small Colorado mountain named Barney Ford Hill.[5]

Henry Stevenson. He was interviewed in 1894 and then again in 1895; he indicated he was about 104 years old, born into slavery in Missouri. In 1895, Stevenson reported that living in Windsor, he never had been more than "50 miles from here" since his arrival. At about the same time, he was included in what became an iconic photograph of "A Group of Refugee Settlers, of Windsor, Ontario."[6]

John Stella Martin. As an orator and abolitionist, Martin visited England three times, and in 1867, he spoke at the Paris Anti-Slavery Conference on behalf of the American Missionary Association. He became famous as a colleague of Frederick Douglass for editing Douglass's newspaper, the *New Era*, in Washington, DC, in the early 1870s. In 1895, Rev. J. S. T. Milligan wrote to Wilbur Siebert about his encounter with John Stella Martin. In the 1850s, Milligan was pastor of a church in Southfield, Michigan, near Detroit. He wrote about his contact with Martin, who stayed at his house for six weeks on his journey to Canada. Milligan wrote that Martin "was the smartest man I have ever met."[7]

James and Narcissa Daniels. James Redpath, an American journalist and abolitionist wrote a warm biography of John Brown shortly after his execution. In this account, he mentions visiting in Canada the twelve freedom seekers about nine months after their arrival. With a brief description of each, he ends by writing of Narcissa and Jim and their three children, living in the country about seven miles from Windsor. He found them working "a farm on shares; they have about sixteen acres of corn, potatoes, &c., part of which are theirs; and they are anticipating the day when they can get a piece of land of their own."[8]

In 1859, local press reports indicated that the group of twelve stayed together for some time in the Windsor area and were prominent participants in that year's twenty-fifth anniversary celebration of the emancipation of slaves in the West Indies. Some seven thousand free people of color joined that celebration in Sandwich, next to Windsor in Canada West.[9]

In 1894, Samuel and Jane Harper were still living in Windsor and were interviewed about John Brown for a Canadian magazine. Sam noted that they were the only ones left, along with John Brown Daniels, Jim and Narcissa's son, who was at the time living in Detroit.[10]

Jim Gray. Part of the fascination with the Jim Gray story is how he disappeared from contemporary and historical accounts as the "Ottawa Rescue Case" gained national attention. The details of the trials and the great speech by John Hossack are part of the build-up to the Civil War, but Jim Gray is gone. All assumed that Jim Gray would simply travel on to safety in Canada. In fact, he stayed in the Midwest, working in the north woods in Wisconsin as a lumber man. He lived there for many years until he became quite ill. In the late 1880s, he indicated that he wanted to come back to Ottawa where he felt so warmly befriended. However, in his effort to return to Ottawa his health continued to decline, and he managed to only reach DeKalb, Illinois, where he died and is now buried.[11]

George Burroughs. George remained in Cairo and continued working for the Illinois Central during the years of the Civil War. He eventually married a woman who had been enslaved in Kentucky. In 1896, he wrote an extended letter to Wilber Siebert reviewing his activities in assisting freedom seekers. Burroughs also mentioned that he met and talked with John Brown, which reinforces the possibility that he worked with the Wagoners and Joneses in Chicago.[12]

Acknowledgments

Appendixes

Notes

Bibliography

Index

ACKNOWLEDGMENTS

Everyone interested in the history and stories of freedom seekers and the Underground Railroad quickly realizes that not only was it all a collaborative effort, but that the study of it is richly collaborative too. It is only through working with a multitude of other folks that we can assemble the puzzles of this part of our national history. I continue to be grateful for the professional and personal help given by so many.

I particularly want to thank and acknowledge the work of my colleagues and friends as we worked together in the Illinois Underground Railroad Association; the Chicago-Calumet Underground Railroad Effort (C-CURE), now the Little Calumet River Underground Railroad Project; and the Chicagoland Underground Railroad Network (CHURN). Also, my thanks to a multitude of local community history organizations and Underground Railroad enthusiasts who have encouraged my work. I am indebted to the insight and support provided over the years by library professionals in Chicago and in communities across northeastern Illinois. I have benefited from the wonderful cooperation of staff and volunteers from historical societies in the region. These included helpful people working with local and regional history in Chicago, Park Forest, Chicago Heights, Ford Heights, Blue Island, Homewood, Robbins, Riverdale, Dolton, and South Holland; Crete, Pembroke, Kankakee, Wilmington, Lockport, Plainfield, Homer Glen, and at Midewin Prairie; Pontiac, Fairbury, La Salle, and Ottawa; Sycamore, Somonauk, Sugar Grove, Aurora, St. Charles, Dundee, and Elgin; Naperville, Downers Grove, Hinsdale, Wheaton, Lombard, and Maywood; Deerfield, Waukegan, Gurnee, and Lake Forest. Also, I express my appreciation for the helpfulness of the staff at the Vivian G. Harsh Collection at the Carter Woodson Regional Library in Chicago; the Chicago Historical Society (now the

Chicago History Museum); the Newberry Library; the Illinois State Historical Library at the Abraham Lincoln Presidential Library; and Historic Fort Wayne and the Wright Museum of African American History in Detroit. I am thankful for the assistance of staff at Fort Maldon Historic Site in Amherstburgh, Canada; the libraries of the University of Windsor and the Buxton National Historic Site and Museum in Ontario, Canada; and in Great Britain, at the British Museum.

In addition, I wish to thank a wide variety of people working in local governments and churches across Chicago and northeastern Illinois who have written and talked to me. Many provided pieces of the story and pointed me toward new documentation. Particular gratitude is due to Glennette Tilley Turner for the enormous amount of material first gathered in her book *The Underground Railroad in Illinois* and for her gracious collaboration as we have worked together on programs and shared ideas and hunches. Special thanks to Diane Banta, now retired from the National Park Service, and to my friend Tom Shepherd for all the good work in the Calumet region. Thanks to Kimberly Simmons for her friendship and the wonderful reflections in regard to her ancestor, Caroline Quarlls; Roy Finkenbine at the University of Detroit Mercy for insightful conversations; Sandy Vasko of the Will County Historical Society; Phyllis Monks and friends in the Crete Area Historical Society, Nancy Schumn of the Ila Township Historical Society; and Bill Goold of Bozeman, Montana, and Charles Stanley for insights related to LaSalle and Livingston Counties. I am grateful to Ed and Harriet (McCoy) Genzler of Crete and Patsy Mighell Paxton of Sugar Grove for time spent in their homes exploring family history. As a friend and colleague, Cheryl LaRoche at the University of Maryland has been extremely helpful in the processes of thinking through our approaches to this complex history. I am grateful for the insight and assistance of colleagues through the National Park Service's Network to Freedom program and particularly for the help of Deanda Johnson and Diane Miller. A special note of thanks to Dr. Bruce Purnell, a descendent of John and Mary Jones, for his permission to use the photograph of them from a family album. During the consideration of this book for publication, I learned so much from editors and readers at Southern Illinois University Press. I simply cannot express how helpful they have been in shaping this work and I am grateful their insights and guidance. In addition, the final presentation of this work was aided by collaboration with the mapmaker Hal Jespersen, and I appreciate his creative work.

Time spent with our dear friend Charlotte Watkins, living in Sandwich, Ontario, and a great-granddaughter of Caroline Quarlls, was enormously helpful in understanding the unique connections for families with histories in the United States and Canada. Sadly, Charlotte passed away before seeing the completion of this book. I appreciate the initial project-approach work on the Underground Railroad in Illinois done more than twenty years ago by graduate students in Early Childhood Education at Governors State University with Professor Diane E. McClellan. This was helpful in beginning the visual expressions of this written work. And, of course, my everlasting thanks to Lil and our blended family for putting up with my spending a few days a week in the nineteenth century over the past several years.

The work on activity south of Chicago is greatly expanded from a paper delivered to the 2005 Symposium of the Illinois State Historical Society. This is fully explored in my book *The Underground Railroad South of Chicago*, published in 2019. On the activity in Chicago, the chapter builds on material presented in its early stages at the State Historical Society's 2007 Symposium. The Will County material was first reflected in a presentation given at the 2007 Annual Meeting of the Will County Historical Society and published as their fall quarterly in 2007, *Will County and the Underground Railroad*. This was expanded for an exhibit on the Underground Railroad in Will County in 2012 and an accompanying publication. Some of my conclusions about the activities of freedom seekers were initially shaped as presentations for national conferences for the National Park Service's Network to Freedom and responses to that work. The presentations were, in 2010, "Freedom Seekers in Illinois"; in 2014, "Women in Chicago working with the Underground Railroad"; and in 2017, "Changes Over Time and Space," a discussion session led with Cheryl LaRoche. The story of Caroline Quarlls is fully explored in *To the River: The Remarkable Journey of Caroline Quarlls, a Freedom Seeker on the Underground Railroad*, written with Kimberly Simmons and published in 2019. Presentations and short courses on the Underground Railroad across the Chicago region led to fascinating conversations and occasional sources of new information.

Part of the fascination of this part of our national history is that most of the activity was illegal and thus it can be challenging to find the usual sorts of details that come from primary sources. We continue to find evidence in unexpected places which serves to reinforce existing assumptions and assertions. On occasion, some fascinating stories shift from being seen as history to being enjoyed as "local tradition," and some move in the other direction.

I have online a guide to web resources leading to locally oriented materials across Illinois. These are available at www.illinoisundergroundrailroad.info.

This is a never-ending story. As you find material that supports or challenges the ideas I have explored in these pages, please join in the collaboration, and help us create a fuller story of this part of our common history.

Peace,
Larry McClellan, 2023

Population Patterns in Northeastern Illinois

Table A.1   Illinois Resident Population

		1810*	1820	1830	1840	1850	1860	
Black	Free	613	457	1,637	3,598	5,436	7,628	
	Slave	168	917	747	331	=	=	
	Total	781	1,374	2,384	3,929	5,436	7,628	
White		11,501	58,837	155,061	472,254	816,034	1,704,291	

*Illinois was a territory at this time.
Bureau of the Census, *Census of Negro Population*, 57.

From the 1820s through 1844, around 500 to 1,000 freedom seekers moved into and through the Chicago-Calumet region, and between 2,500 and 3,500 came through the region from 1845 into 1861. This means that 3,000 to 4,500 freedom seekers passed through the Chicago-Calumet region in the decades before the Civil War.

These estimates grow from tabulations and extrapolations based on a range of sources. Obviously, census data needs to be used carefully, since it was often not in the best personal interests of people of African descent to give details of their families and their background to government officials. However, the summary census data for the region for 1850 reports 493 Black residents and 160,076 white residents; and in 1860, 1,227 Black residents and 394,751 white residents. Earlier, in 1840, the census recorded 49,125 persons in the region including 53 Black residents in Chicago and a small handful in the nearby counties.[1] The estimated numbers of freedom seekers given above appear congruent with this census data. Significantly higher numbers of settled Black residents would suggest a larger number of travelers and refugees.

Through the 1840s and into 1852, from time to time, the *Western Citizen* noted the groups or number of persons who passed through during a particular week. Especially after 1850 and the passage of the Fugitive Slave Act, the movement of freedom seekers through the region increased dramatically. There are a few direct numbers mentioned in the press, including a report in the *Free West*, the successor to the *Western Citizen*, which reported a total of 300 passing through Chicago from July through November of 1854. During the 1850s, the *Chicago Tribune* also made periodic comments about the number of freedom seekers passing through. At the end of 1854, the *Chicago Daily Democrat* reported that from May through November of that year, 482 fugitives had been assisted in getting to Detroit. The funeral comments for both Dr. Dyer and Lewis Isbell mention they had each helped at least 1,000 to escape.[2]

Table A.2   Population by County in Northeastern Illinois, 1850 & 1860

	1850		1860	
	White	Black*	White	Black
Boone	7,618	6	18,676	8
Cook	43,007	378	143,947	1,007
DeKalb	7,539	1	19,079	7
DuPage	9,287	3	14,696	5
Grundy	3,021	2	10,362	7
Kankakee**			15,393	19
Kane	16,697	6	30,024	38
Kendall	7,724	6	13,073	1
Lake	14,187	39	18,248	9
LaSalle	17,799	16	48,272	60
Livingston	,552	0	11,632	5
McHenry	14,975	3	22,085	4
Will***	16,670	28	29,264	57
Totals	160,076	488	394,751	1,227

Federal Census of 1850 and 1860. The Census categories for both were "white," "Black," and "Mulatto".

*For these summaries of both the 1850 and 1860 Census, Black includes mixed race persons identified as "Mulatto".

**Kankakee County was created in 1853 from sections of Iroquois and Will Counties.

*** The summary census materials for Will County in 1850 indicate a total of 33 persons listed as "Black" or "Mulatto." However, the census manuscripts reveal that the Boone household of five persons in Joliet was listed twice, so the official number should be 28.

Table A.3   Chicago's Population before the Civil War

Year	Total	White	Black
1833	350	317	33
1837	4,066	3,989	77
1840	4,470	4,417	53
1843	7,580	7,515	65
1845	12,088	11,948	140
1848	20,028	19,740	288
1850	29,963	29,640	323
1860	109,260	108,305	955

From Census reports and Pierce, *History of Chicago*, 44.

Freedom Seekers and Underground Railroad Sites
in Northeastern Illinois

As reflected in the Map 2 in the Introduction, this research identified over forty places connected to the movement of freedom seekers. Hopefully, over time, further information will come to light and fuller stories can develop around each of the locations. For historical and educational purposes, it is useful to have a set of sites nearby and clearly marked. A recent example is with the installation of a state historic marker in Ottawa, Illinois, noting the controversies with the kidnapping and rescue of Jim Gray.

The National Park Service includes the Network to Freedom program for sites and activities related to the Underground Railroad in American history. In northeastern Illinois, the Network to Freedom program has approved the application of several sites for inclusion on their list of sites of national significance for the Underground Railroad. There are two designated sites in DuPage County: the Sheldon Peck Homestead in Lombard and Blanchard Hall at Wheaton College in Wheaton. Newsome Park in Elgin is a designated site connected to a community of freedom seekers, "contrabands" who arrived there in 1862, and to an early African American family in Elgin. In 2018, in Will County the Crete Congregational Church and Cemetery and the I&M Canal Headquarters in Lockport were added. The engagement of Dutch settlers with the movement of freedom seekers traveling overland on the major road to Detroit was recognized with the addition of the Ton Farm Site to the Network to Freedom register in 2019. Graceland Cemetery in Chicago joined the Network to Freedom listings in 2021. A number of white and Black activists are buried in Graceland, including John and Mary Jones, the Bradfords, Carpenters, Freers, and Pinkertons.

In Chicago

Within the current boundaries of the City of Chicago, documentation supports twenty specific places where freedom seekers received assistance. These included the home of John and Mary Jones (1), near Dearborn and Monroe; the Wagoners' home and mill (2), at the northwest corner of Harrison and Griswald; and the home of Anna and Joseph Hudlin (3), near State and Taylor. It is very probable that fugitives also found welcome in the homes of Emma Jane and Isaac Atkinson and other Black families. From its beginning, the congregation of Quinn Chapel (4), originally located on the southwest corner of Dearborn and Jackson, was deeply involved.[3]

Dr. Charles and Lousia Dyer's home (5), at Dearborn and Monroe, was near to that of John and Mary Jones. Philo and Anne Carpenter's home (6), west of the city center on Morgan between Randolph and Washington, and his drugstore (7), at Wacker and LaSalle, served as places of refuge. Allan and Joan Pinkerton, living in both Chicago and Dundee, in Kane County, often had travelers in their home (8) on Adams Street. When interviewed in 1891, L. C. Paine Freer recalled hosting fugitives in his home (9). Sylvester Lind provided transport from his lumber yard (10) on the south branch of the Chicago River and likely provided some kind of accommodations when it was not possible to immediately place freedom seekers on his boats. Charles and Amanda Cook owned the Mansion House (11), located on Kinzie between Dearborn and Wolcott, which served as a meeting place and for occasional accommodation. Strong local traditions hold that the Tremont Hotel (12) was an established site. Also, the First Congregational Church (13), located on Washington west of Halsted, and Zoar Baptist Church (14), originally on Taylor at Buffalo (just east of Clark), were sites. Zoar became Olivet Baptist Church. South of the original core of Chicago, the Gardner Home and Tavern, also known as Gardner-Wilcox Home (15) in the Morgan Park neighborhood (now 9955 Beverly) was a stopping point on the old Vincennes Trace, also called Hubbard's Trail.[4]

In an area that became part of Chicago at its far southern edge, the Cornelius Kuyper home, on Michigan Avenue in Roseland (16), and the Jan and Aagje Ton Farm (17), near 134th and Indiana, were places of refuge. The Indiana Avenue bridge (18) over the Little Calumet River, near the Kuyper and Ton sites, was the location first of a ferry in 1836, then of a succeeding set of bridges for the historic Chicago to Detroit Road. Over many years, hundreds of freedom seekers crossed this point on their journeys to Canada.

Over time, the offices of James Collins, Calvin DeWolf, and Dr. Dyer were in different locations, but these were used for emergency accommodations (19). Graceland Cemetery (20), on Chicago's northside, is the final resting place for more than thirty activists who participated in the Underground Railroad.

Local traditions, with no available documentation, hold that there were sites in Hyde Park in the late 1850s; at 63rd and Racine in Englewood; and at the "milk stop" on the Rock Island Railroad at 95th near Vincennes.[5]

Potential Significant Sites for Interpretation

The sites identified in Chicago and across the region merit some form of recognition including the use of historical markers. The following are suggested as significant sites for affirming the movement of freedom seekers and the networks of the Underground Railroad. Historic markers and interpretive displays could focus on:

- Chicago's African American Community and the Underground Railroad.

  In the Chicago Loop, at Jackson and Dearborn at the edge of the Federal Plaza is a site that should be recognized. The southwest corner was the site of the original Quinn Chapel. Historic recognition at this place would honor the work of Quinn Chapel and individuals and families in the early Black community who actively assisted freedom seekers who traveled to Chicago. This could be developed in conjunction with Quinn Chapel's current location at Wabash Avenue and 24th Street, and related to Olivet Baptist Church, the descendant of the Zoar Baptist Church, now located at the corner of 31st Street and South Dr. Martin Luther King, Jr., Drive.

- John and Mary Jones and Other Leaders of the Underground Railroad.

  Interpretive materials and signage should be added at Graceland Cemetery on the north side of Chicago, to expand on its designation as a Network to Freedom site. Among the key leaders of the African American community in Chicago for decades from the mid-1840s, John and Mary Jones welcomed many freedom seekers including those traveling with John Brown in 1859. Next to their markers are the graves of Henry and Ailey Bradford. Their stone memorial is a few steps from those of the families of Philo and Ann Carpenter, John's longtime friend, L. C. Paine Freer, Allan Pinkerton and other activist abolitionists.

- The Indiana Avenue Bridge, the Ton Farm, and the Underground Railroad.

At the south edge of Chicago, on the Little Calumet River is the site of a bridge built in 1837 by the Dolton brothers and used for the major road from Chicago to Detroit. Freedom seekers traveling to Canada overland from Chicago used this bridge. A few blocks east of this is the site of the farm of Jan and Aagje Ton, a designated Network to Freedom site. The Tons, the Doltons, and their neighbors aided freedom seekers. This area is at the south edge of Atlgeld Gardens-Murray Homes and connects with other significant elements in the region's Black history. There is an existing Underground Railroad Memorial Garden on the grounds of the First Reformed Church of South Holland, approximately two miles south of the Ton farm site. The Garden honors the heritage of the Tons and their engagement with the Underground Railroad and the Church. The Ton Farm site gained an Illinois State Historical Society marker in 2022; however, this complex of sites needs further recognition.

- Ottawa—Freedom Seekers and the Underground Railroad

In LaSalle County, overlooking the Illinois River, the John and Martha Hassock House still stands (privately owned). Recognizing this site and others in Ottawa would highlight the journeys of Jim Gray and other freedom seekers through LaSalle County, the role of LaSalle County activists and the engagement of the Hossacks and other local abolitionists in the "Ottawa Rescue Case." This would add to the Illinois State Historical Society marker installed in 2022 to recognize the Jim Gray story. In addition, the Hossacks and their children were at the center of a group of activists providing aid to those traveling on and near the Illinois River and the I&M Canal.

- Sycamore and Somonauk—Freedom Seekers and the Underground Railroad.

Both communities in DeKalb County were settled by strong abolitionists. Establishing one or two related commemorative historic sites at the church locations would recognize freedom seekers' journeys and the work of activist abolitionists connected with the Congregational Church in Sycamore and the Presbyterian Church in Somonauk.

- Families and farms along the Sauk Trail and the Underground Railroad.

Reaching across Will County and the southern edge of Cook County, this historic trail was followed by hundreds of freedom seekers. Stories and documentation point to connections and aid in Joliet, New Lenox, Park Forest, South Chicago Heights, and Crete. Particular focus should include the family of John and Sabra McCoy on the Sauk Trail just east of Park Forest, and the family of Elizabeth and Samuel Cushing in Beebe's Grove, now part of Crete.

Prologue

1. *Chicago Tribune*, April 9, 1861, 1; *New York Times*, April 9, 1861, 1. Principal sources on the exodus are in the *Chicago Journal*, *Chicago Tribune*, and *New York Times*. A *New York Times* report said close to one thousand recent refugees left.

2. "Civil War the Great Danger," *Chicago Daily Evening Journal*, March 14, 1861.

3. *Chicago Journal*, March 15, 1861.

4. *Chicago Journal*, April 3, 1861; New-Lisbon, OH, *Anti-Slavery Bugle*, April 13, 1861.

5. *New York Times*, April 4 and 6, 1861.

6. "Man Hunting in the North," *Douglass' Monthly*, May 1861; *Chicago Journal*, April 5, 1861. I first encountered a brief account of these remarkable days in April 1861 in the opening chapter of Drake and Cayton, *Black Metropolis*, 36.

7. *Chicago Tribune*, April 9, 1861.

8. "Death of L. C. Freer, The old settler and veteran lawyer passes away," *Chicago Tribune*, April 15, 1892, 5; Blanchard, *Discovery and Conquests*, 290.

9. *Chicago Tribune*, April 9, 1861.

10. Gettysburg, PA, *Compiler*, April 22, 1861; Dubuque, IA, *Weekly Times*, April 18, quoting from the *Detroit Tribune*; Pittsfield, MA, *Berkshire County Eagle*, April 18; Zanesville, OH, *Daily Courier*, April 9; New-Lisbon, OH, *Anti-Slavery Bugle*, April 13; Raleigh, NC, *Weekly Standard*, April 24, 1861; Great Salt Lake City, UT, *Mountaineer*, April 20, 1861.

11. In *Black Metropolis*, Drake and Cayton referred to this event as "The Great Canadian Exodus," 38. The *Joliet Signal* headlined it as "The Negro Exodus," April 23, 1861; *Chicago Journal*, April 5; *National Republican*, April 10, 1861.

Introduction

1. Washington, *Sojourner Truth's America*, ix; Professor LaRoche and I explored these terms during a program we led together, "Changes over Time and Space," at the Network to Freedom conference, National Park Service, May, 2017.

2. Throughout the book, this term is used, along with the use of Negroes, Blacks, Mullato, African Americans, and people of African descent. This variation is generally in response to the use of terms at the time in primary documents consulted.

3. Harbour, *Organizing Freedom*, 126;

4. LaRoche, "Secrets Well Kept."

5. Owens, *Medical Bondage*, 6.

6. Owens, *Medical Bondage*; and Hurston quoted in Owens, *Medical Bondage*, 120.

7. See also Frost and Tucker, *Fluid Frontier*, 37.

8. See Griffler, *Frontline of Freedom*, chapter 1, "River of Slavery, River of Freedom," 1–11. Assistance to freedom seekers is deeply explored by Cheryl LaRoche in *The Geography of Resistance, Free Black Communities and the Underground Railroad*. See LaRoche, *Geography of Resistance*, especially chapter 1, "Rocky Ford, Illinois: Oral Tradition as Memory," and chapter 2 "Miller Grove, Illinois: Linking a Free Black Community to the Underground Railroad."

9. See the work of Griffler, LaRoche, Harbour, and Owens and also, for example, Sinha, *Slave's Cause*; Foner, *Gateway to Freedom;* Frost and Tucker, *Fluid Frontier*; Blackett, *Captive's Quest for Freedom*; Jackson, *Force and Freedom*; and Masur, *Until Justice Be Done*.

10. Bateman and Selby, *Historical Encyclopedia of Illinois*, 532–7. Drew, *Refugee*.

11. *Chicago Tribune*, June 7, 1854, 2.

12. Heerman, "Great Escape."

13. "Address of Welcome," *Chicago Tribune*, June 10, 1874, 2; see also Gara, "Underground Railroad in Illinois," 508.

14. Siebert, *Slavery to Freedom*, 67.

15. Nida, *Story of Illinois*, 182–3.

16. Siebert, 112.

17. Wellman, "Underground Railroad and the National Register," 11–29. I use distinctions developed in DuPage County, Illinois, with journeys and encounters evaluated as "Verifiable," "Probable," or "Potential"; Angel, *Guide to the Underground Railroad in DuPage County*.

18. The national estimate used by the Lincoln Presidential Library is forty-five thousand. See "African Americans in Illinois," at Illinois Historic Preservation Agency. Earlier estimates ranged from fifty thousand to over one hundred thousand. Verna Cooley records traveling groups of fifteen to twenty through Chicago on a regular basis and notes that the Chicago *Western Citizen* reported on close to five hundred in the last six months of 1854; Cooley, "Illinois and the Underground Railroad," 79. Philo and Ann Carpenter assisted over two hundred; Hammond, *Memorial Sketch of Philo Carpenter*, 6–7. Black activist Lewis Isbell helped as many as one thousand freedom seekers; *Chicago Inter Ocean*, March 18, 1900, 3.

Dr. Charles Dyer also was credited with helping at least 1,000; *Chicago Tribune,* April 25, 1878, 7. Similar numbers were reported in *Voice of the Fugitive,* May 21, 1851 and in Rowe, *Refugees from Slavery in Canada West,* 15; In a late-nineteenth century reference work, an estimate was given that "more than 30,000" found "asylum in Canada;" "Underground Railroad" *American Cyclopedia,* 100. For similar estimates, see Foner, *Gateway to Freedom,* 4; and McPherson, "Fugitives Who Changed America," 69.

19. In a somewhat similar way, we currently use computer language to talk about the brain. It is helpful but may create images of brain function that become too restrictive.

20. Waller, *Waller's History of Illinois,* 70; Blanchard, *Discovery and Conquests,* 282; Cook, *Bygone Days,* 64.

21. Harbour, *Organizing for Freedom,* 4–5.

22. Ransom, "Remembering the Flight to Freedom," 3–7; see the Network to Freedom online at nps.gov/orgs/1205.

23. Gara, *Liberty Line;* Gara, "Underground Railroad in Illinois."

1. Slavery and Freedom in Illinois

1. Federal Census records for James Jackson; 1840 in Lauderdale County, Alabama, and 1820 in Gallatin, Sumner County, Alabama. Tregillis, *River Roads to Freedom,* 36.

2. Tregillis, *River Roads to Freedom,* 59.

3. Tregillis, *River Roads to Freedom,* 27.

4. Tregillis, *River Roads to Freedom,* 90.

5. Shawneetown, IL, *Illinois Gazette* of November 28, 1829.

6. Vandalia, IL, *Illinois Intelligencer* of September 30, 1831.

7. Tregillis, *River Roads to Freedom,* 80.

8. Harris, *History of Negro Servitude,* 2, 4–5.

9. A concise description of this political process and compromise in Ellis, *Founding Brothers.* His chapter on "The Silence" is stunning.

10. In the US Constitution, on ending the slave trade, Article I, Section 9; on enumeration, Article I, Section 1; on the return of fugitives, Article IV, Section 2. See "Completing the Work of the Founders," in Miller, *Arguing About Slavery,* 8–24.

11. *Ordinance for the North-West Territory,* 1787; Bliss, *Illinois,* 30; Harris, *History of Negro Servitude,* 6–15.

12. *Ordinance for the North-West Territory,* 1787, sixth article.

13. Miller, *Arguing About Slavery*, 8–24.

14. Gertz, "Black Laws of Illinois," 463–4.

15. Harris, *History of Negro Servitude*, 22.

16. Parrish, *Romance of Earlier Days*, 320–4.

17. Siebert Papers, "Letter of H. B. Leeper, Princeton, Illinois." Leeper wrote about his father's participation in this early group.

18. Leichtle and Carveth, *Crusade Against Slavery, Edward Coles*, 80, 90; Dexter, *Bondage in Egypt*, 374.

19. Davis, *Frontier Illinois*, 298.

20. Smith, *A Student's History of Illinois*, 220–4.

21. Hamilton, *History of Jersey County, Illinois*, 257.

22. *Proceedings of the Illinois Anti-Slavery Convention*. The delegates from La-Salle County were C. C. Elliot and C. Hatch; from Will County, the delegates were R. E. W. Adams, John J. Miter, E. Beach, and Moses Porter, Jr.

23. Harris, *History of Negro Servitude*, 125.

24. *Proceedings of the Illinois Anti-Slavery Convention*.

25. Cha-Jua, *America's First Black Town, Brooklyn*. On Rev. Quinn, see LaRoche, *Geography of Resistance*, 30–1.

26. LaRoche, *Geography of Resistance*, 30–1.

27. LaRoche, *Geography of Resistance*, 21–42; *History of Madison County*, 310; "Slave Emancipation Registry Book #1 1820-1850," records from the Clerk of Madison County. On the Richardson sisters, see also the family connections outlined in chapter 3 of this book, "Leaders and Travelers."

28. See especially, chapter 2, "Miller Grove, Illinois: Linking a Free Black Community to the Underground Railroad" of LaRoche, *Geography of Resistance*, 43–56.

29. Walker, *Free Frank*, 53.

30. Walker, *Free Frank*, 1–6.

31. Walker, *Free Frank*, 149–51; Shackel, *New Philadelphia*, 184.

32. *Constitution of the State of Illinois*, 1818, Article VI, Section 2; Dexter, *Bondage in Egypt*, 438; Blackett, *Captive's Quest for Freedom*, 152.

33. Brown, *Narrative of William W. Brown*; Farrison, *William Wells Brown*.

34. Ripley, *Black Abolitionist Papers*, 191.

35. Ripley, *Black Abolitionist Papers*, 208; Brown, *Narrative of William W. Brown*, 66.

36. Farrison, *William Wells Brown*, 175.

37. Ripley, *Black Abolitionist Papers*, 210. The vivid description of each panel added to the excitement of the stories Brown told. Wonderfully helpful reference staff at the British Museum looked through a variety of archival databases to see if

the panorama or some of it survived in Great Britain. Sadly, they found nothing. As Ripley et. al. point out, in "typical nineteenth-century fashion," the pamphlet was titled: *A Description of William Wells Brown's Original Panoramic Views of the Scenes in the Life of an American Slave, from His Birth in Slavery to His Death or His Escape to His First Home of Freedom on British Soil.* See Brown, *Narrative*, 70, for the full account of this encounter.

38. Hicks, *History of Kendall County*, 36, describes the activities of Rev. Walker assisted by an interpreter. In the history of Chicago, Jean Baptiste du Sable was the first permanent non-Native resident, and a traditional descriptor says, "the first white resident of Chicago was a Black man." The description of Black Bob is in the first story, "Maud Singleton, A Story of Pioneer Life" in Matson, *Raconteur,15*.

39. Hicks, *History of Kendall County*, 123. In the 1830 Census: for Carnes, *Lancaster, South Carolina*, Series M19, Roll 173, Page 97; for Murray, *Kershaw, South Carolina*, Series M19, Roll 171, Page 25. For the records for Silvie/Jane/Jenny, see 1850 Census: *Ottawa, La Salle, Illinois*, Roll M432_115, Page 180A, Image 10; and see 1860 Census: *Ottawa, La Salle, Illinois*, Roll M653_196, Page 558, Image 561. In 1834, Robert and Mary Ann Carnes arrived with two children and a Black woman named Dinah. 1830 Census records for South Carolina indicate that while there, the Carnes had one slave, a female aged twenty-four to thirty-six. This appears to be a reference to Dinah who was thirty in that year. Dinah appears on the family listing in the 1850 Census for Illinois, a few years older than Robert and Mary Ann. With them settled the family of James and Sarah Murray with a Black woman servant named Silvie. The 1830 Census indicates the Murrays had two male and four female slaves, one of whom could have been Silvie. An 1877 history of the county indicates that Dinah and Silvie were the first Black residents of the county, and both lived there until their deaths; Woodruff, *History of Will County*, 265. This may be Richard Post, a laborer listed in the 1850 Census living with Isaac and Melinda Van Alstine; *1850 Federal Census*; Channahon, Will, Illinois; Roll M432-133; Page 105B.

40. Haines, *Historical and Statistical Sketches of Lake County*, 99. See also *1850 Federal Census*, Place: Warren, Lake, Illinois, roll M432, page 5A, image 15.

41. Siebert Papers, "Letter of Charles F. Buck to W. Siebert, from Lacon, Illinois, February 8, 1932"; Siebert Papers, "Letter of Wm Lewis of the Putnam Anti-Slavery Society, etc."; Matson, *Reminiscences of Bureau County*, 359–63.

42. Reed, *Black Chicago*, 31–44, 71, 73–74; on John Johnson, *Federal Census of 1840*, Place: Chicago Ward 2, Cook County, Illinois, Roll: 57, Page: 215; Reed, "Early African American Settlement of Chicago," 221.

43. Goodspeed and l Healy, *History of Cook County*, 403; *Chicago American*, May 28, 1836; Johnson, *Growth of Cook County*, 81; *Chicago Democrat*, March 16,

1836; Pierce, *History of Chicago*, 253; *Chicago Democrat*, weekly issues, March 9 through June 1, 1836, sheriff's advertisement March 9 through April 13; *Chicago Democrat*, October 12, 1836, 3, and August 16, 1837, 4.

44. Report by Zebina Eastman, in Blanchard, *Discovery and Conquests*, 133.

45. Pierce, *History of Chicago*, 243–55; Andreas, *History of Chicago*, 603; from Calvin DeWolf's presentation at Abolitionists' Reunion, *Chicago Inter Ocean*, June 13, 1874, 9.

46. "Reminiscences of Philo Carpenter," *Chicago Tribune*, July 19, 1882, 1.

47. McClellan, *Underground Railroad South of Chicago*, 109–11. The 1850 Census records for the Doltons note that the mother was born in Maine, the father in Maryland, and children in Ohio; for the Ousterhoudts, all were born in New York.

48. "Steam-Boat Notice," *Chicago Democrat*, June 11, 1834.

49. For a fuller exploration of these concerns see: Masur, *Until Justice be Done*, especially chapter 7 on Illinois; Blackett, *Captive's Quest*, especially chapter 4 on Illinois; and Mahoney, "Black Abolitionists."

50. Robinson, *History of Illinois*, 136.

2. The Underground is Underway

1. Drew, *Narratives of Fugitive Slaves*, 215.

2. Siebert, "Underground Railroad," 155; Cooley, "Illinois and the Underground Railroad"; Muelder, *Underground Railroad in Western Illinois*.

3. Siebert, *Slavery to Freedom*, 82; Buchanan, *Black Life on the Mississippi*, 120.

4. Chicago *Western Citizen*, September 23, 1842, 1; quoted in Cooley, "Illinois and the Underground Railroad to Canada."

5. For this encounter, see the dramatic nineteenth-century expressions by Currey, *Chicago*, 413–4; Andreas, *History of Chicago*, 605–7.

6. Polly's daughter Lucy, late in her life, wrote about their combined story. Delaney, *From the Darkness Cometh the Light*. *St. Louis Republican* of October 1839, as quoted in Goodspeed and Healy, *History of Cook County*, 404.

7. Paul Angle, "Fugitive Slave in Chicago."

8. Chambers, *Trials and Confessions of Madison Henderson*, 1; Buchanan, *Black Life on the Mississippi*, chapter 5.

9. "Old Liners," *Chicago Inter Ocean*, June 13, 1874; Calvin DeWolf's presentation at the Abolitionists' Reunion, *Chicago Inter Ocean*, June 13, 1874, 9.

10. Pierce, *History of Chicago*, 244.

11. Robertson, *Hearts Beating for Liberty*, 26–27, 51–52.

12. Andreas, *Volume II*, 121, 449, 517; Blanchard, *Discovery and Conquests*, 295; *Biographical Sketches of the Leading Men of Chicago*, 73–80; "C. V. Dyer," *Chicago Tribune*, April 25, 1878, 7.

13. "A Generation Ago," *Chicago Tribune*, October 9, 1876, 7; "Mrs. Charles V. Dyer, the Funeral Service," *Chicago Tribune*, April 12, 1875, 8; "Dr. Dyer, the Funeral Service," *Chicago Tribune*, April 27, 1878, 8.

14. Blanchard, *Discovery and Conquests*, 293.

15. "Old Liners," *Chicago Inter Ocean*, June 13, 1874, 9; and articles from June 1874 in the *Chicago Tribune* on the Abolitionists Reunion.

16. "Death of Philo Carpenter – A Memorial Sermon by Dr. Goodwin," *Chicago Tribune*, September 13, 1886, 6.

17. McGiffert, *No Ivory Tower*, 19–21; Blanchard, *Discovery and Conquests*, 274.

18. Blanchard, *Discovery and Conquests*, 289–91.

19. "A Golden Jubilee, 50th Anniversary of the Organization of the First Presbyterian Church," *Chicago Tribune*, June 25, 1883, 1; Spinka, *Congregational and Christian Churches*, 144; *Chicago Tribune*, April 11, 1859,1; *Chicago Tribune*, January 19, 1860, 1; *Chicago Tribune*, November 24, 1862, 4.

20. Blanchard, *Discovery and Conquests*, 275–6, 282–3; "Calvin DeWolf," *Magazine of Western History*, 221–3.

21. 1881 speech by Isaac Arnold, in Lusk, *Politics and Politicians*, 530. *Federal Census of 1850*; Place: Chicago, Ward 1, Cook, Illinois, Roll: 102, Page 139A; and *Federal Census of 1860*; Place: Chicago, Ward 9, Cook, Illinois, Page 236.

22. Reports on the Abolitionist Reunion convention, *Chicago Tribune*, June 11, 1874, 4; Caton, *Early Bench and Bar*, 126–7.

23. "The Manierre Rifles," *Chicago Tribune*, August 17, 1861, 4; *Second Presbyterian Church of Chicago*, 213; Manierre, "Manierre Family," 451.

24. *Biographical Sketches of the Leading Men*, 25–34.

25. Newton and Selby, *History of Kendall County*, 532. At his death, Scammon was memorialized in dozens of newspapers across the Midwest, e.g., from South Dakota, "Jonathan Y. Scammon, A Chicago Pioneer gone to his rest," *Wessington Springs Herald*, March 20, 1890, 3; and Fort Scott, Kansas *Weekly Tribune*, April 3, 1890, 1.

26. *In Memoriam: Isaac Newton Arnold*; *Biographical Sketches of the Leading Men*, 407–5.

27. "Death of William H. Brown," *Chicago Tribune*, July 6, 1867; Brown, *Early Illinois*, 80–86; *Biographical Sketches some of the Early Settlers*, 1–10, 12–18. George Schneider identifies Brown as one of "the most active" in the Underground Railroad but has no specific details. Schneider in Blanchard, *Discovery and Conquests*, 293.

28. Blanchard, *Discovery and Conquests*, 279, 271; Dolinar, *Negro in Illinois*, 18.

29. Evans, *Zebina Eastman Papers, 1840–1885*, 2; Harris, *History of Negro Servitude*, 165.

30. *Charles Cook*, 350–2; "Mrs. Amanda S. N. Cook Dies," *Chicago Tribune*, July 27, 1900, 4.

31. "Lake Reminiscences, The Rival Steamers Illinois and Great Western, their commanders, Capt. Blake and Capt. Walker," *Chicago Tribune*, May 30, 1874, 3; Cooley, "Illinois and the Underground Railroad," 7; *Chicago Tribune*, September 21, 1868, 3.

32. Blanchard, *Discovery and Conquests*, 285–6.

33. *Chicago Democrat*, October 5, 1842, 4, Research Collections, Chicago History Museum.

34. Andreas, *History of Cook County*, 605.

35. Harris, *History of Negro Servitude*, 148; *National Anti-Slavery Standard*, January 20, 1842.

36. *Zebina Eastman Papers*, 1842–4, box 5, v. 15.

37. Gara, "Underground Railroad in Illinois," 513. Quoted from *Minute Book of the Illinois Anti-Slavery Society*, entry for May 26, 1842.

38. "Minutes of the Fifth Anniversary of the Illinois Anti-Slavery Society," Chicago *Western Citizen*, August 5, 1842, 2.

39. Harris, *History of Negro Servitude*, 124–52.

40. Chicago *Western Citizen*, February 1, 13, 1844; See Harris, *History of Negro Servitude*, 154.

41. Notes from Calvin DeWolf's presentation at the Abolitionists' Reunion, *Chicago Inter Ocean*, June 13, 1874, 9.

42. "Old Liners," *Chicago Inter Ocean*, June 13, 1874, 9.

43. Lawrence, *Pioneer of Freedom*; *Lundy Family and their Descendants*.

44. Hoffman, *History of La Salle County*, 105.

45. Eastman, "Early Abolitionism," *Chicago Inter Ocean*, August 31, 1883.

46. For greater details on journeys and aid provided, see McClellan, *Underground Railroad South of Chicago*.

47. This journal is available through the LaSalle County Historical Society. McDonald, "Life and Times of Amos M. Ebersol," 38–44; Siebert Papers, "Letter of J. C. Ebersol," to Siebert, January 23, 1914; and Eastman Papers, "Letter of A. M. Ebersol to Eastman," from LaSalle County, June 9, 1894.

48. *Streator Free Press*, October 24, 1901; Siebert Papers, "Letter from La Salle County, Sam. R. Lewis Letter to W. H. Siebert, Jan. 28, 1896," 2; Siebert Papers, "Putnam County Anti-Slavery Society meeting minutes – 1842-1843," 5; Siebert Papers, John H. Ryan's notes on Underground Railroad activity in Putnam County, Ill.

49. Siebert Papers, "Sam. Lewis Letter to W. H. Siebert," 2. For the list of "conductors" in LaSalle County, including Freeman, see Siebert, *From Slavery to Freedom*, 405. Freeman is also mentioned in the papers of Samuel Lewis, *Streator Free Press*, October 24, 1901, 1.

50. Fitzwilliam, "Chapter XI, The Underground Railroad," 767.

51. Woodruff, *History of Will County*, 740, 521–3.

52. Siebert Papers, William B. Fyfe, "A History: Anti-Slavery Days and Afterward. Chapter X," typescript, 2.

53. *Records of First Congregational Church of Lockport*, 82.

54. Samuel Haven and Allen Denny are listed by Siebert as "conductors." Siebert, *Slavery to Freedom*, 406.

55. *Joliet Sunday Hearld-News* of April 13, 1941, includes a photo of the foundations of the Savage homestead, identified as a site for the Underground Railroad; "Homer Township Family Histories," *Where the Trails Cross*, Vol. XVII: 4, Summer, 1987, 117-8 ; Woodruff, *History of Will County*, 745; Correspondence from Sue Stellen, the Hadley Church, August 2, 2003; "Calvin DeWolf," *Magazine of Western History*, 221–3.

56. Sterling, *Pictorial History of Will County*, plate No. 149, Stewart House; Woodruff, *History of Will County*, 95.

57. Woodruff, *Forty Years Ago*, 100–101.

58. "Underground Railroad Once Flourished Here in Joliet," *Joliet Herald-News*, June 3, 1936, Will County Centennial Edition.

59. *History of Plainfield*; *Joliet Herald-News*, June 13, 1968, 6; "When I Was a Girl: The Memoirs of Louisa Ashley Hammond, 1831–1912."

60. Siebert, *From Slavery to Freedom*, 406; Woodruff, *History of Will County*, 237.

61. Olin, *Record of the John Olin Family*, 82–84, 87; "Hole draws scrutiny as abolitionist site," *Chicago Tribune*, April 13, 2003, Sec. 2, 2.

62. Armstrong, *Lyonsville Congregational Church*, 22; Correspondence with the author from Phyllis Bremer, 2005.

63. Florence McCoy Schumacher interview, July 22, 1980, 2; Interview by the author with Edward and Harriet [McCoy] Genzler, March 1, 2015.

64. Beebe's Grove Congregational Society records, January 31, 1841. With this was a parallel resolution: "Concerning the evils of intemperance, resolved that we require of our members a pledge of total abstinence from the use of and traffic in intoxicating drinks as a beverage." Copies of records are held by the Crete Historical Society. Monks and Triebold, "Underground Railroad," *Crete Remembered*, 14.

65. Demographic information from the Censuses of 1840, 1850, 1860, 1870, 1880, and death records from *Crete Cemetery*. "Crete Township Original Land Owners," *Where the Trails Cross*, vol. 27, no. 2, 35.

66. *Will County Court Record Book, 1843*, 9.

67. Woodruff, *History of Will County*, 263, 557–8.

68. Piepenbrink, *Underground Railroad in Crete Township*; Myrick, "Moses Cook," 19–20; "Many Slaves Sheltered by Crete 'Underground Way,'" *Joliet Sunday Herald*, June 18, 1911, 2; *Federal Census of 1850*, Will County, Crete, Illinois, Roll 432-133, Page 162b; Jenness, "Dr. Mary J. Safford Black," *Cottage Hearth*, 113–4; Monks and Triebold, *Crete Remembered*, vol. 5, 140.

69. McClellan and Simmons, *To the River*; Simmons and McClellan, "Bridging Rivers, Caroline Quarlls' Remarkable Journey," in Frost and Tucker, *Fluid Frontier*.

70. Some details from a version of Goodnow's account in Olin, *Record of the John Olin Family*, XXX-XLI, XXXIV; Freeman is listed among the "conductors" of LaSalle County in Siebert, *From Slavery to Freedom*, 405; he is one of the few African Americans listed by Siebert.

71. Olin, *Record of the John Olin Family*, XXXIV.

72. The full story is in McClellan and Simmons, *To the River*, and today the area of Windsor, Ontario, known as Sandwich includes her story in their public history.

73. Blanchard, *Discovery and Conquests*, 295. See the Gifford paintings at the Elgin History Museum and others at the Sheldon Peck Homestead in Lombard.

74. Joslyn and Joslyn, *History of Kane County*, 827–8; "In the Days of Slavery," *St. Charles Chronicle*, March 29, 1901, 1; "Estate is Fascinating Footnote in Fox Valley history," *Chicago Tribune*, November 28, 1968, Sec. 3A, 12; Letter from Nancy Marshall Fischer, St. Charles to St. Charles Historical Society, June 2, 1991; Siebert Papers, material from *Collections of the Kansas State Historical Society, Vol XIV*, 1918, 208, 222.

75. On Strong, see Siebert Papers, "Letter of Frank L. Woods, Chicago, to Joseph V. Denney, September 29, 1892," 1–2. On Elliott, see *Commemorative Biographical and Historical Record of Kane County*, 649–50; Joslyn and Joslyn, *History of Kane County*, 62. William Thatcher Elliot identified as one who assisted some "to get to Canada." Elliot, *Historical Record of Kane County*, 649–50.

76. Painting of the Wagners at the Aurora Historical Society; "Last Rites for Pioneer Woman Held," *Aurora Beacon-Hews*, September 10, 1928; Buck, *From Slavery to Glory*, 196; Siebert Papers, "Letter of John R. King, Sugar Grove, IL, February 3, 1896."

77. Bateman and Selby, *Encyclopedia of Illinois and History of Kane County*, 720; Paxton, "Underground Railroad," 33–34; Interview by the author with Patsy Mighell Paxton, September 6, 1016; *The Paxton Family*, 241.

78. *Past and Present of Kane County*, 229.

79. Siebert Papers, "Letter of Frank L. Woods, Chicago, to Joseph V. Denney, September 29, 1892," 1–2; Siebert, *From Slavery to Freedom*, 405; Angel, "Friends of the Oppressed," 42–44; *Minutes of the Kane County Anti-Slavery Society*, 5.

80. *Minutes of the Kane County Anti-Slavery Society*, 7.

81. Mackay, *Allan Pinkerton*, 56–65, 83–84.

82. Biggers, *Paper for Aurora University*, letter delivered July 1, 1844.

83. *First Congregational Church, Naperville*, 3–5.

84. Sterba, *Blodgetts of Maple Avenue*, 1–4, 210. The museum is in the restored Blodgett House. Blodgett, *Pioneer Reflections*, 1–4.

85. Calvin DeWolf's presentation at the Abolitionists' Reunion, *Chicago Inter Ocean*, June 13, 1874, 9.

86. Bateman and Selby, *Encyclopedia of Illinois and History of Du Page County*, 629.

87. Bateman and Selby, *Encyclopedia of Illinois and History of Du Page County*, 711, 714, 716; "The Underground Railroad and DuPage County," 3; Federal Writers' Project, *Du Page County*, 77.

88. Quaife, *Chicago's Highways*, 87–104; Cole, *Stagecoach and Tavern Tales*, 129. Today, this site has one of the few memorials for the Underground Railroad in northeastern Illinois. Turner, *Underground Railroad in Illinois*, 91.

89. Federal Writers Project, *Illinois Guide*, 542; Bateman and Selby, *Encyclopedia of Illinois and History of Du Page County*, 711; Dugan, *Village on the County Line*, 62; Obituary for John Coe, *Hinsdale Doings*, February, 17, 1906. For John S. Coe (John Samuel Coe) and adjacent listings for Grants and Fullers: *1850 Federal Census*, Downers Grove, DuPage, Illinois, Roll M432; Page 37A, Image 81.

90. Siebert Papers, "W. B. Williams letter regarding the Underground Railroad, March 25, 1896," 2. "532.

91. On the controversies with "Sukey" Richardson, Pirtle, *Escape Betwixt Two Suns*; Muelder, *Fighters for Freedom*, 145; Matson, *Reminiscences of Bureau County*, 364, 365.

92. Reminiscences of William Nickerson in an article at the time of his death, Sycamore, IL, *Sycamore True Republican*, December 8, 1909, 4; Matson, *Reminiscences of Bureau County*, 368–70.

93. Chicago *Western Citizen*, July 13, 1844; Maas, *Marching to the Drumbeat of Abolitionism*, 16.

94. Spinka, *Illinois Congregational and Christian Churches*, 141.

95. Spinka, *Illinois Congregational and Christian Churches*, 94–95.

96. Spinka, *Illinois Congregational and Christian Churches*, 86, 347, 150.

97. Eastman, "History of the Anti-Slavery Agitation, and the Growth of the Liberty and Republican Parties in the State of Illinois," in Blanchard, *Discovery and Conquests*, 132–5.

98. Known as the "mail book" for each year, these subscription lists are noted by county; see for example the lists from 1842–43 and 1846–47; Eastman Papers, *Western Citizen "Mail-books"* at the Chicago Historical Society.

99. During April, May and June 1843, five articles in the Chicago *Western Citizen in a series: "Tales of the Star-Gazers."* "Jesse and Dysa," April 6; "Frances," April 13; " "History of a 'Chattel,' " April 27; "Not the Star-Led, but the Stream-Led Pilgrim," May 4; and "The Oppressed Widow," June 29. In November and then January of 1844, three articles in a series: *"Tales of the Fugitives."* "Narrative of a Wanderer," November 16; :Conversations with a Chattel," November 30; and a a third article under the general title: *"Tales of the Fugitives," January 4*; Robertson, *Hearts Beating for Liberty*, 169–70; Weiner, "Anti-Abolition Violence," 186.

100. Robertson, *Hearts Beating for Liberty*, 51–52.

101. Chicago *Western Citizen*, September 7, 1843, 2; Robertson, *Hearts Beating for Liberty*, 174, 169.

102. Laux and May, "Susan Short May," 127.

103. These developments are outlined in the previous chapter. LaRoche, *Geography of Resistance*, 28, 44.

3. Leaders and Travelers

1. *Detroit News-Tribune*, July 22, 1894; Quoted in Blassingame, *Slave Testimony*, 529–31.

2. Blassingame, *Slave Testimony*, 531.

3. Siebert Papers, "Henry Stevenson," 3.

4. Siebert Papers, "Henry Stevenson," 4.

5. Siebert Papers, "Henry Stevenson," 4.

6. "Fugitive Slave Case," *Western Citizen*, October 22, 1850, 2; Currey, *Chicago History and Builders*, 413.

7. "Fugitive Slave Case," *Western Citizen*, October 22, 1850, 2; "The First Slave Hunt," *North Star*, October 31, 1850, 3.

8. "Letter from H. O. Wagoner," *Frederick Douglas's Paper*, July 24, 1851, 1.

9. Drake, *Churches and Voluntary Associations*, 35–36.

10. Reed, *Black Chicago's First Century*, 82–85.

11. Quinn's report to the AME Church Conference in 1844 in Payne, *History of the African Methodist Episcopal Church*, 170; Dolinar, *Negro in Illinois*, 70; Wright, *Centennial History*, 301–2.

12. Wright, *Centennial History*, 301–2.

13. *Chicago Daily Journal*, July 29 and November 25, 1850; Drake, *Churches and Voluntary Associations*, 37.

14. Drake, *Churches and Voluntary Associations*, 37. Church traditions suggest three people, John Larmon, Samuel McCoy, and Sallie Jackson, organized as Zenia Baptist on April 6, 1850.

15. Fisher, *History of the Olivet Baptist Church*.

16. "Olivet Baptist Church," *Encyclopedia of Chicago*; Dolinar, *Negro in Illinois*, 74.

17. Henry Bibb, "Hurrah for Chicago!!," *Signal of Liberty*, July 18, 1846

18. Mahoney, "Black Abolitionists," 22–37.

19. Mahoney, "Black Abolitionists," 31.

20. Meites, "1847 Constitutional Convention," 275; Dexter, *Bondage in Egypt*, 273–4.

21. Although directed by this constitution, the legislature did not act on this until 1853. 1848 Constitution of Illinois, Article XIV; Masur, *Until Justice Be Done*, 230; Gertz, "Black Laws," 466–7.

22. Masur, *Until Justice Be Done*, 225–6, 299; Jones, *Black Laws of Illinois*.

23. An early example is the letter from John Jones in Frederick Douglass's *North Star*, June 23, 1848.

24. Gliozzo, "John Jones," 177–88; Foreman, Casey, and Patterson, *Colored Conventions Movement*; *Report of the Proceedings of the Colored National Convention*, 12–16.

25. "The Colored People of Illinois," *The North Star*, October 6, 1848, 1. Earlier, in 1843, there was a delegate from Chicago, Nimrod W. Jones, at the National Convention of Colored Citizens held in Buffalo, New York. He was the only delegate from Illinois in a convention mostly of men from eastern states and was elected as one of the Vice Presidents for the meeting. See *Minutes of the National Convention of Colored Citizens, 1843*, 10. The convention was called to consider their "moral and political conditions as American citizens."

26. Bell, "Chicago Negroes," 153–5. Reed, *Black Chicago's First Century, 43 - 58*; Reed, "The Early African American Settlement of Chicago," 211–65.

27. Abolitionist records of the time also mention John W. Jones, an African American in Elmira, New York, who was active with the Underground Railroad. At times, the two "Johns" are mistaken for one another. "John Jones, Social Honors to Chicago's Favorite Colored Citizen, Thirtieth Anniversary of His Residence in the City," *Chicago Tribune*, March 12, 1875, 2; *Chicago Evening Journal*, March 11, 1875: "Mr. Jones speaks in the highest terms of the friendships of L. C. Paine Freer and Dr. Chars. Dyer"; Dolinar, "John Brown's Friend," *Negro in Illinois*, 41–50; Gliozzo, "John Jones," 177–88; Letter of Lavinia Jones Lee, April 21, 1905.

28. Blanchard, *Discovery and Conquests*, 297.

29. Foner and Walker, *Black State Conventions*, 63; "The Haytien Emigration Movement," *Chicago Tribune*, April 26, 1859, 1; "Colored Men in Council," *Chicago Tribune*, November 20, 1857, 2.

30. See Census records for 1850, 1860, and 1870 and death records for Henry and Ailey, and for Diza Richardson, mother of Ailey and Mary. Diza Morris Richardson came to Chicago and lived her final years with her daughters until her death in 1880.

31. "Famous with His Race," *Chicago Inter Ocean*, March 18, 1900, 6; Reed, "Early African American Settlement," 221; Foner and Walker, *Black State Conventions*, 63, 69.

32. They were married July 14, 1849. Marriage Records, Madison County, Illinois, at Ancestry.com; *Illinois, U.S., County Marriage Records, 1800–1940. Federal Census of 1850*, Chicago Ward 3, Cook, Illinois, Roll M432_102, Page 218B, Image 209. On the Isbell family, see also Reed, "Early African American Settlement," 71–74; Alfred Richardson, *US Census of 1840;* Alton, Madison, Illinois, Roll: 64, Page: 138; Family History Library Fil: 0007643; *History of Madison County, Illinois*, 310; "Famous with His Race," *Chicago Sunday Inter Ocean*, March 18, 1900, 3; "He May Shave Dewey," Chicago *Sunday Inter Ocean*, April 29, 1900, 37. See the North Star Lodge discussed later in this chapter.

33. Simmons, *Men of Mark*, 679–784; "Amid Stirring Scenes, Mr. Waggoner's Recollection of John Brown and Days of Slavery," *Spokane Review*, September 2, 1892; Wagoner's obituary, *Rocky Mountain News*, January 28, 1909, 5; Advertisement, *Chicago Tribune*, December 13, 1859, 4.

34. Talmadge and Gilmore, *Barney Ford*, 68–69; Parkhill, *Mister Barney Ford*.

35. Talmadge and Gilmore, *Barney Ford*, 109–13.

36. For example, "Colored Men in Council," *Chicago Tribune*, November 20, 1857, 2, with Ford as chair and Wagoner leading Resolutions Committee; and "Meeting of the Colored Citizens," *Chicago Tribune*, August 16, 1858, 1, with both serving as secretaries.

37. "Meeting of Colored Citizens," *Chicago Tribune*, January 8, 1852; "Mass Meeting of Colored Citizens," *Chicago Tribune*, December 28, 1853; "Colored Men in Council," *Chicago Tribune*, November 20, 1857; "Meeting of the Colored Citizens," *Chicago Tribune*, August 16, 1858; "The Haytien Migration Movement," *Chicago Tribune*, April 26, 1859; "An Appeal from Colored Citizens," *Chicago Tribune*, July 13, 1860.

38. Simmons, *Men of Mark*, 682; "H.O. Wagoner," typescript, 4; Dolinar, *Negro in Illinois*, 46–47.

39. "From the Pike's Peak Gold Region," *Douglass' Monthly*, April, 1861; Letter from H. O. Wagoner about Johnson; *Federal Census for 1850*, Place: Chicago Ward 9, Cook, Illinois, Roll: 102, Page: 415A; Fisher, *History of the Olivet Baptist Church*, chapter 1.

40. Lloyd Augustus Hall, in Haber, *Black Pioneers*, 103–11; Reed, *Black Chicago's First Century*, 83; *Chicago Tribune*, April 27, 1878, 1; "Hall, Abraham Thomson," *Centennial Encyclopedia of the African Methodist Episcopal Church*, 103.

41. Reed, *Black Chicago's First Century*, 54, 78. Family records indicate their move to Chicago in 1847; however, information from Census records of 1860, 1870, and 1880 suggests they were living in New York. See the Grace Mason Papers; and Lyon, "Generations," 156 (an article on the Atkinson family with historic photos).

42. Advertisements in *Frederick Douglass' Paper*, January through April 1854; "Plan of the American Industrial School," *Frederick Douglass' Paper*, May 5, 1854; "A Good Man has Fallen," *Frederick Douglass' Paper*, December 14, 1855; McCaffrey, "James Bonner."

43. Others involved included R. H. Rollins, William Smith, and Alexander Smith. See Reed, *Black Chicago's First Century*, 48, 98. See also letter from John Jones, *Frederick Douglass' Paper*, November 18, 1853. On James Green, see Reed, *Black Chicago's First Century*, 48.

44. Their son, also Joseph H., was born in that house in 1858 and followed his father into work as the chief custodian at the Board of Trade; he shared stories of the family's work with the Underground Railroad. See "Faithful," *Chicago Tribune*, February 5, 1928, 105; Andrews, *Masonic Abolitionists*, 59; Brown, *Homespun Heroines*, 141–4. See Reed, *Black Chicago's First Century*, 55, 57–58.

45. *1860 Federal Census*: Place: Galesburg, Knox, Illinois, Page: 1005; Muelder, *Underground Railroad in Western Illinois*, 113. On attending the conventions, Foner and Walker, *Black State Conventions*, 63, 69.

46. Harris, Jr., "H. Ford Douglas," 217–34; Foner and Walker, *Black State Conventions*, 69.

47. *Centennial Encyclopedia*, 360–461; Salem, IL, *Weekly Advocate*, May 25, 1854, 3. On Parker raising funds for Quinn Chapel in Wisconsin see the Racine, WI, *Advocate*, May 28, 1853.

48. Noyes, "Byrd Parker," 59, quoting an 1858 Wisconsin editor; "Meeting of Colored Citizens," *Chicago Tribune*, June 29, 1853, 2; Foner and Walker, *Black State Conventions*, 63; Ripley, *Black Abolitionist Papers*, vol. 4, 174.

49. Byrd and Jane had three children. They left Chicago in 1857 and he served congregations in Wisconsin. Byrd died while preaching in 1860 and is buried in Oshkosh. For Jane, see *Federal Census of 1860*, Place: Oshkosh, Ward 4, Winnebago, Wisconsin, Page: 681.

50. "Rev. Byrd Parker," *Chicago Tribune*, February 13, 1954, 2.

51. Drake, *Churches and Voluntary Associations*, 42.

52. Davidson, "The African Methodist Church in the Chicago Area," 7. Mahoney supports evidence for Emma Atkinson and Reed suggests that these four are likely choices; see Mahoney, "Black Abolitionists," 23; and Reed, *Black Chicago's First Century*, 67.

53. Kirkland, *Chicago Yesterdays*, 94–95.

54. Reed, *Black Chicago's First Century*, 59; "A Generation ago, Reminiscences of Chicago Forty Years Ago," *Chicago Tribune*, October 9, 1876, 7; "Lake Reminiscences," *Chicago Tribune*, May 30, 1874, 1.

55. Moses and Kirkland, "Aaron Gibbs," 652–4; Obituary, *Chicago Inter Ocean*, August 4, 1890.

56. "The 'Underground Railroad' and Those Who Operated It," Massachusetts *Springfield Republican*, March 11, 1900; "Henry B. Hurd," 330–341; "Relive Old Times," *Chicago Inter Ocean*, October 6, 1895, 3.

57. Blanchard, *Discovery and Conquests*, 305–6.

58. *Biographical Sketches of the Leading Men*, 537–43.

59. Halsey, *History of Lake County, Illinois*, 1912; Marshall, "North to Freedom."

60. "Refuge of the Slaves, How Chicagoans helped to get them to Canada," *Chicago Tribune*, September 21, 1890, 33. Without attribution, this article was based upon an interview of Lind by a student at Lake Forest College. Danforth, "The Underground Railway," 185–8; Mackay, *Allan Pinkerton*, 56–65, 83–84.

61. Selby, "George Schneider," 331–4; Blanchard, *Discovery and Conquests*, 293.

62. *Chicago Times-Herald*, June 9, 1895, cited in Meites, *History of the Jews in Chicago*, 83–84; Cutler, *Jews of Chicago*, 19, 26; Whiteman, "Jews in the antislavery movement," 93–95; Wolf, *American Jew as Patriot*, 425–6. On Greenebaum, see *Biographical Sketches of the Leading Men*, 257–60.

63. *The Liberty Tree*, August 1, 1846, no. 10, 129–56.

64. Harris, *History of Negro Servitude*, 162–76.

65. *Western Citizen*, September 1, 1846, 1.

66. *Western Citizen*, September 23, 1842, 1; Quote from the St. Louis *Organ* in Verna Cooley, "Illinois and the Underground Railroad to Canada," 7.

67. Zebina Eastman, "Lake Reminiscences," *Chicago Tribune*, May 30, 1874, 1.

68. "One Thousand Dollar Reward," *St. Louis Republican*, November 1844, quoted in article "Pro-Slavery," *National Anti-Slavery Standard*, November 28, 1844.

69. From the Library of Congress, Prints and Photos Division, Image LC-USZ62-62797.

70. *Belleville Advocate*, July 17, 1851,

71. Bushnell, *Biographical Sketches of Early Settlers*, 26–31; *Chicago Tribune*, June 11, 1874, 4.

72. Bushnell, 30; *Chicago Tribune*, June 11, 1874, 4; Andreas, *History of Chicago*, 607.

73. Andreas, *History of Chicago*, 607.

74. Andreas, *History of Chicago*, 607.

75. *Western Citizen*, November 3 and 10, 1846; Pierce, *History of Chicago*, vol. 1, 252; Gara, *Liberty Line*, 109–10; Junger, "God and Man Helped Those Who Helped Themselves,' John and Mary Jones," 113–4.

76. "C.V. Dyer, His Death Yesterday, A Brief Sketch of an Eventful Life," *Chicago Tribune*, April 25, 1878, 7; Zebina Eastman, "Hunting," *Chicago Tribune*, April 5, 1874, 7.

77. Siebert Papers, "James H. Collins Letter to George W. Clark, Nov. 7, 1846."

78. "Kidnappers," *Chicago Tribune*, June 16, 1848; "Slavery in Chicago," *Sunday Inter Ocean*, June 28, 1891, 2.

79. Olin, *Olin Family History*, lxxiv; Siebert Papers, "Dr. Charles Voleny Dyer, Underground Railroad, Chicago," 2.

80. Siebert Papers, "Interview with Mrs. Lucinda Seymour of Windsor, Ont., Canada, Monday, July, 1895," 4.

81. "'Man-Hunters' Foiled," *Chicago Tribune*, May 8, 1850,

82. From Calvin DeWolf's presentation at the third day of the Abolitionists' Reunion, *Chicago Inter Ocean*, June 13, 1874, 9.

83. Blackett, *Captive's Quest for Freedom*, preface, xii–xiii.

84. *Chicago Daily Journal*, October 3, 1850, as noted in "The Railroad to Freedom," WPA Papers, Vivian Harsh Collection, Chicago Public Library, Box 7, Folder 2; Milwaukee *Daily Free Democrat*, October 12, 1850; Gara, *Liberty Line*, 102; Junger, "'God and Man Helped Those Who Helped Themselves,'" 118; Andreas, *History of Chicago*, 333.

85. Andreas, *History of Chicago*, 608.

86. Andreas, *History of Chicago*, 333; Blanchard, *Discovery and Conquests*, 298; Goodspeed and Healy, *History of Cook County, Illinois*, 408; Blackett, *Captive's Quest for Freedom*, 165.

87. Resolutions by the Common Council on October 21st, quoted in Currey, *Chicago History and Builders*, 415; Blackett, *Captive's Quest for Freedom*, 23.

88. This controversy is in most Chicago histories, for example, Pierce, *History of Chicago*, 195–7.

89. "Minutes of meeting of November 11, 1850," in the Zebina Eastman Papers, Box 1, folder 1, items 37 and 39; Mahoney, "Black Abolitionists," 33.

90. From *Chicago Democrat*, as quoted in Douglass' *North Star*, October 31, 1850; Griffler, *Front Line of Freedom*, 121, 149; *Western Citizen*, November 5, 1850.

91. Patten, *History of Somonauk Church*, 61–62.

92. "Editorial Letter," *Voice of the Fugitive*, July 30, 1851.

93. *Minutes of the Christian Anti-Slavery Convention*, 2–3.

94. "Letter from H. O. Wagoner," *Frederick Douglass' Paper*, July 24, 1851, 1.

95. Blanchard, *Discovery and Conquests*, 308; *Chicago Daily Democrat*, June 4, 5, 7, 1851; Pierce, *History of Chicago*, 198; *The Liberator*, July 11, 1851, 4; *The Liberator*, and July 13, 1851, 4. Goodspeed and Healy, *History of Cook County*, 411–2.

96. "Slavery in Chicago, An Interesting Interview with L. C. P. Freer," June 28, 1891, *Chicago Inter Ocean*, 2. In Goodspeed and Healy, *History of Cook County*, 412, the man is identified as Jones's brother, but that is unlikely.

97. "John Jones, General Intelligence Office," *Frederick Douglass' Paper*, September 8, 1854.

98. "Meeting of Colored Persons in Chicago," *Chicago Tribune*, December 30, 1852, 2.

99. Foreman, Casey, and Patterson, *Colored Convention Movement*, 115; *Chicago Tribune*, June 6, 1853, 2; *Chicago Tribune*, June 29, 1853, 2.

100. Goodspeed and Healy, *History of Cook County*, 412–3; Lusk, *Politics and Politicians*, 331–3.

101. Harrison, "We are Here Assembled," 326; Foner and Walker, *Black State Conventions*, 63–65.

102. *Chicago Tribune*, December 28, 1853, 3; Ripley, *Black Abolitionists*, vol. 4, 180–2.

103. *Frederick Douglass' Paper*, November 18, 1853.

104. Andrews, *Masonic Abolitionists*, 59.

105. "Masonic Festival, The Members of North Star Lodge No. 12," *Chicago Tribune*, December 28, 1857, 1.

106. Blackett, *Captive's Quest for Freedom*, 143.

107. Andrews, *Masonic Abolitionists*, 70. Other early members Joseph Hudlin and Robert Gray, see "Robert Gray," *Chicago Inter Ocean*, October 16, 1892. See the parallel history of the Knights of Tabor, established in 1846 in St. Louis by free men of color, but not organized in Chicago until after the Civil War. "Knights of Tabor," *Chicago Inter Ocean*, August 13, 1879, 8.

108. "Meeting of North Star Lodge," *Chicago Tribune*, December 25, 1858, 1.

109. Otis, *The First Presbyterian Church*, 35; Reed, *Black Chicago's First Century*, 96; "Recalls Old Days," *Chicago Tribune*, January 9, 1893, 9.

110. Barton, *Joseph Edwin Roy*, 21.

111. Williams, *Congregationalism in Illinois*, 86–88.

112. *Congregational Herald*, May 7, 1853, 1; *Congregational Herald*, July 2, 1853, 3; *Congregational Herald*, August 11, 1853, 1.

113. "A Dark Affair," *Chicago Tribune*, May 31, 1853, 2.

114. "A Dark Affair," *Chicago Tribune*, May 31, 1853, 2.

115. "Abolitionism in Missouri," *Chicago Tribune*, November 22, 1853, 1.

116. *Chicago Tribune*, June 7, 1854, 2.

117. *Chicago Tribune*, September 11, 1854, 2; *Chicago Tribune*, September 19, 1854, 3.

118. *Chicago Tribune*, September 19, 1854, 3.

119. *Chicago Tribune*, September 19, 1854, 3.

120. *Chicago Tribune*, September 12, 1854, 2.

121. *Chicago Tribune*, September 14, 1854, 2 and September 19, 1854, 3. *Chicago Tribune*, "Outrageous Conspiracy, Escape of the Kidnappers," September 21, 1854, 2. Quotes from *St. Louis Republican*, as carried in *Chicago Tribune*, September 28, 1854, 2

122. Siebert Papers, "Letter of H. C. Burnham, living in Havana, Mason County, February 3, 1896."

123. "Slave Hunt in Chicago, Great Excitement, Military Called Out," *Free West*, December 14, 1854, 2.

124. *New York Daily Times*, December 9, 1854.

125. *New York Daily Times*, December 9, 1854.

126. *Chicago Tribune*, September 15, 1854.

127. *St. Louis Republican*, August 30, 1854; Reprinted in Chicago *Tribune*, September 2, 1854; and in *New York Daily Times*, September 6, 1854; Merkel, "Underground Railroad and the Missouri Borders," 278–85; St. Louis, MO, *Daily Intelligencer*, August 31, 1854.

128. This is more fully explored in McClellan, *Underground Railroad South of Chicago*.

129. Siebert Papers, "Letter from W. B. Fyfe, Stockton, Calif., Jan 30th, 1896," 2; "Death of W. B. Fyfe," *Pontiac Sentinel*, June 20, 1899; Siebert Papers, W. B. Fyfe, "A History, Anti-Slavery Days and Afterward." The articles for the *Pontiac Sentinel* are outlined in Appendix One in McClellan, *Underground Railroad South of Chicago*.

130. Siebert Papers, "John Hossack Memoriam" and "John Hossack Dead," Ryan, "A Sketch of the Sturdy Abolitionist, John Hossack, 27–28; *1860 Federal Census*, Place: Ottawa, LaSalle, Illinois, Roll: M432_115, Page: 184A, Image: 18.

131. Shufelt, "When Lisbon Was a Prairie"; Siebert Papers, W. B. Fyfe, "A History: Anti-Slavery Days and Afterward," 3–6.

132. *History of Livingston County*, 713; "To the Radical Abolitionists of Illinois," *National Era*, December 18, 1856.

133. "Attempt to Kidnap in Illinois," New-Lisbon, OH, *Anti-Slavery Bugle*, July 29, 1854, 1.

134. Siebert Papers, Edmund Seeley, "Unsigned letter to Siebert, December 17, 1895," 1, 5.

135. Siebert Papers, Edmund Seeley, "Unsigned letter to Siebert, December 17, 1895," 1, 5.

136. Siebert Papers, "Letter of Lucius Whitney, Helena, Montana, April 27, 1896," 2–3. He is listed by Siebert as a "conductor" in Kendall County.

137. Siebert Papers, "Letter of Lucius Whitney, Helena, Montana, April 27, 1896," 4.

138. Bateman and Selby, *Historical Encyclopedia of Illinois and History of Kendall County*, 769; Siebert Papers, "Letter of Nathaniel Sherrill, August 4, 1892," 3–4.

139. *Ottawa Free Trader*, January 3, 1845, 3; *Ottawa Free Trader*, January 17, 1845, 5; *Ottawa Free Trader*, February 7, 1845, 3.

140. Foner and Walker, *Black State Conventions*, 52–85.

141. Woodruff, *History of Will County*, 281, 261; *Forty Years Ago*, 94–98; *Genealogical and Biographical Record of Will County*, 29; Rajala, *Black and White Together*, 10–11; *Proceedings of the Illinois Anti-Slavery*; "Underground Railroad Once Flourished Here in Joliet," *Joliet Herald News*, June 3, 1936, Will County Centennial Edition.

142. Also known as the Gardner-Wilcox home, a historical marker noted this site in the 1930s. *Chicago Tribune*, September 12, 1937, 45; Cutler, *Chicago, Metropolis of the Mid-Continent*, 118; Barnard-Wilcox family records at the Ridge Historical Society. On the Dyer properties, Flowers, *Cook County, Illinois* (map).

143. Further details in McClellan, *Underground Railroad South of Chicago*, chapter 4; Andreas, *History of Chicago*, 609.

144. Paul Petraitus, "Crossroads to Freedom," 2; Petraitus, "UGRR in the Chicago/Calumet Area: A Brief History"; Petraitus and Kelliher, "Timeline," *Chicago/Calumet Underground Railroad Effort (C/C.U.R.E.)*; Brennan, *Wonders of the Dunes*; *Chicago Tribune*, July 4, 1948, 8.

145. Beasley, *Underground Railroad in DeKalb County*.

146. Gross, *Past and Present of DeKalb County*, 101; Beasley, *Underground Railroad in DeKalb County*, 15.

147. Boies, *History of DeKalb County*, 451; *Federal Census of 1850*, Place Sycamore, DeKalb, IL, Roll M432-104, Page 385A, Image 443.

148. Beasley, *Underground Railroad in DeKalb County*, 189, 92, 100. Correspondence with the author from descendent, Mary Kelsey Benson, through the Sycamore Historical Society, May 27, 2016.

149. Patten, *History of the Somonauk United Presbyterian Church*, 59–61.

150. Boies, *History of DeKalb County*, 522.

151. Gross, *Past and Present of DeKalb County*, 101. Reminiscences of William Nickerson in an article at the time of his death, *Sycamore True Republican*, December 8, 1909, 1.

152. Gross, *Past and Present of DeKalb County*, 98.

153. "The Underground Railroad," *Sycamore True Republican*, March 12, 1884, 1–4. Reminiscence by a resident of Ogle County who accompanied Uncle Sol, originally published in the *Polo Press* and later in the *Sycamore True Republican*.

Shaver is listed by Siebert, *From Slavery to Freedom*, under "Ogle County, Illinois" in his appendix of "Underground Railroad Operators," 405.

154. This and other quotes from the article in the *Sycamore True Republican*.

155. "The Underground Railroad," *Sycamore True Republican*, March 12, 1884, 4.

156. Dupre, "Misc. Notes on Congregational Churches of Elgin and Dundee."

157. On Phoebe and Gill: *Federal Census of 1850*, Aurora, Kane, Illinois, Roll M432_112, Page 190B, Image 495; Buck, *From Slavery to Glory*, 30–31; Joslyn and Joslyn, *History of Kane County*, Letter from Rev. Miller to the book authors, 130–2.

158. Joslyn and Joslyn, *History of Kane County*, 131.

159. Joslyn and Joslyn, *History of Kane County*, 131.

160. Joslyn and Joslyn, *History of Kane County*, 131, quotes from 132.

161. Joslyn and Joslyn, *History of Kane County*, 571; Buck, *From Slavery to Glory*, 73.

162. Joslyn and Joslyn, *History of Kane County*, 571–2.

163. Maas, *Marching to the Drumbeat of Abolition*, 14–17.

164. Advertisement for the Institute in *True Wesleyan*, March 31, 1853, as noted in Maas, *Marching to the Drumbeat of Abolition*, 15.

165. Maas, *Drum Beat of Abolition*, 17; Federal Writers' Project, *Du Page County*, 170.

166. "Anti-Slavery Meetings," *Chicago Tribune*, October 3, 1859, 1. On lectures in Wheaton and Babcock's Grove (Lombard) by Jones and Douglas.

167. Two traditional county histories do not mention the Underground Railroad: *Historical Encyclopedia of Illinois and History of Boone County*, and *Past and Present of Boone County, Illinois*. Ephraim Nichols, who later was active in DeKalb County, moved to Boone County in 1837 and then on to Mayfield township in DeKalb in 1845. *Past and Present of DeKalb County*, 351.

168. *History of McHenry County, Illinois*, 674, 827–8, 877–8; *Biographical Directory of the Taxpayers of McHenry County*, 113. Census records have Samuel and Laura Terwilliger in McHenry County in 1840, 1850, and 1860 and the family of John and Mary Janes McHenry County in 1850 and 1860. The Terwilliger House was placed on the National Register of Historic Places in 1979. Siebert, *From Slavery to Freedom*, 405, includes one person, a man named "Russel," for McHenry County in his list of Conductors. This may be a reference to the Russell in Caroline Quarlls's story.

169. Jackson and McDonald, *Finding Freedom*.

170. Dretske and Westerman, "Incredible Story of Amos Bennett," 1–3; Siebert, *From Slavery to Freedom*, 405. In his list of Conductors, Seth Paine is listed for Cook County.

171. Bateman and Selby, *Encyclopedia of Illinois and History of Lake County*, 631. On Eratus and Wealthy Rudd, *1850 US Census*, Warren, Lake, Illinois, Roll M432-114, Page 1B. The Warren Township Historical Society maintains a museum in the Mother Rudd House.

172. Brainerd, *Earliest History of the Church*, 5. At times, the church and community have been spelled "Milburn."

173. Brainerd, *Earliest History of the Church*, 5. The reference to the appearance of Sojourner Truth appears in several church histories, but this is not confirmed from any other source Halsey, *History of Lake County*, 93; "Millburn Congregational Church," 10–11.

174. "Millburn Congregational Church," 24. "Laying Tracks, Countians Helped Fugitive Slaves," *Waukegan News-Sun*, June 24, 1981, 9A.

175. Bateman and Selby, *Encyclopedia of Illinois and History of Lake County*, 679. "Seth Paine, Reminiscences of a Remarkable Career," *Chicago Tribune*, July 7, 1872, 5. Interview with Nancy Schumn, President of the Ila Township Historical Society, April 7, 2016.

176. Barbara Apple, "Laying Tracks, Countians helped fugitive slaves, Picture this 20-ton rock in hiding," *Waukegan News-Sun*, June 24, 1981, 9A.

177. *Little Fort* [Waukegan] *Porcupine and Democratic Banner*, November 8, 1845, 1; Letter of Edward E. Link, for the Waukegan Historical Society, to Open Secrets and Railroads Virginia A. Johnson, August 14, 1996, in archives of the Open Secrets and Railroads society; Blodgett, *Autobiography of Henry W. Blodgett*, 59; Portrait and Biographical Album of Lake County, 227. A potential report on Blodgett is in *Waukegan Herald*, January 28, 1876, 10.

178. *Portrait and Biographical Album of Lake County*, 789; Lola A. Shephard, "History of Lake County, 1928," *Waukegan Daily Sun*, July 27, 1928; Typescript on Waukegan, 8–9; "Mrs. Sarah Stafford is Dead at 100," July 20, 1937, obituary in archives of the Waukegan Historical Society.

179. *Federal Census of 1850*, Waukegan, Lake, Illinois, Roll M432_114, Pages 141A, Image 287; 149B, 304; 150A, 305.

180. Mary Ann Shadd, "A Short Letter," *Provincial Freeman*, March 8, 1856, 2. She mentions "enjoyed the hospitality of Mr. and Mrs. Ibell"—note the spelling, neither Ibell or Isbell found in Waukegan census records.

181. "Negroes vs. Horses," *The North Star*, October 27, 1848.

182. *Voice of the Fugitive*, August 12, 1852. Emphases in the original.

183. *Western Citizen*, September 28, 1852, 3.

184. Jackson, *Force and Freedom*.

185. From *Chicago Tribune*, quoted in *New York Daily Times*, June 14, 1854, 6.

186. *Chicago Tribune*, June 14, 1854, 6.

187. A report from the Muscatine, Iowa *Journal* as noted in the *Daily Missouri Republican*, September 8, 1854, 2.

188. Kirkland, *Chicago Yesterdays*, 95.

4. Open Secrets and Railroads

1. On the southern opinion, *St. Louis News*, as quoted in the *Chicago Tribune*, November 11, 1859, 1; Reynolds, *John Brown*, 278–87.

2. DeRamus, *Forbidden Fruit*, 92–93.

3. Details of the traditional story from Reynolds, *John Brown*, 278–87.

4. Soike, *Necessary Courage*, 152; "Brown's Rescued Negroes Landed in Canada," *Anti-Slavery Bugle*, March 26, 1859, 2, reprinted in *Douglass' Monthly*, April, 1859; Siebert, *From Slavery to Freedom*, 190; Soike, *Necessary Courage*, 118; Reynolds, *John Brown*, 261.

5. "Amid Stirring Scenes, Mr. Waggoner's Recollection of John Brown and Days of Slavery," *Spokane Review*, September 2, 1892, 4; Account of Wagoner's life, "Recall role of 'Forgotten' man in fight for freedom," *Daily Defender*, March 28, 1959, 11; Accounts by Mary Jones and William Pinkerton in Blanchard, *Discovery and Conquests*, 297–305; Letter of William Pinkerton to F. F. Hall, April 8, 1916, in archives of the Dundee Historical Society; "Recall John Brown's Rendezvous in Chicago 100 Years Ago," *Daily Defender*, March 21, 1959, 11..

6. *Chicago Daily Democrat*, December 5, 1859, noted in Cooley, "Illinois and the Underground Railroad to Canada," 10.

7. "A Long and Unprofitable Slave Hunt," *Chicago Tribune*, February 15, 1855, 2; "Colored People Flogging Slave Hunters," *Provincial Freeman*, March 10, 1855, 2; "He May Shave Dewey," *Chicago Inter Ocean*, April 29, 1900, 37.

8. "Colored People Flogging Slave Hunters," *Provincial Freeman*, March 10, 1855, 2.

9. "A Long and Unprofitable Slave Hunt," *Chicago Tribune*, February 15, 1855, 2.

10. *Chicago Tribune*, August 15, 1855, reprinted in New-Lisbon, OH, *Anti-Slavery Bugle*, August 25, 1855, 3; *Chicago Daily Democrat*, March 30, 1855, quoted in Dolinar, *Negro in Illinois*, 20. *Chicago Daily Democrat*, August 14, 1855.

11. "Anti-Slavery Society of Chicago," *Chicago Tribune*, March 7, 1855, 2.

12. *Daily Missouri Republican*, October 15, 1860, 4.

13. Mary Ann Shadd, *Provincial Freeman*, May 17, 1856, 2.

14. Fisher, "History of the Olivet Baptist Church," 7. Zoar eventually became Olivet Baptist.

15. Harrison, "We are Here Assembled," 331–2; Foner and Walker, *Proceedings of the Black State Conventions.* On the importance of conventions as an environment for planning and practical issues in aiding freedom seekers, see LaRoche, "Secrets Well Kept," 246–60.

16. "Underground," *Douglass' Monthly*, January 1859.

17. "An Attempt to Kidnapping," *Provincial Freeman*, February 9, 1856, 2.

18. Siebert Papers, "Letter of John G. Weiblen, Fairview, Penn., November 26, 1895."

19. Siebert Papers, "C. E. Cory Address to Kansas State Historical Society, January 21, 1902," 1–2; Oertel, "Blazing a Path to Freedom"; *Nashville Democrat*, quoted in the *Chicago Tribune*, July 16, 1857, emphasis in the original.

20. Woodruff, *History of Will County*, 268.

21. Schmidt, *Der rothe doktor von Chicago* [The Red Doctor of Chicago].

22. "Lovejoy, Singleton, Lombard and Old Mose," *Chicago Tribune*, February 15, 1859, 2; "Old Mose on the Carpet Again, Passage in the House between Messrs. Lovejoy of Ill. and Singleton of Miss.," *Chicago Tribune*, February 15, 1859, 2.

23. "Speech on the Fanaticism of the Democratic Party, February 21, 1859" by Owen Lovejoy, in Moore and Moore, *Owen Lovejoy*, 176–8.

24. "Law Intelligence, Rodney v. Illinois Central Railroad," *Chicago Tribune*, January 13, 1858. 2. "Rodney v. ICRR," *Report of Cases Determined of the Supreme Court of the State of Illinois, Vol. XIX, November 1857–April 1858*, 42–45.

25. "Fugitive Slave Excitement," *Chicago Tribune*, September 1, 1857, 1; Blackett, *Captive's Quest for Freedom*, 170-171.

26. Regosin and Shaffer, *Voices of Emancipation*, 42.

27. "What does it mean?," *Chicago Tribune*, January 18, 1858, 1.

28. "U. G. R. R.," *Chicago Tribune*, September 24, 1858, 1.

29. *Chicago Tribune*, February 26, 1859, 1.

30. "Negro Stampede," Glascow, MO, *Weekly Times*, November 17, 1859, 3.

31. *St. Louis News*, reported in the *Chicago Tribune*, November 11, 1859, 1; *Chicago Tribune*, November 19, 1859, quoted in Goodspeed and Healy, *History of Cook County*, 416.

32. Reminiscence by a policemen involved, told to reporters writing on the notorious "Levee" area of Chicago, *Chicago Inter Ocean*, June 9, 1901, 41.

33. *Chicago Tribune*, January 7, 1860, 1.

34. Goodspeed and Healy, *History of Cook County*, 417.

35. From an article in the *St. Charles Valley Chronicle* in 1891 by "J.P.B." Interview with Patsy Mighell Paxton, September 6, 1016.

36. *Chicago Tribune*, November 13, 1860, 1; *Chicago Tribune*, November 16, 1860, 21 and *Chicago Tribune*, December 5, 1860, 18. The story of Eliza before Chicago is in Soike, *Necessary Courage*, 122–34.

37. *Nebraska City News*, November 24, 1860, 1.

38. Barton, *Joseph Edwin Roy*, 26, 29.

39. Barton, *Joseph Edwin Roy*, 33; Siebert Papers, "Letter from Rev. J. E. Roy, April 9, 1896," 4.

40. Siebert Papers, "Letter from Rev. J. E. Roy, April 9, 1896," 2.

41. "The Underground Railroad in Chicago," *New York Daily Herald*, October 5, 1859, 3.

42. Details of Andrew Jackson's story from Samuel Ott, who lived in Deerfield. In 1918, Deerfield Grammar School produced a local history of Deerfield as a state centennial project. Deerfield Grammar School, *1918 School Histories*; Reichelt, *History of Deerfield*, 107–8.

43. *Federal Census of 1860, Slave Schedules*, Marshall County, Mississippi, "Andrew Jackson, Slave Owner," T3, R1&2 West, Page 108.

44. On the Wilmonts: *Federal Census of 1860*, Deerfield, Lake County, Illinois, Roll M653, Page 676, Image 281.

45. Deerfield Grammar School, *1918 School Histories*; Reichelt, *History of Deerfield*, 107–8. It is probable that Samuel Ott remembered direct conversations with Jackson about his journey but also possible that the reconstruction of Jackson's first-person account was a fanciful effort by Ott or the earnest children and teachers of the Deerfield Grammar School.

46. Reminiscences of William Nickerson, *Sycamore True Republican*, December 8, 1909, 4; Beasley, *Underground Railroad in DeKalb County*, 163

47. Nickerson, *Sycamore True Republican*, December 8, 1909, 4.

48. Boies, *History of DeKalb County*, 451; *Federal Census of 1860*, Sycamore, DeKalb, Illinois, Roll M653-173, Page 9, Image 9. On Mary's origins and arrival in De Kalb County, see Beasley, *Underground Railroad in DeKalb County*, 163–4.

49. Listing for the Dickersons: *Federal Census of 1860*, Grand Rapids, Meridian, LaSalle County, Illinois; Roll M653-196; Page 348 ; See "Arrest of a Free Negro on Suspicion of being a Fugitive," *Joliet Democrat*, May 7, 1859, 2.

50. "A Free Negro from Illinois is Sold into Slavery and Makes His Escape," *Douglass' Monthly*, November, 1859, 1.

51. *History of LaSalle County*, 444–6.

52. *Jonesboro Gazette*, September 17, 1859, noted in *Chicago Tribune*, November 4, 1859.

53. "The Ottawa Rescue Case," *Chicago Tribune*, December 31, 1859, 2.

54. "The Ottawa Rescue Case," *Chicago Tribune*, December 31, 1859, 2.

55. Siebert Papers, "Letter of H. D. Hickok to Siebert, January 6, 1914," 4; "U. S. District Court," *Chicago Tribune*, December 22, 1859; Siebert Papers, "Letter from

M. B. Fyfe to the *Pontiac Sentinel*, November 15, 1891," 2; Youmans, *Historical and Genealogical Notes of the Youmans*, 2.

56. Ryan, "A Sketch of the Sturdy Abolitionist, John Hossack," 27–28.

57. *Ottawa Free Trader*, October 15, 1859; *Ottawa Free Trader*, October 22, 1859 and *Ottawa Free Trader*, November 19, 1859.

58. Karamanski, *Rally 'Round the Flag*, 45–46.

59. *Anti-Slavery Tracts*, "Speech of John Hossack, Convicted of a Violation of the Fugitive Slave Law, before Judge Drummond, of the United States District Court, Chicago, ILL," 11.

60. "The Union in Danger," *Chicago Tribune*, October 21, 1859, 1; *Chicago Daily Democrat*, December 15, 1859.

61. "Slavery in Illinois," *Chicago Tribune*, January 14, 1860, 1; "The Kidnapping Business, Letter from the Kidnapper-in-Chief," *Chicago Tribune*, January 13, 1860, 1.

62. *Carlinville Free Democrat*, February 3, 1860, quoted in "Whisky and Kidnapping, Awful Death of John B Jones and J. Curtly, the Union County Kidnappers," *Chicago Tribune*, February 11, 1860, 2.

63. "A Flagrant Case of Kidnapping," *Chicago Tribune*, June 9, 1860, 2.

64. *Free West*, December 14, 1854, 1; Mackay, *Allan Pinkerton*, 84; Harris, "Early Railroading in Michigan and Wisconsin."

65. *Frederick Douglass' Paper*, March 9, 1855, 3; Bordewich, *Bound for Canaan*, 409.

66. *Cairo City Times*, February 1855, quoted in Dolinar, *Negro in Illinois*, 32; Federal Writers' Project, *Cairo Guide*, 30.

67. *St. Louis Intelligencer*, September 6, 1855, cited in Merkel, "The UGRR and the Missouri Borders," 278–85.

68. Siebert Papers, "George Burroughs letter"; Siebert, *From Slavery to Freedom*, 70; Ripley, *Black Abolitionist Papers*, 306–9; On True Bands in Drew, *Narratives of Fugitive Slaves*, 336–7.

69. His age is calculated from data in the *Federal Census of 1880*, Roll 175, Page 26C, Enumeration District 002, Image 0509.

70. Siebert Papers, "Burroughs Letter."

71. Siebert Papers, "Burroughs Letter."

72. Siebert Papers, "Burroughs Letter."

73. Siebert Papers, "Letter of James Wilson, January 17, 1896," 2.

74. Siebert Papers, "Illinois Underground Railroad description," 1.

75. "The Underground Railroad," *Anti-Slavery Bugle*, June 11, 1859, 2.

76. Banks, J. H. *I Am a Witness Against American Slavery*.

77. Blassingame, *Slave Testimony*, 734; Autobiography by John Sella Martin, originally published in an Edinburgh monthly, *Good Words* 8 (May and June 1867).

78. Blassingame, *Slave Testimony*, 702–35.

79. Siebert Papers, "Emma M. Chapin, Geneseo, Il., January 11, 1896," 8.

80. Soike, *Necessary Courage*, 71–75.

81. Chapman, *History of Knox County*, 211; Soike, *Necessary Courage*, 60–65; Muelder, *Underground Railroad in Western Illinois*, 149–59.

82. Siebert Papers, "Letter of Roderick B. Frary, Bureau County, IL, August 3, 1896."

83. Siebert Papers, "The Life and Poems of John Howard Bryant excerpt."

84. Cooley, "Illinois and the Underground Railroad to Canada," 42; Woodruff, *Forty Years Ago*, 98–99; Woodruff, *History of Will County*, 281.

85. "Underground Railroad," *Daily Missouri Republican*, May 28, 1855, 2.

86. This is seen in headlines of the *Chicago Tribune*, with titles like "Kidnapping in Iowa," February 3, 1860, and "The McDonough Kidnapping Case," December 27, 1859.

87. "The McDonough Kidnapping Case," *Chicago Tribune*, December 27, 1859, 2; "About Negro-catching," *Chicago Tribune*, December 27, 1859, 2.

88. *Chicago Tribune*, August 7, 1860, 1.

89. "Daring Rascality Defeated," *Chicago Tribune*, August 23, 1860, 1; "Excitement in 'Egypt,' A Chicago Irishman arrested under the Black Laws, He is held as a Fugitive Slave," *Chicago Tribune*, November 30, 1859, 2; "A Panic Among the Kidnappers," *Chicago Tribune*, December 13, 1859.

90. This story is in a series of front-page articles in the *Chicago Tribune*, including: "Excitement among Colored Residents-An Alleged Kidnapper's Agent stored in jail," *Chicago Tribune*, July 20, 1859; "Successful-Three Fugitive Slaves, Sent back to Servitude from Chicago-The Price of Blood Paid Over," *Chicago Tribune*, July 21, 1859; "The Case of the Negro Catchers," *Chicago Tribune*, July 25, 1859; "The Colored Citizen Meeting," *Chicago Tribune*, July 25, 1859; "The Kidnapping Case," *Chicago Tribune*, July 27, 1859; [front page, no title], *Chicago Tribune*, August 3, 1859; *History of Livingston County*, 713.

91. It is unlikely that this is the same Turner who escaped kidnapping in 1854, as mentioned in chapter 4.

92. *Chicago Tribune*, July 25, 1859, 1; *Chicago Tribune*, July 27, 1859. 1.

93. *National Anti-Slavery Standard*, August 27, 1859.

94. "Infamous Attempt to Kidnap Free Negroes from Chicago," *Chicago Tribune*, March 24, 1860, 2.

95. "Kidnapping at Clifton, Ill.," *Chicago Tribune*, July 4, 1860; "A Trilling and True Story," *Douglass' Monthly*, October, 1860, 1.

96. "Kidnapping at Clifton, Ill," *Chicago Tribune*, July 4, 1860; "The Last Great Outrage," *Chicago Tribune*, July 6, 1860; "No More Kidnapping," *Chicago Tribune*,

July 10, 1860; "Is Illinois a Free State, Finale of a Late Kidnapping Case," *Chicago Tribune*, August 15, 1860.

97. *Chicago Tribune*, April 9, 1861, 4. A report by telegraph from Detroit.

98. "Man Hunting in the North," *Douglass' Monthly*, May, 1861.

99. "The Fugitives in Canada," *Chicago Tribune*, April 11, 1861, 2.

100. "Underground Railroad," *Daily Missouri Republican*, April 13, 1861.

101. "The Negro Exodus," *Chicago Times*, April 11, 1861, 1.

102. *Chicago Tribune*, April 11, 1861, 1.

103. *Chicago Tribune*, April 4, 1861, 1.

Epilogue

1. Walker, *Free Frank*, 172.

2. Drew, *Narratives of Fugitive Slaves*, 219; Brown-Kubisch, *Queen's Bush Settlement*, 215.

3. See Brown-Kubisch. A brief version of their story in DeRamus's *Forbidden Fruit*, 125–8.

4. See the series of publications from Applewood Books on *Slave Narratives from the Federal Writers' Project, 1936–1938* [for each of seventeen states] and online materials of the American Memory project of the Library of Congress at *memory.loc.gov/ammem/snhtml/snhome.html*. The quote is from Drew, *Narratives of Fugitive Slaves, 201–2*.

5. "From the Pike's Peak Gold Region," *Douglass' Monthly*, April 1861; See Talmadge and Gilmore, *Barney Ford: Black Baron*; and Parkhill, *Mister Barney Ford*.

6. *Detroit News-Tribune*, July 22, 1894; Blassingame, *Slave Testimony*, 529–31; Siebert Papers, "Henry Stevenson," 4–5; Turner, *Underground Railroad in Illinois*, 58–59; Siebert Papers, "Escape of Henry Stevenson from Odrain Co., Mo. through Illinois."

7. Siebert Papers, "Letter of J. S. T. Milligan's, December 5, 1895," 5.

8. James Redpath, *Public Life of John Brown*, 229.

9. "Seven thousand Negroes Celebrate," *St. Joseph Weekly Free Democrat*, August 20, 1859, 2.

10. Hamilton, "John Brown in Canada," 6.

11. Ibid.

12. Siebert Papers, "George Burroughs"; Siebert, *From Slavery to Freedom*, 70.

Appendixes

1. Forstall, *Population of the States and Counties*, 45–48.

2. *Chicago Daily Democrat*, December 16, 1854, August 10, 1859; *Free West*, December 21, 1854; *Chicago Inter Ocean*, March 18, 1900, 3; Chicago Tribune, April 25, 1878, 7; and Cooley, "Illinois and the Underground Railroad to Canada," 31.

3. Reed, *Black Chicago's First Century*, 98–99; Anna Hudlin in Brown, *Homespun Heroines*. John and Mary Jones lived initially in a house and workspace they built at 119 Dearborn, later in a house at 9th and Plymouth, near the Mary Richardson Jones Park, at 1240 S. Plymouth Court.

4. On Carpenter, see McGiffert, Jr., *No Ivory Tower*, 20; Interview with Freer, "Slavery in Chicago," Chicago *Inter Ocean*, June 28, 1891; Advertisement in *Chicago Tribune*, March 19, 1857; Reed, *Black Chicago's First Century*, 98– 99, 184; "Old and New, the Tremont from 1833 to 1874," Chicago *Tribune*, February 2, 1874, 5; Turner, *Underground Railroad in Illinois*, 99, 184. In the 1930s, the Gardner-Wilcox home was marked with a historical marker; Cutler, *Chicago, Metropolis of the Mid-Continent*, 118. Local family records at the Ridge Historical Society identified the house and barn as sites.

5. On the Gardner-Wilcox home and "milk stop," see Petraitus, Crossroads to Freedom. On Englewood, see Polk and Dumke, "A Brief History of Englewood."

Newspapers

Anti-Slavery Bugle (New Lisbon, OH)
Aurora Beacon-News
Berkshire County Eagle (Pittsfield, MA)
Cairo City Times
Carlinville Free Democrat
Chicago American
Chicago Democrat
Chicago Tribune
Compiler (Gettysburg, PA)
Congregational Herald (Chicago, IL)
Daily Courier (Zanesville, OH)
Daily Defender (Chicago, IL)
Daily Missouri Republican
Daily St. Louis Intelligencer
Detroit Tribune
Douglass' Monthly (Rochester, NY)
Frederick Douglass' Paper
Free West (Chicago, IL)
Genius of Universal Emancipation (Lowell, IL)
Illinois Gazette
Illinois Intelligencer
NeJoliet Democrat
Joliet Herald-News
Joliet Signal
Jonesboro Gazette
The Liberator (Boston, MA)
The Liberty Tree (Chicago, IL)
The Mountaineer (Salt Lake City, UT)

National Anti-Slavery Standard (Washington, DC)
National Republican (Washington, DC)
Nebraska City News
New York Daily Herald
New York Times
The North Star (Rochester, NY)
Ottawa Free Trader
Pontiac Sentinel
Provincial Freeman (Windsor, Ontario)
Signal of Liberty (Ann Arbor, MI)
St. Charles Valley Chronicle
St. Louis Republican
Streator Free Press
Sunday Inter Ocean (Chicago, IL)
Sycamore True Republican
Washington Springs Herald (WA)
Weekly Times (Glasgow, MO)
Weekly Tribune (Fort Scott, KA)
Western Citizen (Chicago, IL)

Online Sources

Ancestry.com. "Census and Voter Lists." Accessed December 31, 2016. https://
    www.ancestry.com/search/categories/35/
Chicago History Museum. "Online Resources." Accessed April 30, 2006. https://
    www.chicagohistory.org/online-research-resources/
Colored Conventions Project. "Digital Records." Accessed September 1, 2022.
    https://omeka.coloredconventions.org/
Illinois State Library. "Illinois Digital Archives." Accessed May 1, 2011. https://
    www.idaillinois.org/digital/custom/bySubject
Library of Congress. "Chronicling America." Accessed November 6, 2011. https://
    chroniclingamerica.loc.gov/McCaffrey, Hope. "James Bonner." Black
    Organizing in Pre-Civil War Illinois: Creating Community, Demanding
    Justice. Accessed September 1. 2022. https://coloredconventions.org/black
    -illinois-organizing/delegates/james-bonner/.
Madison County Circuit Clerks Office. "Slave Emancipation Registry Book #1
    1820-1850." Clerk of Madison County, Illinois. Accessed June 16, 2018. https://
    madisoncountycircuitclerk.contentdm.oclc.org.

Minutes of the National Convention of Colored Citizens Held at Buffalo. 1943 New York: Peircy & Reed, 1843. Accessed September 1, 2022. https://omeka.colored conventions.org/items/show/278

Newspapers.com. "Chicago Tribune." Accessed December 19, 2017. https://www .newspapers.com/papers/.

Oertel, Kristen. "Blazing a Path to Freedom: African Americans and Their White allies in Bleeding Kansas." *BlackPast*, March 7, 2011. Accessed October 3, 2018. Blackhistory.org.

Ohio Historical Society. "Wilbur H. Siebert Underground Railroad Collection," Accessed April 26, 2006. https://www.ohiomemory.org/digital/collection /siebert

Pro Quest. "Chicago Tribune." Accessed July 11, 2007. https://www.proquest .com/.

Schomburg Center for Research in Black Culture, New York Public Library. "Digital Schomburg." Accessed September 10, 2025. https://www.nypl.org/about /locations/schomburg/digital-schomburg

"When I Was a Girl: The Memoirs of Louisa Ashley Hammond, 1831–1912." Accessed May 10, 2018. http://www.ljhammond.com/essays/memoirs.htm.

University of Detroit Mercy. *Black Abolitionist Archive.* Accessed March 3, 2008. https://www.udmercy.edu/academics/special/black-abolitionist.php

University Library of the University of North Carolina at Chapel Hill. "Documenting the American South." Accessed March 11, 2010. docsouth .unc.edu.

Interviews and Correspondence

Benson, Mary Kelsey. Correspondence with the author through the Sycamore Historical Society, May 27, 2016.

Bremer, Phyllis. Correspondence with the author, January 2005.

Fischer, Nancy Marshall. Letter to St. Charles Historical Society, June 2, 1991.

Genzler, Edward, and Harriet [McCoy]. Interview by the author March 1, 2015

Paxton, Patsy Mighell. Interview by the author, September 6, 1016.

Schumacher, Florence McCoy. Oral and typescript interview, July 22, 1980. *OH Park Forest!: The Park Forest Oral History Project*, Park Forest, IL: 1980.

Schumn, Nancy. President of the Ila Township Historical Society, interview with the author, April 7, 2016.

Stellen, Sue. Correspondence from church staff member, the Hadley Church, August 2, 2003.

Primary Sources

"The Underground Railroad." *American Cyclopedia*. New York: A. D. Appleton, 1879.

An Ordinance for the Government of the Territory of the United States, North-West of the River Ohio, Article the Sixth, 1787. Found at https://guides.loc.gov/northwest-ordinance

Andreas, A. T. *History of Chicago from the Earliest Period to the Present Time, Volume II: From 1857 Until the Fire of 1871*. Chicago: A. T. Andreas, 1884.

———. History of Cook County, The Earliest Period to the Present Time. Chicago: A. T. Andreas, 1884.

Armstrong, J. C. "The Lyonsville Church at Three Score Years and Ten." *Lyonsville Congregational Church, Seventieth Anniversary Celebration, May 13, 1913*. Copy given to the author in 2005.

Banks, J. H. *I Am a Witness against American Slavery and All Its Horrors: A Narrative of Events of the Life of J. H. Banks, an Escaped Slave, From the Cotton State, Alabama, in America*. Liverpool: M. Rourke, Printer, 1861. With introduction by J. W. C. Pennington, D. D., who interviewed Banks.

Barton, William E. *Joseph Edwin Roy, 1827–1908, A Faithful Servant of God and of His Own Generation*. Oak Park: Puritan Press, 1908.

Bateman, Newton, and Paul Selby, eds. *Historical Encyclopedia of Illinois and History of Kane County*. Chicago: Munsell Publishing Company, 1904.

———. *Historical Encyclopedia of Illinois and History of Kendall County*. Chicago: Munsell Publishing, 1914.

———. *Historical Encyclopedia of Illinois and History of Du Page County, Volume II*. Chicago: Munsell Publishing, 1913.

———. *Historical Encyclopedia of Illinois and History of Lake County*. Chicago: Munsell Publishing, 1909.

Bentley, R. L., and Lorraine Rodgers. *Records of First Congregational Church of Lockport, IL., Compiled from Original Records*. Lockport: Typescript, 1985.

Biggers, Alice E. "The Abolition Movement in Three Kane County Communities: Batavia, Geneva, and St. Charles, 1840–1865." Paper for Aurora University, 1986.

Biographical Directory of the Tax-payers and Voters of McHenry County. Chicago: C. Walker, 1877.

Biographical Sketches of the Leading Men of Chicago. Chicago: Wilson & St. Clair, 1868.

Blanchard, Rufus. *"The Underground Railroad," The Discovery and Conquests of the Northwest and the History of Chicago, Volume II*. Chicago: Rufus Blanchard, 1900.

Blassingame, John. *Slave Testimony*. Baton Rouge: Louisiana State University Press, 1977.

Blodgett, Henry W. *Autobiography of Henry W. Blodgett*. Waukegan, IL: privately printed, 1906.

Blodgett, Julia Wygant. *Pioneer Reflections of Avis Dodge Blodgett*. Du Page County: Printed booklet, June 1915.

Boies, Henry L. *History of DeKalb County*. Chicago: O. P. Bassett, Printer, 1868.

Brainerd, E. J. *Earliest History of the Church* (Ivanhoe Congregational Church). Typescript from the Church, c. 1973.

Brennan, George. *The Wonders of the Dunes*. Indianapolis: Bobbs-Merrill, 1923.

Brown, Hallie. *Homespun Heroines and Other Women of Distinction*. Xenia, OH: Aldine, 1926.

Brown, William H. "Early History of Illinois." *Early Illinois*. Chicago: Fergus Printing, 1881.

Brown, William Wells. *Narrative of William W. Brown, a Fugitive Slave, Written by Himself*. Boston: The Anti-Slavery Office, 1848.

Bureau of the Census. *Census of Negro Population 1790–1915*. Washington, DC: Government Printing Office, 1918.

Burgess, Daniel. *Map of the Western States Designed to Accompany Smith's Geography for Schools, 1840*.

Bushnell, William. *Biographical Sketches of some of the Early Settlers of the City of Chicago*. Chicago: Fergus Printing, 1876.

"Calvin DeWolf." *Magazine of Western History* 13 (November 1890–April 1891): 221–5.

Caton, John Dean. *Early Bench and Bar in Illinois*. Chicago: Chicago Legal News, 1893.

Centennial Encyclopedia of the African Methodist Episcopal Church. Philadelphia: Book Concern of the A. M. E. Church, 1916.

Chamberlain, Everett. *Chicago and Its Suburbs*. Chicago: T. A. Hungerford, 1874.

Chambers, A., ed. *Trials and Confessions of Madison Henderson, alias Blanchard, Alfred Amos Warrick, James W. Seward and Charles Brown*. St. Louis: Chambers & Knapp, 1841.

Chapman, Charles C. *History of Knox County, Illinois*. Chicago: Chas C. Chapman, 1878.

"Charles Cook." *Magazine of Western History* 13, November 1890–April 1891.

Clark, Charles M., ed. *The History of the Thirty-Ninth Regiment, Illinois, Volunteer Veteran Infantry in the War of the Rebellion, 1861–1865*. Chicago: Veteran Association of the Regiment, 1889.

Collections of the Kansas State Historical Society. Vol. 14. Topeka: Kansas State Printing Plant, 1918.

Commemorative Biographical and Historical Record of Kane County. Chicago: Beers, Leggett, 1888.

Cooley, Verna. "Illinois and the Underground Railroad to Canada." *MA Thesis, University of Illinois*, 1917. At https://archive.org/details/illinoisundergrooocool /page/n3/mode/2up

Currey, J. Seymour *Chicago: Its History and Its Builders*. Chicago: S. J. Publishing, 1912.

Constitution of the State of Illinois, 1818. Illinois State Library, Illinois Digital Archives. Accessed May 1, 2011. https://www.idaillinois.org/digital/collection /isl2/id/167/

Crete Cemetery. South Holland: South Suburban Genealogical and Historical Society, 1979.

Danforth W. E. (W. E. D.). "The Underground Railway." *Lake Forest College Stentor* 3 (May 1890).

Davidson, Olga. "The African Methodist Church in the Chicago Area." Typescript in Federal Writers' Project Papers, Abraham Lincoln Presidential Library, Folder FWP 184, June 26, 1941.

Delaney, Lucy A. *From the Darkness Cometh the Light: Or, Struggles for Freedom*. St. Louis: Publishing House of J. T. Smith, 1891.

Deerfield Grammar School. *1918 School Histories, Deerfield Township, Deerfield Grammar School*. Handwritten paper report, 1918, at Lake County Discovery Museum.

Drake, St. Clair. *Churches and Voluntary Associations in the Chicago Negro Community*. Chicago: Institute for Juvenile Research, 1940.

Drew, Benjamin. *The Refugee or The Narratives of Fugitive Slaves in Canada*. Boston: J. P. Jewett, 1856. Reprinted as *The Narratives of Fugitive Slaves*. Toronto: Prospero Books, 2000.

Dupre, Irma. "Misc. Notes on Congregational Churches of Elgin and Dundee." *Scrapbook of Dundee Township Historical Church Material*. C. 1940. Archives of the Dundee Township Historical Society.

Eastman Papers. Zebina Eastman Papers, Research Center, Chicago History Museum. Linda J. Evans, *Zebina Eastman Papers, 1840–1885*. Descriptive Inventory for the Collection at Chicago History Museum, Research Center, rev. 2009.

First Congregational Church, Naperville, Illinois, History, 1833–1933, Centennial Celebration, July 13 & 16, 1933. Naperville: privately printed, 1933.

Fischer, Nancy Marshall. Letter to St. Charles Historical Society, June 2, 1991. 2 pages, typescript, at the archives of the St. Charles Historical Society.

Fisher, Miles Mark. *The History of the Olivet Baptist Church of Chicago*. Chicago: MA thesis, Divinity School, University of Chicago, 1922.

Fitzwilliam, Sarah Raymond. "Chapter XI, The Underground Railroad." In Newton Bateman and Paul Selby, *Historical Encyclopedia of Illinois, and History of Kendall County*. Chicago: Munsell Publishing, 1914.

Flinn, John J. and John Elbert Wilkie. *History of the Chicago Police*. Chicago: Chicago Police Book Fund, 1887.

Flowers, W. L., surveyor. *Cook County, Illinois*. Map. Chicago: S. H. Burhans & J. Van Vechten, 1862.

Foner, Philip S., and George E. Walker, eds. *Proceedings of the Black State Conventions, 1840–1865*. Philadelphia: Temple University Press, 1980.

Forstall, Richard L. *Population of the States and Counties of the United States: 1790–1990*. Washington, DC: Department of Commerce, US Bureau of the Census, 1996.

"The Fugitive Slave Law and Its Victims, 1856," *Anti-Slavery Tracts, No. 18*. New York: American Anti-Slavery Society, 1856. Accessed October 3, 2008. www .accessgenealogy.com/african/anti_slavery_tracts.htm.

Genealogical and Biographical Record of Will County, Illinois. Chicago: Biographical Publishing Company, 1900.

Grace Mason Papers/Franklyn Atkinson Henderson Photograph Collection. Chicago Public Library, Woodson Regional Library, Vivian G. Harsh Collection of Afro-American History and Literature.

Gross, Lewis M. *Past and Present of DeKalb County, Illinois*. Vol. 1. Chicago: Pioneer, 1907.

Goodspeed, Weston A., and Daniel Healy. *History of Cook County, Illinois*. Chicago: The Goodspeed Historical Association, 1909.

Haines, Elijah M. *Historical and Statistical Sketches of Lake County, State of Illinois*. Waukegan, IL: E. G. Howe, 1852.

Halsey, John J. *A History of Lake County, Illinois*. Chicago: Roy S. Bates, 1912.

Hamilton, James Cleland. "John Brown in Canada." *Canadian Magazine* (December 1894).

Hamilton, Oscar B. *History of Jersey County, Illinois*. Chicago: Munsell Publishing, 1919.

Hammond, Rev. Henry L. *Memorial Sketch of Philo Carpenter. February 27, 1805–August 7, 1886. Read before the Chicago Historical Society, July 17, 1888*. Chicago: Fergus Printing Company, 1888.

"Henry B. Hurd." *Transactions of the Illinois State Historical Society for 1906*. Springfield: Illinois State Historical Library, 1906.

Hicks, E. W. *History of Kendall County.* Aurora, IL: Knickerbocker & Hodder Steam Printers and Blank Book Makers, 1877.

History of LaSalle County, Illinois. Vol. 1. Chicago: Inter-state Publishing, 1886.

History of Madison County, Illinois. Edwardsville: W. R. Brink, 1882.

History of McHenry County, Illinois. Chicago: Inter-State, 1885.

History of Plainfield as told Through Newspaper Clippings and Photos, Book II. Assembled 1992–93, Plainfield Public Library.

Hoffman, U. J. *History of La Salle County, Illinois.* Chicago: S. J. Clarke Publishing, 1908.

"H.O. Wagoner." Typescript. Vivian Harsh Collection, Chicago Public Library, WPA Collection, Box 07–Strangers–UGRR, File 20.

In Memoriam: Isaac Newton Arnold. Chicago: Fergus Print, 1885.

Jenness, Carrie L. "Dr. Mary J. Safford Black." *The Cottage Hearth* [Massachusetts] 3, no. 5 (May 1876): 113–4. University of Mississippi, Special Collections: Dr. Anne Gowdy/Sherwood Bonner Collection, Folder 2-6.

Johnson, H. U. *From Dixie to Canada, Romances and Realities of the Underground Railroad.* Orwell, OH: H. U. Johnson, 1896.

Jones, John. *The Black Laws of Illinois and a Few Reasons Why They Should be Repealed.* Chicago: *Chicago Tribune,* 1864.

Joslyn, R. Waite, and Frank Joslyn. *History of Kane County, Ill. 1908.* Vol. I. Chicago: Pioneer Publishing, 1908.

Kirkland, Caroline. *Chicago Yesterdays, A Sheaf of Reminiscences.* Chicago: Daughaday, 1919.

Laux, James B., and Susan Short May. "Susan Short May: The Story of Her Ancestry and of Her Early Life in Illinois." *Journal of the Illinois State Historical Society* 6, no. 1, (April 1913).

Lawrence, George A. *A Pioneer of Freedom, an Address upon the Life and Services of Benjamin Lundy.* Annual Meeting of the Illinois Historical Society, May 15, 1913.

Lee, Lavinia Jones. Letter to Caroline McIlvaine, Librarian of the Historical Society, April 21, 1905, John Jones Collection, Research Center, Chicago Historical Society.

Link, Edward E. Letter from the Waukegan Historical Society, to Virginia A. Johnson, August 14, 1996. In archives of the Waukegan Historical Society.

The Lundy Family and their Descendants of Whatsoever Name, with a Biographical Sketch of Benjamin Lundy. New Brunswick, NJ: J. Heidingsfeld, Printer, 1902.

Lusk, D. W. *Politics and Politicians of Illinois.* 3rd rev. ed. Springfield: H. W. Rokker, Printer, 1889.

Manierre, George. "The Manierre Family in Early Chicago History." *Journal of the Illinois State Historical Society* 8, no. 3 (October, 1915). Matson, Nehemiah.

Raconteur: four romantic stories relating to pioneer life, scenes in foreign countries, religious fanaticism, love, murder, &c., all of which are founded on facts. Chicago: G. K. Hazlitt, 1882.

———. *Reminiscences of Bureau County.* Princeton, IL: Republican Book and Job Office, 1872.

"Millburn Congregational Church." Manuscript. Untitled. In the archives of the Waukegan Historical Society.

Minutes of the Christian Anti-Slavery Convention, Held July 3rd, 4th, and 5th, 1851, at Chicago, Ill. Chicago: Office of the Western Citizen, 1851.

Minutes of the Kane County Anti-Slavery Society, July 14, 1842. Transcribed in Alice E. Biggers, "The Abolition Movement in Three Kane County Communities: Batavia, Geneva, and St. Charles, 1840–1865." Paper for Aurora University, 1986.

Moses, John, and Joseph Kirkland. "Aaron Gibbs." *History of Chicago.* Vol. 1. Chicago: Munsell, 1895.

Myrick, Mrs. George. "Moses Cook." *Papers Read at the Local History Day Meeting.* Crete, IL: Women's Club of Crete, 1922.

Olin, Chauncey C. *A Complete Record of the John Olin Family.* Indianapolis: Baker-Randolph, 1893.

Otis, Philo Adams. *The First Presbyterian Church, 1833–1913.* Chicago: Fleming H. Revell, 1913.

The Paxton Family, The Paxtons: We Are One. Platte City, MO: Lankmark Print, 1903.

Parrish, Randall. *Historic Illinois, The Romance of Earlier Days.* Chicago: McClurg, 1905.

Past and Present of Boone County, Illinois. Chicago: H. F. Kett, 1877.

The Past and Present of Kane County, Illinois. Chicago: Wm. LaBaron, Jr., 1878.

Patten, Jennie M. *History of the Somonauk United Presbyterian Church, near Sandwich, DeKalb County, Illinois.* Chicago: James A. Patten and Henry J. Patten, 1928.

Payne, Daniel A. *History of the African Methodist Episcopal Church.* Nashville: Publishing House of the AME Sunday School Union, 1891.

Pinkerton, William. Letter to F. F. Hall, April 8, 1916, in archives of the Dundee Historical Society.

Portrait and Biographical Album of Lake County, Illinois. Chicago: Lake Publishing, 1891.

Proceedings of the Illinois Anti-Slavery Convention Held at Upper Alton on the 26th, 27th and 28th October, 1837. Alton: Park & Breath, 1838.

Redpath, James. *The Public Life of John Brown.* Boston: Thayer and Eldridge, 1860.

Report of the Proceedings of the Colored National Convention, Held at Cleveland, Ohio, on Wednesday, Sept. 6, 1848. Rochester, New York: John Dick, at the North Star Office, 1848.

Ripley, C. Peter, ed. *The Black Abolitionist Papers: The British Isles, 1830–1865.* 4 vols. With Jeffery S. Rossback, Roy E. Finkenbine, Fiona E. Spiers, and Debra Susie. Chapel Hill: The University of North Carolina Press, 1985.

Robinson, L. E. *History of Illinois.* New York: American Book Company, 1909.

Rowe, S. G. *The Refugees from Slavery in Canada West, Report of the Freedmen's Inquiry Commission.* Boston: Wright & Potter, Printers, 1864.

Ryan, John H. "A Chapter from the History of the Underground Railroad in Illinois: A Sketch of the Sturdy Abolitionist, John Hossack." Journal *of the Illinois State Historical Society* 8 (April, 1915): 6, 27–28.

Scott, Emma. *The Underground Railroad.* "Prepared for the Woodford County Historical Society and read at the Society's Annual Picnic on the Freese farm, August 30, 1934." Booklet. 42 pages.

The Second Presbyterian Church of Chicago. Chicago: Knight, Leonard, 1892.

Shufelt, Mrs. John L. "When Lisbon Was a Prairie." *Kendall County Record,* January 24, 1917. With a letter from H. L. Hossack, Ottawa, January 1, 1917. Kendallkin.org.

Siebert Papers. Wilbur H. Siebert Collection, Ohio State Historical Society. Ohio Memory. ohiohistory.org.

Siebert, Wilbur. "The Underground Railroad." *New England Magazine* 27 (September 1902–February 1903).

Simmons, William J. *Men of Mark: Eminent, Progressive and Rising.* Cleveland: Geo. M. Rewell, 1887.

Smith, George W. *A Student's History of Illinois.* Carbondale: printed for the author, 1907.

Smuskiewicz, A. J. "'The Man for the Occasion,' Peter Stewart, Wilmington Developer." *Quarterly of the Will County Historical Society* (Spring 2020). Lockport: Will County Historical Society, 2020.

"Thomas Rodney v ICRR." *Report of Cases Determined of the Supreme Court of the State of Illinois: November 1857–April 1858.* Vol. 19. Chicago: Callaghan & Co., 1877.

Tregillis, Helen. *River Roads to Freedom, Fugitive Slave Notices and Sheriff Notices found in Illinois Sources.* Maryland: Heritage Books, 1988.

Waukegan (Typescript) Compiled by the Daughters of the American Revolution, c. 1940. on In the archives of the Waukegan Historical Society

Will County Court Record Book, 1843 Archives of the Will County Historical Society, Lockport, Illinois.

Wright, Richard R. *The Centennial History of the African Methodist Episcopal Church.* Philadelphia: Book Concern on the A. M. E. Church, 1916.

Woodruff, George. *The History of Will County, Illinois*. Chicago: Wm. Le Baron, Jr., 1878.

———. *Forty Years Ago, a contribution to the early history of Joliet and Will County*. Joliet, IL: Republican Steam Printing House, 1874.

Youmans, Louis Irwin. *Historical and Genealogical Notes of the Youmans and Underhill Families and Connected Family Lines*. Chicago: handwritten family history, 1936. Copy held by La Salle County Historical Society.

Secondary Sources

Andrews, Daryl Lamar. *Masonic Abolitionists, Freemasonry and the Underground Railroad in Illinois*. Chicago: Andrews Press, 2011.

Angel, Jeanne Schultz. *A Guide to the Underground Railroad in DuPage County, IL*. DuPage Community Foundation, 2014–16. Program material developed for the Lombard, IL Historical Society.

———. "Friends of the Oppressed: An Investigation of the Kane County Anti-Slavery Society." MA Thesis, Illinois State University, 2004.

Angle, Paul. "A Fugitive Slave in Chicago." *Chicago History*, Vol. 2, no. 12, Summer, 1951, Chicago: Chicago Historical Society, 1951, 364-66. Barton, William E. *Joseph Edwin Roy, 1827–1908: A Faithful Servant of God and of His Own Generation*. Oak Park: Puritan Press, 1908.

Beasley, Nancy. *The Underground Railroad in DeKalb County, Illinois*. Jefferson, NC: McFarland, 2013.

Bell, Howard H. "Chicago Negroes in the Reform Movement, 1847–1853." *Negro History Bulletin* 21, no. 7 (April 1918): 153–5.

Blackett, R. J. M. *The Captive's Quest for Freedom*. New York: Cambridge University Press, 2018.

Blassingame, John W. "Autobiographies Published in Books and Periodicals, 1828–1878." In *Slave Testimony: Two Centuries of Letters, Speeches, Interviews, and Autobiographies*, ed. John W. Blassingame. Baton Rouge: Louisiana State University Press, 1977.

Blight, David. *Passages to Freedom: The Underground Railroad in History and Memory*. Washington, DC: Smithsonian Books, 2004.

Bliss, Roger. *Illinois: A History of the Land and Its People*. DeKalb: Northern Illinois University Press, 2005.

Bordewich, Fergus M. *Bound for Canaan: The Underground Railroad and the War for the Soul of America*. New York: Harper Collins, 2005.

Brown, Hallie. *Homespun Heroines and Other Women of Distinction*. Freeport, NY: Free Library Press, 1971.

Brown-Kubisch, Linda. *The Queen's Bush Settlement: Black Pioneers 1839–1865.* Toronto: Natural Heritage Books, 2004

Buchanan, Thomas C. *Black Life on the Mississippi: Slaves, Free Blacks, and the Western Steamboat World.* Chapel Hill: University of North Carolina Press, 2004.

Buck, Dennis. *From Slavery to Glory: African Americans Come to Aurora, Illinois, 1850–1920.* Aurora, IL: River Street Press, 2005.

Campbell, Tom. *Fighting Slavery in Chicago: Abolitionists, the Law of Slavery and Lincoln.* Chicago: Ampersand, 2009.

Cha-Jua, Sundiata Keita. *America's First Black Town: Brooklyn, Illinois, 1830–1915.* Urbana: University of Illinois Press, 2000.

Cole, Harry Ellsworth. *Stagecoach and Tavern Tales of the Old Northwest.* Cleveland: Arthur H. Clark, 1930.

Cook, Frederick Francis. *Bygone Days in Chicago: Recollections of the "Garden City" of the Sixties.* Chicago: A. C. McClurg, 1910.

Cooley, Verna. "Illinois and the Underground Railroad to Canada." *Transactions of the Illinois State Historical Society,* 23 (1917).

Cutler, Irving. *Chicago, Metropolis of the Mid-Continent.* Dubuque: Kendall Hunt, 1982.

Davis, James E. *Frontier Illinois.* Bloomington: Indiana University Press, 1998.

DeRamus, Betty. *Forbidden Fruit: Love Stories from the Underground Railroad.* New York: Atria Books, 2005.

Dexter, Darrel. *Bondage in Egypt: Slavery in Southern Illinois.* Cape Girardeau, MO: Center for Regional History, Southeast Missouri State University, 2011.

Dolinar, Brian. *The Negro in Illinois: the WPA Papers.* Urbana: University of Illinois Press, 2013.

Drake, St. Clair, and Horace R. Cayton. *Black Metropolis A Study of Negro Life in a Northern City.* New York: Harcourt, Brace, 1945.

Dretske, Diana, and Al Westerman. "The Incredible Story of Amos Bennett." *LCMA Historian* 21, no. 4 (Winter 1993). Newsletter of the Lake County Museum Association.

Dugan, Hugh G. *Village on the County Line: A History of Hinsdale, Illinois.* Hinsdale: privately printed, 1949.

Ellis, Joseph. *The Founding Brothers: The Revolutionary Generation.* New York: Alfred A. Knopf, 2004.

Farrison, William E. *William Wells Brown: Author and Reformer.* Chicago: University of Chicago Press, 1969.

Federal Writers' Project. *Cairo Guide.* Cairo, IL: Cairo Public Library, 1938.

———. *Du Page County, A Descriptive and Historical Guide, 1831–1939.* Elmhurst, IL: Irvin A. Ruby, Distributor, 1948.

———. *Illinois, A Descriptive and Historical Guide.* Chicago: A. C. McClurg, 1939.

Foner, Eric. *Gateway to Freedom: The Hidden History of the Underground Railroad.* New York: W. W. Norton, 2015.

Foreman, P. Gabrielle, Jim Casey, and Sarah Lynn Patterson, eds. *The Colored Conventions Movement: Black Organizing in the Nineteenth Century.* Chapel Hill: University of North Carolina Press, 2021.

Frazier, Harriet C. *Runaway and Freed Missouri Slaves and Those Who Helped Them, 1763–1865.* Jefferson, NC: McFarland, 2004.

Frost, Karolyn Smardz, and Veta Smith Tucker. *A Fluid Frontier: Slavery, Resistance, and the Underground Railroad in the Detroit River Borderland.* Detroit: Wayne State University Press, 2016.

Gara, Larry. *The Liberty Line, The Legend of the Underground Railroad.* Lexington: University of Kentucky Press, 1961.

———. "The Underground Railroad in Illinois." *Journal of the Illinois State Historical Society* 56, no. 3 (Autumn 1963): 508–28.

Gertz, Elmer. "The Black Laws of Illinois." *Journal of the Illinois State Historical Society* 56, no. 3 (Autumn 1963): 454-73. 463–4.

Gliozzo, Charles A. "John Jones, A Study of a Black Chicagoan." *Illinois Historical Journal* 80 (Autumn 1987).

Griffler, Keith P. *Frontline of Freedom: African Americans and the Forging of the Underground Railroad in the Ohio Valley.* Lexington: University Press of Kentucky, 2004.

Haber, Louis. *Black Pioneers of Science and Invention.* New York: Harcourt, Brace, 1970.

Harbour, Jennifer R. *Organizing Freedom: Black Emancipation Activism in the Civil War Midwest.* Carbondale: Southern Illinois University Press, 2020.

Harris, N. Dwight. *The History of Negro Servitude in Illinois and of the Slavery Agitation in That State.* Chicago: A. C. McClurg, 1904.

Harris, Robert L., Jr. "H. Ford Douglas: Afro-American Antislavery Emigrationist." *Journal of Negro History* 62, no. 3 (July 1977).

Harris, Samuel. "Early Railroading in Michigan and Wisconsin." *Old Lighthouse News* 7, no. 3 Michigan City, (September 1981).

Harrison, Victoria L. "We are Here Assembled: Illinois Colored Conventions, 1853–1873." *Journal of the Illinois State Historical Society* 108, no. 3/4, (Fall/Winter 2015).

Heerman, M. Scott. "The Great Escape: Runaway Slave Narratives in Chicago's Antislavery Press." Paper at the January 2015 conference of the American Historical Association.

Jackson, Kellie Carter. *Force and Freedom: Black Abolitionists and the Politics of Violence.* Philadelphia: University of Pennsylvania Press, 2019.

Jackson, Ruby West, and Walter T. McDonald. *Finding Freedom: The Untold Story of Joshua Glover, Runaway Slave*. Madison: Wisconsin Historical Society Press, 2007.

Johnson, Charles. *Growth of Cook County*. Vol. I. Chicago: County Board of Commissioners, 1960.

Junger, Richard. "'God and Man Helped Those Who Helped Themselves,' John and Mary Jones and the Culture of African American Self-Sufficiency in Mid-Nineteenth-Century Chicago." *Journal of Illinois History* 11, no. 2 (Summer 2008).

Karamanski, Theodore J. *Rally 'Round the Flag: Chicago and the Civil War*. Chicago: Nelson-Hall, 1993.

Kubisch, Linda Brown. *The Queen's Bush Settlement: Black Pioneers, 1839–1865*. Toronto: Natural Heritage Books, 2004,

LaRoche, Cheryl J. *The Geography of Resistance, Free Black Communities and the Underground Railroad*. Urbana: University of Illinois Press, 2014.

———. "Secrets Well Kept: Colored Conventioneers and Underground Railroad Activism." In *The Colored Conventions Movement: Black Organizing in the Nineteenth Century*, ed. P. Gabrielle Foreman, Jim Casey, and Sarah Lynn Patterson. Chapel Hill: The University of North Carolina Press, 2021.

Leichtle, Kurt E., and Bruce G. Carveth. *Crusade Against Slavery: Edward Coles, Pioneer of Freedom*. Carbondale: Southern Illinois University Press, 2011.

Lusk, D. W. *Politics and Politicians, A Succinct History of the Politics of Illinois*. Springfield: D. W. Lusk, 1889.

Lyon, Jeff. "Generations. a quiet quest to honor a family's memory" *Chicago Tribune Magazine*, February 23, 1992, 14-20. On Isaac and Emma Atkinson and their descendants.

Mackay, James. *Allan Pinkerton, the first Private Eye*. New York: John Wiley, 1996.

Mahoney, Olivia. "Black Abolitionists." *Chicago History* 20, no. 1/2 (Spring/Summer 1991): 22–37.

Maas, David E. *Marching to the Drumbeat of Abolitionism: Wheaton College in the Civil War* Wheaton, IL: Wheaton College, 2010.

Marshall, Jonathan. "North to Freedom." *North Shore Magazine*, June 2003.

Masur, Kate. *Until Justice Be Done, America's First Civil Rights Movement, from the Revolution to Reconstruction*. New York: W. W. Norton, 2021.

McClellan, Larry A. *The Underground Railroad South of Chicago*. Crete, IL: Thorn Creek Press, 2019.

McClellan, Larry A., and Kimberly Simmons. *To the River, the Remarkable Journey of Caroline Quarlls: A Freedom Seeker on the Underground Railroad*. Crete, IL: Thorn Creek Press, 2019.

McDonald, Jeanne Gillespie. "The Life and Times of Amos M. Ebersol: A Practical Abolitionist and Illinois Farmer." *Illinois Heritage,* July-August 2021. Magazine of the Illinois State Historical Society.

McGiffert, Arthur., Jr. *No Ivory Tower: The Story of the Chicago Theological Seminary.* Chicago: The Chicago Theological Seminary, 1969.

McPherson, James M. "The Fugitives Who Changed America." *The New York Review of Books.* June 4, 2015.

Meites, Hyman L. *History of the Jews in Chicago.* Chicago: Chicago Jewish Historical Society, 1990. Reprint of 1924 edition.

Meites, Jerome B. "The 1847 Constitutional Convention and Persons of Color." *Journal of the Illinois State Historical Society* 108, no. 3/4 (Fall/Winter 2015).

Merkel, Benjamin G. "The Underground Railroad and the Missouri Borders, 1840–1860." *Missouri Historical Review* 37 (April 1943).

Miller, William Lee. *Arguing About Slavery: The Great Battle in the United States Congress.* New York: Alfred A. Knopf, 1996.

Monks, Phyllis, and Carol Triebold. "Article 4 – Underground Railroad." *Crete Remembered.* Vol. 1. Crete: Crete Historical Society, 2003.

———. *Crete Remembered.* Vol. 5, *A Glimpse of the Early Days of Crete, Illinois.* Crete: Crete Historical Society, 2003.

Moore, William F., and Jane Ann Moore. *Owen Lovejoy: His Brother's Blood, Speeches and Writings, 1838–64.* Urbana: University of Illinois Press, 2004.

Muelder, Herman. *Fighters for Freedom: A History of Anti-Slavery Activities of Men and Women Associated with Knox College.* New York: Columbia University Press, 1959.

Muelder, Owen. *The Underground Railroad in Western Illinois.* Jefferson, NC: McFarland, 2008.

Nida, William L. *The Story of Illinois and Its People.* Chicago: O. P. Barnes, Publisher, 1910.

Owens, Deirdre Cooper. *Medical Bondage: Race, Gender, and the Origins of American Gynecology.* Athens: The University of Georgia Press, 2018.

Parkhill, Forbes. *Mister Barney Ford: A Portrait in Bistre.* Denver: Sage Books, 1963.

Paxton, Patsy Mighell. *Sin-qua-sip, Sugar Grove, A History of Sugar Grove Township, Kane County, Illinois.* Sugar Grove, IL: privately printed, 2000.

Petraitus, Paul. "Crossroads to Freedom: The Underground Railroad in the Western Calumet Region." Presentation for Wolf Lake Initiative Conference, January, 2011.

———. "UGRR in the Chicago/Calumet Area: A Brief History." Printed report, 2012.

Petraitus, Paul, and Marion Kelliher. "Timeline for the *Chicago/Calumet Under-ground Railroad Effort (C/C.U.R.E.)."* Printed for C-CURE Conference, September 2002.

Piepenbrink, Howard. *The Underground Railroad in Crete Township, Will County, Illinois.* 2004. Self-published booklet from a family in Crete Township settled since the 1840s.

Pierce, Bessie Louise. *A History of Chicago.* Vol. 2. New York: Alfred A. Knopf, 1940.

Pirtle, Carol. *Escape Betwixt Two Suns: A True Tale of the Underground Railroad in Illinois.* Carbondale: Southern Illinois University Press, 2000.

Polk, Chanel, and Mick Dumke. "A Brief History of Englewood." *Chicago Reporter.* December 1999.

Population of the States and Counties of the United States: 1790–1990. Washington, DC: Department of Commerce, US Bureau of the Census, 1996.

Quaife, Milo. *Chicago's Highways, Old and New.* Chicago: D. F. Keller, 1923.

"The Railroad to Freedom." WPA Papers, Vivian Harsh Collection, Chicago Public Library, Box 7, Folder 2.

Rajala, Hope. *Black and White Together.* Joliet: Will County Historical Society, 1970. Reissued in 2004.

Ransom, Terry. "Remembering the Flight to Freedom, The Underground Railroad in Illinois." *Historic Illinois* 22, no. 6 (April 2000): 3–7.

Reed, Christopher R. *Black Chicago's First Century.* Columbia, MO: University of Missouri Press, 2005.

———. "The Early African American Settlement of Chicago, 1833–1870." *Journal of the Illinois State Historical Society* 108, no. 3/4 (Fall/Winter 2015).

Regosin, Elizabeth A., and Donald R. Shaffer. *Voices of Emancipation: Understanding Slavery, the Civil War, and Reconstruction through the U. S. Pension Bureau Files.* New York: New York University Press, 2008.

Reichelt, Marie Ward. *History of Deerfield, Illinois: For Deerfield Post, 738, American Legion.* Lake County: Glenview Press, August 1928.

Reynolds, David. *John Brown, Abolitionist: The Man Who Killed Slavery, Sparked the Civil War, and Seeded Civil Rights.* New York: Alfred A. Knopf, 2005.

Robertson, Stacey M. *Hearts Beating for Liberty: Women Abolitionists in the Old Northwest.* Chapel Hill: University of North Carolina Press, 2010.

Saunders, Delores. *Illinois Liberty Lines (The History of the Underground Railroad).* Farmington, IL: The Farmington Shopper, 1982.

Selby, Paul. "George Schneider." *Transactions of the Illinois State Historical Society for 1906.* Springfield: Illinois State Historical Library, 1906.

Shackel, Paul A. *New Philadelphia: An Archaeology of Race in the Heartland.* Berkeley: University of California Press, 2011.

Siebert, Wilbur H. *The Underground Railroad from Slavery to Freedom*. New York: Macmillan, 1898.

Sinha, Manisha, *The Slave's Cause: A History of Abolition*. New Haven: Yale University Press, 2016.

Soike, Lowell J. *Necessary Courage: Iowa's Underground Railroad in the Struggle against Slavery*. Iowa City: University of Iowa Press, 2013.

Spinka, Matthew. *A History of Illinois Congregational and Christian Churches*. Chicago: The Congregational and Christian Conference of Illinois, 1944.

Sterling, Robert E. *A Pictorial History of Will County*. Vol. 1. Joliet: Will County Historical Publications, 1975.

Sterba, Lois. *The Blodgetts of Maple Avenue*. Downers Grove Park District Museum, 2010.

Struve, Walter, Book review *The Red Doctor* for from book review by Walter Struve of the Graduate Center, City University of New York. www.h-net.org /reviews. Review of Schmidt, Axel W. O. *Der Rothe Doktor von Chicago, 1830–1900* [The Red Doctor of Chicago 1830–1900]. Frankfort am Main: Peter Lang, 2003.

Talmadge, Marian, and Iris Gilmore. *Barney Ford: Black Baron*. New York: Dodd, 1973.

Turner, Glennette Tilley. *The Underground Railroad in Illinois*. Glen Ellyn, IL: Newman Educational, 2001.

———. *Running for Our Lives*. Glen Ellyn, IL: Newman Educational, 2004.

"The Underground Railroad and DuPage County." Booklet. Lombard, IL: Lombard Historical Society, 2010.

Walker, Juliet E. K. *Free Frank: A Black Pioneer on the Antebellum Frontier*. Lexington: University Press of Kentucky, 1983.

Waller, Elbert. *Waller's History of Illinois*. 7th ed. Galesburg: Wagoner Printing Company, 1920.

Washington, Margaret. *Sojourner Truth's America*. Urbana: University of Illinois Press, 2009.

Weiner, Dana E. "Anti-Abolition Violence and Freedom of Speech in Peoria, Illinois." *Journal of Illinois History* 11, no. 3 (Autumn, 2008).

Wellman, Judith. "The Underground Railroad and the National Register of Historic Places: Historical Importance vs. Architectural Integrity." *Public Historian* 24, no. 1 (Winter 2002): 11–29.

Where the Trails Cross. Journal of the South Suburban Genealogical and Historical Society. Hazel Crest, IL: South Suburban Genealogical and Historical Society.

Whiteman, Maxwell. "Jews in the Antislavery Movement." Introduction to *The Kidnapped and the Ransomed: The Narrative of Peter and Vina Still after Forty*

Years of Slavery, by Kate E. R. Pickard. Philadelphia: The Jewish Publication Society of America, 1970.

Williams, John M. "History of the Chicago Congregational Association during Its First Quarter Century." *Congregationalism in Illinois*. Chicago: Illinois Society of Church History, 1895.

Wolf, Simon. *The American Jew as Patriot, Soldier and Citizen*. Philadelphia: Levytype, 1895.

Italicized page numbers indicate figures.

abolitionists: Chicago leadership, 52;
defined, 16; the Liberty Party, 88;
women, 89; work of Rev. John Cross,
86
Adams County, 32
African American Freemasons. *See*
Prince Hall Freemasons
African Methodist Episcopal Church
(AME Church), 13, 35, 44, 96, 98.
See Quinn, Bishop William Paul
Alton, Illinois, 13, 48
Anderson, Washington and James,
201
Anthony and Margaret, 91
anti-slavery, 16; resolutions, 66–67, 70,
72, 75, 89, 158; supported in 1824, 31;
Wesleyan Methodist Church, 156
Anti-Slavery Reunion, National, in
1874, 12
Anti-Slavery Society, 53. *See* Illinois
Anti-Slavery Society
American, 72; Jersey County, 32; Kane
County, 82, 153, 235; Lake County,
159; Will County, 34
Armstrong, Tom and William, 202
Arnold, Isaac and Harriet, 56, 62, 109,
119, 189
Atkinson, Isaac and Emma, 109, 101,
110–11, 221, 239, 268

Aunt Charlotte, 116
Aurora, Illinois, 67, 74–75, 81, 154–55

Bagsby, Joseph, and Lewis Isbell, 169
Baltimore, Priscilla "Mother," 35, 115
Banks, Jourden, 196
Barnard, George, 146
Barquet, Joseph and Maria, 101, 114,
135, 172
Bascom, Rev. Flavel and Ruth, 43, 53,
58, 82, 158
Beach, Deacon Reuben, 74, 80
Beach, Ebenezer, 82
Beebe's Grove Congregational Society,
75–76, 80, 132, 224, 233. *See* Crete
Congregational Church
Belt, Henry, 73
Belvidere, Illinois, 157
Bennett, Amos, 39, 132, 158, 160
Berkley, 184–85, 188
Beveridge, George and Ann, 151
Beveridge, John, Governor, 11
Bibb, Henry, 97, 122, 131–32
Biggers, Alice E., 263
biracial collaboration, 16, 54, 130, 133,
181
Black Bob,, 39, 229
Black Codes (Black Laws), 9, 30, 98,
129, 135–36

Sauk Trail, 22, 37, 73, 75, 80, 147, 224
Savage, Deacon Levi and Melinda, 73, 233
Scammon, Jonathan Y. and Mary Ann, 61–62
Schmidt, Ernst, 174
Schmidt, Oscar, 151
Schneider, George, 121, 232, 240
Seymour, Lucinda, *94*, 127
Shadd, Mary Ann, 161, 171
Shawneetown, Illinois, 23–24, 30, 37
Shepherd, Tom, 214
Siebert, Wilbur H., 12, 144, 211, 264
Signal of Liberty, 97
Silvie, 229
Simmons, Kimberly, 214–15
Slain, Victor, 76
"A Slave Hunt," *25*
Smith, Alexander, 133, 239
Smith, Charles W., 201
Smith, Elijah, 40
Smith, William, 239
Sojourner Truth, 159, 246
Somonauk, Illinois, 131, 151, 224; Presbyterian Church, 151, 224
South Carolina, 1, 39
South Grove Township, DeKalb County, 152–53
South Holland, Illinois, 213, 223, 260; First Reformed Church, 223
St. Charles, Illinois, 81, 150, 152, 213, 234, 258, 263
Stevenson, Henry, 91, 94, 211; journey, *92*
Stewart, Peter and Elizabeth, 73–74, 76, 174
St. Louis, Missouri, 26, 32, 41, 77, 121, 136, 142
St. Louis Republican, 51, 123, 143

Story of Illinois and Its People, 12
Stout, Joseph and James, 119, 188–89
Strawn, William, 187
Strong, Deacon William J. and Caroline, 81
Sugar Grove, Illinois, 213, 234
Sycamore Congregational Church, 150, 224

Taylor, George, 140
Taylor, William, 132
Tennessee River, 23, 46, 182
Terwilliger, Samuel and Laura, 157, 245
Thomas, Wilson, 24
Thompson, Samuel, 176
Titus, 42
Ton, Jan and Aagje Vander Syde, 148–49, 223; their farm, *149*, 221, 223
Townsend, Joshua, 152
Tremont, Indiana, 149
True Band societies, 193, 250
Tubman, Harriet, 8, 35
Turner, Glennette Tilley, 214
Turner the accomplice, 201
Turner with Capt. Taylor, 140

Underground Railroad: Black leadership, 18, 101; as journeys to freedom, 18; in late 1840s, 125; Memorial Garden, 223; misperception, 17; railroad imagery, 17; seen as a business, 207; seen as success, 162; women and men, 18
Union County, 185–86, 189, 191
Upper Alton, Illinois, 35

Vigilance Committees, 100, 129, 131, 202
Vincennes Trace, 70, 221
Virginia, 28–29, 31, 38, 114

Larry A. McClellan, emeritus professor of sociology and community studies at Governors State University, has been instrumental in adding listings to the National Park Service Network to Freedom register of the Underground Railroad. McClellan helped create GSU, was the mayor of University Park, and was a consultant for the Northeastern Illinois Planning Commission. He is the author of *The Underground Railroad South of Chicago* and *To the River: The Remarkable Journey of Caroline Quarlls, a Freedom Seeker on the Underground Railroad.*